THANK YOU FOR HAVING ME

THANK YOU FOR HAVING ME

MAUREEN LIPMAN

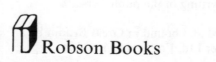
Robson Books

First published in Great Britain in 1990 by
Robson Books Ltd, Bolsover House,
5–6 Clipstone Street, London W1P 7EB

Copyright © 1990 Dramatic Licence Ltd
The right of Maureen Lipman to be identified
as author of this work has been asserted by her
in accordance with the Copyright, Designs and
Patents Act 1988

British Library Cataloguing in Publication Data
Lipman, Maureen
  Thank you for having me.
  1. Acting – Biographies
  I. Title
  792.028092
  ISBN 0 86051 679 2

Typeset, printed and bound in Great Britain by
Butler & Tanner Ltd, Frome and London

To the enduring memory of two unique men, Maurice Julius Lipman, my father, and Philip Sayer, my friend. It's a lot less fun without them.

Grovelling thanks and a pint of shandy to:

JEREMY ROBSON: He has the soul of a poet and the elbow of a tennis player.

CAROLE ROBSON: For insisting Jack put half a tomato on the finger he trapped in her car door. It worked and so can he.

LOUISE DIXON, my editor: for the job of patience and the gift of mirth.

LIZ ROSE: For editing during a three-legged race.

CHERYLL ROBERTS: For her P.R. and her T.A.C.T.

CLAUDETTE: For saving my life with kettle, water and bag.

LAYLA, my secretary: For typing up the scrawl and saving me from enraged committee members.

AMY: For typing up at the weekends whilst Layla recovers (see above).

JACK: For his wisdom and his ear.

OPTIONS: For the airspace.

SHE: For more airspace.

BT, MC and CTV: For continuing to employ me after reading this book.

ZELMA: For her input.

ADAM: For not being put out.

MY FAX: For my fiction.

Contents

Introduction

Dear Reader

For those of you who may have spent the last few years on a YTS scheme in St Petersburgh or in a queue for designer jeans in Omsk, may I take the liberty of introducing you to the dramatis personae of this my fourth and faintly familial book. I'll start as I mean to go on. Incoherently.

The cast so far: Maureen, age forty-mumble, a moderately emaciated artistc, known throughout the land for a certain sharpness of tongue and feature and a close affinity with a grey wig and several telephones.

This part will be essayed by Mrs M D Rosenthal, née Lipman, late of Hull, E Yorks, lately Humberside, now residing in up-and-gazumping Muswell Hill, Borough of Haringey (left-wing council, highest poll tax in England, move yer own rubbish bags or we'll dump 'em in yer ornamental urn).

Jack, her long-suffering, as in twenty years – for four of which he avoided matrimony with the fortitude, if not the pout, of a Manchester Warren Beatty, only to succumb after the wife-to-be's acquisition of one brown suit, two pink rabbis and a mother in a floral hat. A successful writer, he now devotes the greater part of his creative life to creating after-theatre suppers for his exhausted thespian wife and smiling wanly when greeted with 'Hello, Mr Lipman, is she in?' The role could be played by George Cole, unless the said wife has a hand in the casting, in which case Jeff Bridges would be just *perfect*.

Next is Amy, their chip-off-the-old-block sixteen-year-old, known to the Old Block herself as Amele, Trog, Boll or Blue Peter – this latter to describe her resourcefulness and practicality ...

QUESTION: 'What would you do if the sole fell completely off your shoe in Oxford Street?'

AMY'S ANSWER: 'Hop.'

QUESTION: 'Why can't you take the bus to school like other girls?'

AMY'S ANSWER: 'I'd forget which stop to get off and get kidnapped and it's not fair.'

This teenager hates boys, pop music, discos and any clothes which aren't her mother's Nicole Farhi's. She is currently sitting GCSEs in Astrology and Henna. Jamie Lee Curtis would not be suitable casting.

Adam, her thirteen-year-old brother, whose passions are Cricket, Astronomy and LATIN! His last note to his father (in Latin) read: 'Dear Dod, Your joyfulness is even more beautiful than your left testicle.' Nice. His father was thrilled. His mother is too dumb to understand one word he says and relies entirely on sign-language to say 'Your ears need descaling' or 'Kindly remove your skateboard from my bidet.' He regards her as a harmless eccentric. Was it not she who washed his anorak, which had been doubling as a sledge for some months, without checking the pockets? You should see what a No 5 fast-coloured wash/spin can do to two satsumas and a Pontefract Cake. Any actor who's ever played Adrian Mole, Just William or Just Mole would suffice. As a last resort Patrick Moore in short trousers would do.

Various housekeepers to the aforementioned Munsters, all suffering the classic symptoms of severe shock. It's not just that the house is a bacon-free zone, full of telephones and weirdos (one of whom, Zelma, the wife's mother, wears a bag on her head in the mornings and rearranges utensil cupboards out of all recognition, whilst they've just slipped out for a sly gammon). Nor is it the fact that one child eats only peas and gravy, the other anything that hasn't been in the same room as gravy, the husband lives on herrings – probably with gravy – and the wife is allergic to bread, chocolate, cheese and housework. Ms M Poppins should not apply.

And, last but not pleased, Pushkin the agoraphobic mog, aged seventy in cat-years and purchased as a sop to Amy for her parents' heartless temerity in bringing a baby boy into the house to spoil her life, her liberty and apparently it wasn't fair either. Pushkin has allied herself to her mistress's cause by unerringly depositing her deposits on typewriter, vegetable rack and piano stool – which is quite a literary gag when you think about it. Pushkin will play herself.

References will be made at decidedly odd intervals to Les the Fireman (Wednesdays), Christine, the feather-duster-wielder (Tuesdays and Thursdays), David, the beloved soil expert (Fridays), Layla, secretary (most days) 'No, Miss Lipman's not home at the moment, can I lie *for* her?', and Esperanza, their delightful Colombian housekeeper who can't believe what she daily stumbles into. Just a run-of-the-mill, every day middle-class Still Life. By Salvador Dali.

Readers, this is the time to write to your bookseller, your MP and Mother Teresa of Calcutta to protest against the intrusion of this bizarre lifestyle on to your respectable bookshelves.

1

Domestos-city

The Door to my House is Always Open

The front door of my house is probably the costliest item in it. It's probably the costliest front door in North London, if not in the Northern hemisphere. Yet only a few months ago it was one of the least financially demanding items on which our lives ever hinged. Let me explain.

When my publisher Jeremy Robson made his tri-monthly call to discuss the states of both our lives, he managed to end the conversation with a sentence which chilled my plasma. 'So,' he said, with a cheery mixture of timidity and aggression, 'what's the new book going to be called?'

It was news to me that there was going to BE a book, since writing one is the second hardest thing I've ever been forced to do, and this is not the time to discuss childbirth.

Still, I'm a trained improviser and respond like whatsit's dogs – Anna Pavlova's – you know, she did ballet, desserts and dogs – to a challenge. I just open my mouth and provocation comes out like fumes from a Fiat. The next thing I know about it, somebody is reading me a quote from the *Sun* which came from almost anybody's lips but mine.

'Erm. It's going to be called *Holding Your Own*,' I said.

There was a pause and, I thought, a slightly embarrassed giggle.

'Well, maybe *Holding My Own* then? And on the cover I'll be holding out my arms and all my friends and associates will be standing on them. My arms I mean. Very small.'

I could tell by Jeremy's silence that he was totting up the cost of the trick photography. Another tack was called for.

'How's about you photograph me outside the phone box in the garden and we call it *I'm IN the Book*? Funny, yes?'

'Very funny,' said Jeremy. 'Er – how closely do you want to be associated with BT?'

If I'd had a drawing board I'd have gone straight back to it.

'Got it,' I eureka'd. 'We paint the front door like a *trompe l'œuil* and I wear a party dress and we call it *Thank You For Having Me*.'

'Er . . . yees,' said Jeremy, understanding as much of what I'd just said as you have. I was in my designer's hat and the brim was covering most of my brain.

'I'll ask Chris Clark to paint marble veins running through the door – he's a brilliant stage painter – and we can subtitle it *Maureen the same vein*, I yelled. ' "More in" – gettit? Ben Frow can make me a backless dress from this wonderful piece of mottled pink and blue chiffon he showed me once, and we'll have balloons and streamers and lilac wistaria in the same colours, then on the back we can have the same shot only I'll be leaving drunk as a skunk and–'

'Fine, it sounds – er – great,' said Jeremy.

'Lovely,' said Chris Clarke.

'When do I start?' said Ben Frow.

'Must remember to bring some film,' said Anthony Grant, photographer.

'I'll pick up the wistaria,' said Steve Ridgeway, the jacket designer.

'*WHOSE DOOR ARE YOU USING?*' said Jack Rosenthal, flattening himself protectively against his own.

Well, we talked about doing it in a studio like proper professionals, and I looked out for suitable front doors on my way to the swimming-pool and even contemplated ringing the doorbell of one particularly entrancing portal hung with claret clematis, and offering them a few readies. In my heart, however, I knew whose front door was about to be pillaged – the writing was on the door. After all, *How Was It For You?* featured my bathroom, *Something To Fall Back On*, my dining-room curtains – I was following a tradition as old as Prince Harry.

'It'll just be for a day, love. Then we'll have it painted back. Whatever colour you like.'

'I like it the colour it *is*,' he wailed. He likes a nice brown door, does Jack.

Two days before the shoot we had a dress rehearsal. Chris

Clarke, who'd been working on the door for several days, had painted seven or eight hardboard door samples, using all the pinks and blues in the scrap of fabric which Ben had left for him. The door was now sporting a deep blue undercoat and Steve Ridgeway was cutting out cardboard covers for the stained glass panels, which were also to be painted, and Madam was framed against the lintel wearing all she had of the halter neck – a small silk collar and the contents of a pin-cushion. Steve and Ben held up some plastic clematis, I smiled into the sunshine and Anthony Grant took the polaroids. 'OK. We have a cover.'

The next day, I was working at Elstree on the British Telecom 'Anniversary' advert. My main concern was my hair. Not only was it lying under Beattie's wig all day, but it was generally in revolt against the treatment, or lack of it, meted out to it all year. Carmen-rollered and lacquered for my one-woman show, *Re:Joyce*, every day and twice on Saturdays, brown in some places, grey and coarse in others and burnt brass in the places where the henna misfired, it had all the gloss and consistency of a bag of potting compost.

Robert came to my rescue – Robert being the exquisitely handsome Scots make-up artist who assists Lorna on the BT shoots. He promised to whiz round to me the following morning and reassemble my head. He arrived about midday and we agreed that the cut would be the thing and we'd paint the grey out later. I wonder if the public realizes how haphazard and home-spun most personal appearances are? Or is it just me? Do the other lady writers (and presumably Jeffrey Archer) have the services of John Frieda and Barbara Daly for their photographic shoots? Is Joan Collins to be found like me, scrabbling through sticky make-up bags in search of a stick of kohl which turns out to be stuck all over the inside of the bag? Suffice it to say Robert cut my hair beautifully, and with a good haircut everything else just falls into place. Like your face.

It was to be a late afternoon shoot, to give the impression of leaving a party at dusk. Ben arrived at three o'clock with the dress. It was a thing of great loveliness, clingy where it should cling and wide where it should hide. The young genius knows my body better than my osteopath does.

The doorbell – which by now was the only thing left on the door apart from cardboard, veins, stippling, spongeing, marble-izing, three balloons and a colourless glaze – rang. It was John Henderson, director of the television series *About Face*, calling to keep the appointment I'd forgotten to cancel, to discuss Series Two. He admired the new door and my backless dress rather quizzically, and asked who was having the party. Since John never drinks tea, or anything else as far as I can see, I couldn't stall him with a cuppa whilst I slipped into something with a back (and a bit more front), so I pushed him into Jack's study for a chat.

At 4.30 I excused myself again, took off the clothes I'd just put on for modesty's sake, and carefully painted my face to match the rest of me. Ben came back, Steve arrived replete with the plastic clematis and more balloons, and Anthony Grant zoomed into the driveway with lights and cameras ready for action.

Whereupon the heavens went black. Then they opened up, emptying fourteen thousand litres of baleful, hailful rain on our halter-necked shoot, halting any chances we ever had of shooting anything.

Anthony, undaunted, donned a kagoul and laid his cables through the front living-room window. The rest of us huddled indoors, whilst Amy, clutching a packet of henna, told us the exact shade of red she intended to dye her hair. Many cups of tea later, the skies cleared, we wiped down the door, and I stood shiveringly on the steps, improvising vivacity.

At which point a man arrived in a van carrying a crate of wine. It was my fee for writing an article on My Favourite Tipple. The 'vin driver' surveyed the scene before staggering through the door scattering balloons and streamers in his wake. 'I like your vine,' he said as I signed something. 'Oh, it's not real,' I smiled cheerily, 'it's just plastic. We stuck it on.' He looked at me and left.

'He said, "I like your *wine*", I think,' hissed Ben, as he left. We returned to the shoot. I smiled, I grinned, I looked meaningful, I drank fake champagne, I donned a party hat and blew a party blower. Then the sky blackened and it tossed it down again. Out of the blackness ran a small drenched figure in white carrying a cricket bag.

'We were rained off, Mod,' he mumbled. 'I scored nine. I'm wet – what are you doing?'

'Change your clothes and dry your hair,' I muttered without moving my lips or my vivacious position.

'S'all right, they'll dry on me.'

'Excuse me, Anthony, for a minute – I have to dry my son.'

I came back, wet, and somehow we did it. There were twenty-six mugs in the sink when everyone left, and I felt like one of them.

In the following days everyone who came to the house commented on the loveliness of the front door. Everyone except the door owner. Finally Les came round for his weekly handymanning, sighed, removed the cardboard and sanded all the paint down. 'What colour do you want it?' he asked. 'Same as before or different?

'Same' – 'Different,' said Jack and I, at the same time.

Les produced a chart.

'French Navy,' I said, 'with cream on the mouldings.' Jack looked mournfully at me. 'You'll love it, darling. It's smart.' I went out.

Les undercoated. ''S'funny,' he said. 'The paint's drying immediately. I don't understand it.'

'It looks a bit bright, Les.'

'Yeah. It's only the undercoat though.'

'Yeah. Bye, Les.'

I was out for most of the following day. When I arrived home it was to find Les putting the finishing touches to a door which was the colour of a packet of cornflour.

'I hate it.'

'I thought you would.'

The cream had run into the blue.

''S'funny,' said Les. 'The paint just sits on the surface like. . . .'

'Like paint on a glazed finish?'

'Yeah.'

'Yeah.'

I rang Chris Clarke, who explained that he'd explained to

me about the glaze and how the door would need a lot of work on it.

'Oh. Yeah, I remember now.'

Les went home. I said I'd think about it. I thought about it. The next day Layla phoned a French Polisher she knew. Paul. He came over.

'Yeah, I could do it. The door will have to be taken away and dipped in acid. It'll come up very nice.'

I swallowed. 'All right, Jack?' I said.

'Why can't you paint it brown?' said Jack for the seventeenth and final time.

'It's a good old wooden door,' I argued. 'It would look wonderful stripped and stained. It's probably mahogany.'

'The burglar alarm's in the door, you know, you'll have to ring George the burglar.' (He's our Cypriot burglar-alarm man, and not an easy chap to pin down.)

I rang him. 'He can come on Tuesday,' I told Paul. Paul consulted his diary. 'Yeah. Should be all right.'

On Monday Paul rang to say the people with the acid bath could only do it on Friday.

I rang George. He could only do it Tuesday.

I rang Paul. Paul rang another firm. They rang me. They'd pick it up tomorrow.

When I got up in the morning the door had gone. We all wore a lot of woollies, through a somewhat breezy day.

George arrived back at 3.30 to re-fix the alarm. He waited. By 5.30 the door was still not back. George left for his next appointment.

At 6 o'clock the door came back, looking bleached but far from perfect. The good old wood turned out to be a pine surround, one fruitwood panel, two old planks and a piece of hardboard. Jack did not say 'I told you so'.

Paul arrived Friday and so did the first firm of strippers, whom he'd forgotten to cancel.

'Whoever did this has got no bloody idea,' said the stripper. 'How much did this cowboy charge you, eh?'

Paul stripped the rest of the paint off by hand and started patching up the cracks and holes with filler. It took most of the day. And the next day.

A few days later he came back and started staining the

wood. 'These mouldings are in terrible shape,' he said. 'If I were you I'd have new mouldings made.'

We had new mouldings made.

A week later Paul returned with the new mouldings and continued staining. He brought his son Duran, aged seven, with whom I immediately fell in love. He is solemn and his straight blond hair is cut straight round like a pudding basin.

He wandered into the room where I was pretending to write. I work with Radio 2 on. 'Would you like a coke?' I asked.

'No, thank you,' he said. 'Do you have any Pavarotti records?' I was hooked. His dad paints and stains. Duran and I talked.

'You will bring him with you next time, won't you?' I asked anxiously.

'Yeah,' says Paul. 'Looking better, isn't it? You know the stained glass is cracked, don't you?'

'Yeah.' I look up 'Stained Glass' in the Yellow Pages.

He finished staining and varnishing. The next time he called and replaced the letter box and house numbers. Once they were screwed back the door began to look lovely.

Jack said, 'The brass bits should have been polished before they were screwed back.'

Paul unscrewed them. Jack and Duran polished the door furniture. Paul replaced them. I watched.

Then, out of the blue, a strange red-faced man in a back-pack wandered down the pathway and stood in front of the door. He surveyed it for a while. Jack and I surveyed his surveillance from behind the wooden blinds.

'What's going on with this door, then? Eh? One minute it's brown, the next minute it's mauve, then it's blue, then it's nothing. What is it now, eh?'

Paul continued varnishing and said, 'I'm varnishing it now.'

'Oh yes,' the man droned, 'very nice. Better, much better. I couldn't understand what was going on. One minute it was brown, then it was blue, I thought, whatever next? Eh? But this is it, is it? This is how it's going to be, is it?'

'Er, yes,' Paul reiterated, varnishing away.

'Very nice. Yes.' He stood back. 'I like it. Better, much

better.' He paused. 'I couldn't understand it. Brown, then blue, then something else. Whatever next I thought. Eh?'

Jack and I got a serious attack of the giggles. We slid down the study wall and heaved silently. With the occasional squeak. 'Right, then,' said Paul, 'best get on.'

'I'll say,' said our over-interested party. 'Me, too.' He took a step backwards and returned. 'Friend of mine. Now, he's got a door. Now, that's what I call a door. Stained glass! Stained glass! From top to bottom. Top and bottom. All glass. All stained. Beautiful. Mind you, this one looks a lot better now. I thought to myself, "Hello," I thought, "what's it going to be today?" '

I left them to it. I don't know how Paul got rid of him and finished the finish as t'were, but he did. All right, so he varnished over the spy-hole. What the hell? You can only see who's out there if they're exactly five foot one anyway.

So folks, we have a nice front door. And a cover. Like I said, it cost a mere arm and a mere leg and several weeks of several people's lives. Still, at least it's framed.

P.S. The lower door panel has now cracked straight across in two places. Paul says it's shrinking and we'll have to wait till it stops shrinking before we re-fill and re-stain it. The way I look at it, if the cat diets, in a couple of weeks she'll have a built-in cat-flap. Every cloud . . .

The Battle of What Loo

As Jack quietly buffed a rhino, I asked him, 'Have I done the toilets?'

He looked up as only he or the late Eric Morecambe *could* look up, and said, 'Done what in the toilets?'

'Written about them,' I replied.

'No, love,' he said, breathing on to a bronze flank-fold, 'but I expect you will.'

As I headed fools-capwards, I thought I heard someone mutter, 'She's scraping the bottom of the b—,' but I didn't catch whether it was Jack or his little endangered friend.

I must say, for a convenience item, your average lavatory leaves a fair amount to be desired. Travelling around the country recently, I was constantly struck by the mechanization which has gone on behind my back, so to speak. First, there's the unspeakable horror of the new super-loo, that giant padlock in the street which locks secretly behind you and relentlessly plays *Raindrops Keep Falling On My Head* while you attempt to wee to the beat, and boils its own walls after you've escaped. Just.

Then there's the new jumbo-sized toilet-roll dispenser. A plastic disc so jam-packed with the legendary stuff that only one sheet can be prised from it, and any attempt to remove more results in your hand being bitten by a set of serrated dentures.

I see they've left the large gaps under the door and walls, though. For what purpose, limbo dancing not being what it was in legendary days, I fail completely to grasp. I'm always convinced that the moment I'm ensconced in what the world of Laboratory Testing calls 'mid-stream', an arm and hand will appear underneath, snatch my handbag and disappear for ever as I struggle with my jumpsuit and my tights. Of

course, if there were a place to put one's handbag other than
on the floor or the top of the cistern, the thieving arm would
be waggling around for long enough to stamp on it and pinch
its watch.

'Kindly wash your hands,' patronizes the sign on the door.
It should add, 'And kindly reserve half an hour for them
to dry.' This snide aside refers to the introduction of the
automatic drying machine which has taken the place of the
now defunct, antiquarian and labour-consuming device we
affectionately called 'a towel'. In fairness, the machine *is*
probably more hygienic than the towel. It requires no laun-
dering and never needs replacing. It does however, have two
major disadvantages. One is that it can't, won't and doesn't
dry a human hand. Certainly not in less than five minutes,
which feel like five hours when your husband/lover has kept
the waiter waiting, notebook in hand, because you said, 'Back
in two shakes.' Two, the machine is generally out of order,
both before and after you've kicked it, and you end up drying
your hands on the carpet, the doily under the pot-pourri
bowl, your Thai silk cami-knickers or the lavatory attendant.

I mustn't forget the other thrilling part of public toiletries –
the door which *nearly* locks. The scenario here is that the
lock slides round to say 'AGED' and 'VAC', which you assume
means 'safe for a while'. Big mistake. No sooner have you let
it all hang out than the door is pushed sharply inwards,
causing you to shout in a hysterical soprano, 'Sorry! Someone
in here! Won't be long. Sorry!' while simultaneously shooting
your foot up against the incoming door, crashing your coccyx
into the toilet rim and peeing on your other foot.

Toilets terrified me in childhood. Particularly scaring were
those tiny replicas of grown-up bowls, specially reserved for
primary schools. They were meant to be comforting, but
they didn't fool me for a second. I knew, as sure as I knew
sherbet-dip cost tuppence ha'penny, that they still had a
climbing spider in the bowl. Just a smaller spider, that was
all.

It was in these tiny toilets that the really serious bullying
went on. Not to mention those other great British sports.
'You show me yours and I'll show you mine' and fart-
lighting. I was so scared of the big girls in those loos that I

rarely went in them, and thus had to run home at four o'clock with clenched knees. We had a storm porch (there's posh) in Northfield Road, outside our front door, and on one such occasion I remember standing there for an outrageously long time, while my mother took her time coming to the door. When she finally arrived the relief was too much for me and she was confronted by her daughter standing damply in what passed for a steam cabinet.

My paternal grandmother had an outside toilet. I can see it now. Neat squares of newspaper hanging on a string while the wind whistled through your navy knickers. The mad scurry past the bogeyman, back to the scullery to wash your hands in the big, old sink, and the inevitability of your mother's, 'Did you wash your hands?' in front of a roomful of relatives, who now knew exactly where you'd been and why. Red-faced by the grate, to sulk over a handful of coloured spills ... Ey-up! You can almost hear the Hovis music.

Finally, I shall cite body stockings without snap-crotches, leotards, body stockings *with* snap-crotches when you're short sighted, all-in-one sodding jumpsuits and the sort of padding I sport when playing sixty-five-year-old grand-mothers in telephone commercials or Margaret Thatcher. All are arch-enemies of the conventional tinkle.

One fond memory. A longish car journey with Jack and Amy, then a recently toilet-trained toddler. At her per-emptory request we stopped in a lay-by and her doting dad volunteered to do the grid watering. Through the window, I watched him hold her out before him as she none-too-deftly performed both over the grid and her father's shoes. Then, through misty orbs, I watched him do the most natural act. He shook her. Just a few times. Carefully. For all the world as if she were an extension of himself, which, of course, she was.

Actually I've just had a new downstairs lavatory installed chez Rosenthal. It was no trouble. The new built-in cup-boards went in easily and came out just as easily once we'd realized you had to crouch down on all fours to open them. We've come to love the fact that the sink is almost large enough to hold one piece of hotel soap, and the dried-blood shade I chose for the paintwork really does grow on you. After a while.

When we bought the house six years ago, my mother's only comment was, 'It's got no downstairs toilet. What if someone with colitis comes to visit?' At the time this didn't seem too much of a problem, and we've managed to survive ever since on the two upstairs toilets and to keep a colitis-free visitors' book.

However, the wedge-shape under the stairs containing three bicycles, one trampoline, five roller-skates (assorted sizes), a plastic bag full of plastic bags, one-and-a-half punctured bags of cat-litter and a shopper on wheel (sic) was obviously in desperate need of a transformation scene. Indeed, the words 'Please let me become a toilet' were the understair wedge equivalent of 'I must go to Moscow' in a Chekhov play.

Well, now it's done. Its window has a posh venetian blind and I've learned to unlock it through a series of patient lectures and several on-site demonstrations from my husband, who pretends to understand these things. There is now a smart pinch-pleated curtain where the built-in cupboards used to be, and behind it, are a trampoline, five roller-skates, a plastic bag full of plastic bags etc etc ('Where are the bikes?' I hear you ponder. 'Everywhere,' I hear me reply.) We have a folding door with brass knob, a mahogany seat and pipework discreetly covered to make it flush – no, not that kind of flush – with the dried-blood walls. All that was completed two months ago. Since then I've continued, through force of habit, to use the upstairs toilets and only ever think of the downstairs one when passing the hardware store, when I think, 'I must buy a toilet-roll dispenser.'

The only problem now is the flooring. Something has to be done. Let's face it, there's no pleasure in using a room where the eye and the feet are met by torn, ancient, Araldited, brick-look lino, interspersed with concrete screed and bits of mock-marble. All in the space of four-foot-square(ish). Something has indeed to be done. But what? The wedge leads into the hall, the hall has an intricate parquet floor so old, so neglected, and so squeegee'd and Flashed by my cleaning lady that what used to be its grain is now its open fretwork. To rip it up and start again means having men in, and men in means dust, and dust means conjunctivitis and conjunctivitis means no mascara and no mascara means 'TV Jewish Mother Checks Incognito into Cosmetic Clinic'.

Jack's all in favour of Amtico-ing the lot – porches, loo, et 'hall – with the black-and-white tiled Stately Home look. (His aristocratic background in Cheetham Hill, Manchester 8, rearing its crested head again.) Certainly, the Amtico random-plank wood-look in my kitchen has worked a treat. In fact, our Christine, who has been mopping it for five years, only realized last week that it wasn't wood. But to cover oak parquet with a man-made fibre would hurt, wooden it? Loyd Grossman would call round and sneer in his Transylvanian accent. It's not worth it.

'Carpet it!' says Zelma, the Oracle. 'You can't beat a nice carpet. Patterned so's it won't show anything. Fitted right through. It's warm, it's practical and, above all, you can Hoover it every day.'

For some reason this doesn't thrill me as it thrills her, although in my deepest heart I know she's right.

Jack's doubts go even deeper. When challenged, he prevaricates. 'It's not in the style of the house ... It won't match the stair carpet ... It's a crime to cover parquet' (though not with vinyl tiles, apparently, be they black and white or taupe and bleedin' tartan). It was obvious what a doting father's objection was to a carpeted hall. Well, it was to me. Number One Son, destined to lead the England team out in their MCC whites or his Manchester United strip (notwithstanding the sudden groin strain if he doesn't score immediately), was the issue. How was the lad to practise his impeccable ball-sense on an 80/20 wool-mix twist-pile and tread-air underlay with as much bounce as Duncan Goodhew's hair? It was a serious consideration. We return to Square(ish) One.

Tiles. *Real* tiles are a thing of beauty nowadays. Works of art. They're cool in summer and ... er ... cooler still in winter. Balls bounce on them. Squeegee mops rinse them. You can break almost anything you drop on them, including the fragile joints of elderly visitors racing frenetically on their colitic way to your new downstairs toilet. Feeling mildly excited, I popped round to the local 'Tile of Two Cities' and returned with twelve enormous slabs of tiny tile samples stuck on hardboard. Jack points out to me that they all look like the inside of a swimming pool. I scoff scornfully and remind him of the beauty of small mosaic tiles laid in a traditional pattern. He turns over the samples to reveal labels which say: 'Suitable for any kind of swimming pool or garden pond.' I ponder that perhaps if Number One Son took up scuba-diving I could tile the hall floor – and walls – and please everybody.

The best bit is when you ring the flooring people for the estimate. The advert reads: 'Free estimates given. No waiting. We call and measure at your convenience.' Which, in my case, is more or less where it's at. You call them and have an animated chat with their musical answering-machine. You make an appointment for them to come and measure up. Three or four appointments later, they come at a time roughly similar to the one you arranged, or at least in the same month, and it happily coincides with the day you're not in Madagascar. They measure up, they have a cuppa and a chat and another cuppa, they show you their wares, and photos of their children, you express interest and wave them off with a cheery 'We look forward to hearing from you Tuesday, then!' And the rest is silence. A silence that implies their flooring advert was a cover for a sophisticated form of Market Research into house-measurements and that you'll end up as nothing more than a statistic in a floppy-disc on an obsolete Apple in Anstey Cuckfield.

Now, according to an article I have in front of me, a certain Professor Rudi van Wahrenz, a doctor of Behavioural Psychology, believes that violence on the football field, dizziness in the office, and even romantic feelings in the bedroom are caused by the surfaces on which we stand. His study on 'Surface Psychosis' shows that astro-turf calms soccer hooligans, thick-pile carpet imparts a womb-like feeling to the office, and marble flooring in shopping centres gives women in high heels panic-attacks. Apparently, bizarre behaviour can be witnessed in one Milan shopping centre where people start spinning round in different directions. The reason is there's a mosaic of a bull on the floor. And tradition has it that if you spin on a bull's testicles you will become fertile. (If you're a cow, of course, you'll just be disappointed, which may explain mad cow disease.)

One might presume, therefore, that my patchwork thinking may be entirely due to my patchwork flooring. That the reason for my lack of organization lies beneath my soles. My dithering about is surface-linked and my inability to finish what I've started and never reach a real conclusion is, well – well grounded, really. Or is it just a load of old bull?

I've never known a good First Night not to come out of an appalling mess of a dress rehearsal; the best holidays follow an insane, last-minute, hysterical departure; and the best parties are impromptu muck-ins. Still, as Mandy Rice-Davies is wont to say, 'I would say that, wouldn't I?'

PS George the Irish builder and I took a van ride to the tile shop to finish off the bathroom with a set of terracotta tiles. On the way he said 'I'm terrible at maths. What's nine feet in inches?'

'Erm ...' I mumbled (I got 8 per cent for my maths 'O' level.) 'Well, erm ... nine tens are ninety ... so ... er ... nine twos are ...' Much finger work, then, triumphantly, '108 inches!'

'A hundred and eight inches,' he said ruminatively, 'and what would that be in inches?'

If I wasn't violently opposed to prejudicial humour, I would describe that as an Irish joke.

And to finish, an *ablution* joke:

There's a nun in the bath. Suddenly there's a knock at the door and a man's voice says: 'Blind man.' The nun leaps out of the bath and opens the door, saying 'Come in dear man, come in.'

'Nice boobs,' says the man, 'now, where do you want the blind?'

Pass-over the Joint, Please

'Don't worry about a thing, darling,' I assured my hospital-bound spouse. 'Yvonne and I will manage everything. The house will manage without you, I promise.' Little did I know the house was listening.

He looked sweet, propped up in his narrow bed waiting for his hip operation, and I could tell that the worry-lines on his forehead were more to do with what he'd left behind than what he faced ahead.

I ran down the six flights of steps to the door of the hospital and made a bargain with my legs as they moved so easily up and down. 'I'm going to walk up these six flights every time I visit instead of using the lift,' I vowed. That way I'd be sharing the leg-ache. It was a decision I came to regret but never to abandon, even when after leaving three vital items in the car, I arrived the last time on all fours grabbing at nurses' ankles and gasping for an oxygen cylinder.

During the two weeks of post-operative care I cheered Jack up with tales of how well the house was running without him. It was, of course, a lie. It began the minute I got home from the hospital. On walking out of my walk-in cupboard, I closed the door behind me and noticed that the doorknob was still in my hand. This would have been fine except that I was now in the bathroom – where the toilet had packed in doing the one thing you most want a toilet to do – flush – and instead was making a wheezy, asthmatic sound reminiscent of me on the fifth floor hospital landing. Almost simultaneously, the dishwasher died of an illness known to service engineers as 'built-in obsolescence' (Rest in Pieces).

Then suddenly it came to pass that it was Passover. The plan was that we would share the ceremony and the dinner with our friends, the Shindlers, and I was to cook the lamb and the roasties and take them over early evening.

I looked at the cooked shoulder of lamb and realized it had shrunk to the size of an elbow of vole. Hastily, I left our then housekeeper Yvonne a note saying: 'Cook another one, please, and we'll take them both. For fear.' I then left the house to go hospital-visiting (or peak-scaling, depending on your point of view), where the patient was making dazzling progress for someone trapped in a hothouse filled with rotting fruit and asphyxiating foliage.

When I got home I felt something was missing. Jack's car was missing. So was Yvonne. The children were in the house, warming up the TV for *Neighbours*, having got in through the OPEN back door. I remained calm – and headed for the kitchen to look at the lamb. The oven was emptier than an NHS deposit account. I still remained calm. 'Where's me meat?' I inquired calmly.

The children looked sideways from Ramsay Street. 'What?'

'I said, "*Where's me meat?*" ' This time a little louder.

They turned back to the real domestic tragedy and ignored the fictional one.

'*Where's me meat?*' I shrieked at the cat, lying somewhat obscenely across the chopping board in search of placid wasps. Before she could confess, the phone rang – surely my poor, captive housekeeper, gagged and bound with a well-cooked roast potato in each ear. I snatched the receiver and bellowed, 'Where's me meat?'

The man at the other end sounded puzzled. 'I beg your pardon,' he stammered, 'I think we must have a crossed line. This is Peter Hayward of the *Sunday Telegraph*, I wanted to ask you if you'd write an article on ...'

'Certainly I will. I'll write a novelette if you tell me what you've done with my frigging meat!' He rang off.

'What we're dealing with here,' I told the children, 'is a very unusual burglar. He leaves the Rosenthal heirlooms and steals a housekeeper and two shoulders of lamb.' Sex starved, in one sense of both words.

It all came out right in the end, of course. Yvonne returned, breathless. At 3 pm she'd gone to check the lamb and found it sitting there as pink and chilled as it had been an hour and

a half before when she'd put it in. It was practically bleating!
Rosemary's baby – with real rosemary! The disintegrating
domestic scenario continued. It was as plain as the face
around my nose. The oven loved Jack. The oven missed
Jack's tender, loving ministrations with fish and grill pan.
And eventually the oven had had a breakdown and cracked
its little thermostat. Pausing only to kick it, Yvonne had
bundled spuds for nine and lambs in assorted states of cook-
ability into the car and thrust them into the Shindlers' gas
oven. Ten Brownie points and a clove of garlic for initiative!

The lamb was still cooking when we hit the Shindlers. It'd
been in and out more times than the Kray Twins and was
beginning to look institutionalized. Finally it came out of the
oven of its own volition and baa-ed, 'I've had it – it's hell in
there,' and Colin carved it while I covered both eyes with a
sheet of Matzo.

It was, of course, a Miracle. The meat was perfect! Ah, all
right then, the spuds were on the crunchy side – well, let's
face it, they were guerrilla ammunition – but the lamb . . .
you couldn't fault. Agneau what I mean?

So. Remember: the Lipman way to perfect roast lamb. 1
Pre-cook joint in electric oven – $1\frac{1}{2}$ hours. 2 Leave in cold
oven – 2 hours. 3 Re-ignite oven. 4 Blow out after 20 minutes.
5 Carry joint through pouring rain – 15 minutes. 6 Stick into
warmish gas oven – several more hours. Carve and serve.
Voilà!

I could tell Jack was feeling better. He'd begun to wax
lyrical about the nurses, one in particular. Kept telling me
how wonderful they were and how hard they all worked. I
just sat there puffing and serving out leftover lamb, and the
evening just . . . well, passed over, really.

When I drove him home on crutches, two pillows and
black plastic bin-liner to assist the sliding-in-car process, he
gazed at London like a man who'd spent six years in Alcatraz.
Or Brent Cross. 'It's so . . . so . . . WONDERFUL, isn't it? It's
so bloody wonderful.' I showed him the house. I showed the
house him. They both sighed and gazed at each other like
stark-lost lovers. And, triumphantly, of its own accord, the
toilet flushed.

Salmon Chanted Evening

I gave a dinner party last week. Pause for effect. Now, those of you who know me will be picking themselves up off the parquet and thumbing through their 1982 diaries in search of my last one, and the other twelve will be saying 'How does this affect the price of liverwurst in Cirencester?'

It was a fairly impromptu affair. So much so that at least three of the guests didn't realize they'd been invited, and didn't turn up. 'But I thought you were ringing back to confirm!' said a flustered one when I phoned just as he was welcoming guests at his own front door. 'Oh, I thought *you* were!' I laughed. 'No, honestly, it's my fault, don't worry, some other time, I'll ring you.' But don't hold your breath, I nearly added under mine. The second call unearthed a man just about to take his mother to see *Hamlet* at the National. Now, I get exasperated with *my* mother often enough, particularly when I'm up to my armpits in dinner-party and she's up to hers in my tights drawer, but I'd never dream of treating her *that* badly!

Suddenly the fresh salmon looked like Orca the Whale and the potatoes could have fed the extras in *The Last Emperor*. Jack had cooked the salmon, so everyone but he pronounced it perfect. Friend Astrid had brought her cucumber in yoghurt, and the pudding was a triumph. In honour of Astrid's father, who's Norwegian, I had prepared 'Norwegian Bombe'. It took me a while to prepare because I'm recipe-blind. I can look at a list of ingredients for twenty-five minutes and get no further than 'Grease an eight-inch pie-dish'. This requires another twenty-five minutes' searching for a tape to measure the dish and a further fifteen to fathom whether it's the outside or the inside you grease. Anyway, the 'Norwegian Bombe' was pronounced first-rate.

'Are those currants?' inquired Peg, Astrid's mum, who's a foodaholic from Massachusetts.

'No, no currants in it.' I was on fairly sure ground here because if the recipe had said currants I'd have had to go out and pick 'em, this not being a currant-conserving kitchen.

'Well, what the hell are they, then?' demanded Peg, picking a few dozen out of her dental-work.

'I'll get the recipe.' The book opened naturally at the page, owing to the black, sticky wodge of food I'd left in it. 'There you are. No currants. Just butter and sugar and cream and ... oh, yes! Mincemeat!'

As six mouths mouthed 'Mincemeat!!' in unison, I observed that the recipe I'd followed was on the wrong side of the page – and far from being 'Norwegian Bombe' (very far, in fact), was 'Anzac Christmas Pudding'. About 11,000 miles far, as it happens. So, Australia – Norway – It's all the same to someone whose geography teacher had no roof to her mouth.

Still, a good smirk was had by all, and at 2 am the Bombe disposal squad began picking over the salmon whilst returning what looked like the set of *Cats* into a passable version of my kitchen.

The following morning, my mother was flying to Geneva. I ordered a taxi to take her to Victoria, then spent the rest of the morning cancelling the second cab she'd booked in case the first one didn't turn up. Meanwhile, I dictated some letters into the tape-recorder. 'Dear Miss Littman,' said one I had received, scribbled on lined paper, 'for my class project we can write about a museum or a prominent Jew. I chose the Jew. I have chosen you.' Presumably he thought I tend to make an exhibition of myself. Later I realized it said a *Muslim* or a Jew. Just as well I re-read it before someone accused me of blasphemy against the V & A.

I took out the Carmen rollers, phoned a girlfriend with problems, waved my mother off, defrosted some herrings and dressed for three functions on the same day, all in one fell swoop. Eat your heart out, jugglers everywhere (and those who do that boring thing with Indian Clubs, in particular).

The first function was a charity luncheon. On the way I

wrote my speech – a fact which gave the committee-member who drove me there more terror than *Nightmare on Elm Street*. I was wearing my new outfit, a fine wool dress and coat, sort of *Breakfast at Tiffany's* – or, in my case, *Brunch at Garfunkel's* – in lilac and black, and clutching my black cloak. The Audrey-Hepburn-Meets-Agnes-Moorehead look. I began my speech by asking the whole audience to get it out of their systems by saying together, 'Oooh, doesn't she look thinner in real life!' This stops the hissing of the said sentence throughout the first ten minutes. (There's a lovely story of the sister of Gladys Cooper giving up the stage in despair because she was convinced the audience always hissed when she came on. In fact, what she always heard was 'ThatsGladysCooperssisterthatsGladysCooperssister . . .')

Incidentally, the lunch was fresh salmon. I vaguely began to feel as though I was swimming upstream.

Afterwards, I headed straight to my son's school for his parent-teacher afternoon. In the car I took off the coat and put on the black cloak. Catch me looking like someone who's just spoken at a luncheon and not like a proper mother! We queued up to see the individual teachers. At both our children's schools this can take up to two hours – two and a half if you get a really chatty teacher who can't quite place your child but loved the last show you did.

Anyroad up, the boy was doing fine, particularly at anything he enjoyed doing. (Funny, that.) I told his Latin teacher that I had to stop him conjugating under the bedclothes by torchlight. He said he wasn't a bit surprised! It was probably his age. We scurried back to the car, had a quick change of coat and earrings and a packet of crisps (salmon-flavoured?) and tottered off to our third and final gig, the First Night of a West End play . . . with attendant First Night audience – you know, witches and warlocks and weirdos – and that was only the critics.

In the foyer, the Press had gathered. What's the collective noun for the Press – a 'rabble', a 'goggle', a 'fleet', perhaps a 'bevy' of photographers? And, for once in my life, I didn't feel like beaming good-naturedly only to see my beloved dress and most of my back fillings, tongue and uvula unamusingly captioned in the Sunday 'Where are they now?' section.

Later, we drove to the First Night party. It was a jubilant affair and – as you've guessed – Jack and I ate our fresh salmon with alacrity . . . which is an unusual way to serve it, when you think about it.

The next night we decided to have another dinner-party. Himself and me, a mug of tea, beans on toast and the BBC.

And maybe just a blob of Hellman's for the withdrawal symptoms.

How Ya Gonna Keep 'Em Down In Paris – After They've Seen The Farm?

I've sent my mother to a health farm. Against her will, of course. 'What will I do there? I won't know anybody. Will they make me swim? Should you have massages if you've got varicose veins? I'll miss all what's going on at your house. Who'll give your father his pills?'

Finally we packed her protestingly on to the 4.15 pm to Newbury, assuring her repeatedly that a hot jalopy would whisk her to the waiting luxury of Inglewood Health Hydro. We then returned home, to wait for the phone to explode.

Dad was finding it difficult to understand the whole concept of a health farm. 'What's wrong with her health?' he wanted to know.

'Well,' I explained, 'her blood pressure's high but it's not just that. She'll have a rest and massage and fresh air and, well – it'll do her good . . .'

'Yes, but where does she sleep?' he wanted to know. 'When she's not on the farm?'

I realized in a blinding flash that I now had to abolish all thoughts of cows and pigs – *particularly* pigs – from his mind and lean heavily on the hotel side of the proceedings. The *all-female* side.

By 6 am Monday I'd lost a bit of my assurance. I cast my mind back to my last trip to Inglewood. Sharing a moist jacuzzi with my fellow flabbies, being pummelled by Tommy, the ex-boxer masseur, aerobicking myself into a sweaty, leotarded heap. How could I do this to my own flesh and blood pressure? Matricide, thy name is Maureen. Inexorably my mind raced towards the possibility of springing her through the sauna roof. Should I look up the SAS in Yellow Pages?

The phone rang. Excitedly. I grabbed it. It was she. In a

state. 'Well. I can't believe it. Maureen. IT IS... Well. What can I say? IT IS ... Well. I've never known anything like it. IT IS ... unbelievable!'

'You like it, then?'

'Like it? Are you mad? Like it?? It's the most ... It's like ... It's – well – it beats Fuengirola into a cocked hat!'

I breathed again for the first time in many minutes. Greater praise hath no resort, healthy or otherwise in Zelma's estimation, than to reduce the Costa del Sol to half-cock.

'So what have you done?' I asked.

'Done? I've not stopped talking since I got here. I know everyone's life story – ooh, I love it! It's so *palatial!* And the food – '

'What diet are you on?'

'*Diet!!!* They said I could fast, or go on fruit, or go on the light diet or whatever I like – '

'So what did you choose?'

'I went on the *heavy* diet. Ooooh, it's fabulous! The salad stuffs and the tongue – well – I've not stopped eating and talking. Ooooh, there's some *lovely* people here. There's a lovely couple from Wales with their daughter. She's only twenty-two and she's had glandular fever ...'

'Yes, Mother, but what treatments have you had?'

'*Treatments?!* Oh, well. I had a massage – oooh, isn't it wonderful? I don't know how I've managed to go all those years without having one. And I've had a G5 and a peat bath. I'm just in my room now but I can't wait to go downstairs again. Ooooh, Maureen, I absolutely love it! I could stay here for ever. How's the kids?'

'Fine. Your husband's fine too.' I waited for her to say 'Who?' then left her to it.

The following day I went out shopping. For a commercial. And what was I playing? A sixty-five-year-old Jewish Grand Momma. And what did that entail buying? Knitted suits, sensible court shoes, Thatcher handbags, firm-control corselettes, support stockings, blue-grey wig, and glasses. I came back more than a little depressed by the sight of myself in so much Crimplene in so many two-way mirrors. Meanwhile, somewhere in Berkshire the prototype was phoning in with details of *her* day.

'Well, I'm still *loving* it. I've just had my yoga class. I'm wearing your brown tracksuit. I look marvellous in it. I might go out for a bike ride with some of the girls in a bit.'

Standing in front of the long mirror in a simple emerald and black jersey dress with neck bow and brooch, rehearsing my lines in a querulous mezzo, I told her to be careful for God's sake, she wasn't as young as she felt.

'I feel bloody marvellous, love. I've seen every bedroom here. They all know how much I love it. I had the two cleaners in here this morning, sitting on my bed telling me everything. They've shown me all the rooms. Ooh, mine's the nicest one I've seen.'

So there we are. Role reversal run riot. I'm thinking of knitting socks on four needles in front of the telly. Playing maybe a little bridge ... which reminds me, my bridge-work's beginning to loosen up nicely, a single hair has shot out of what I thought was a beauty spot, and I'm wearing one pair of glasses to look for the other. I've doled out braised steak and apple pie to the family. Washed up in rubber gloves and taken a Bisodol. I'll probably watch the ten o'clock news, rub some cream on my neck and turn in with a cup of tea and a Ruth Rendell.

While somewhere in leafy Kintbury a tracksuited tearaway with clear unspectacled eyes and all her own teeth is probably, even as we speak, abseiling through the hills of Berkshire with a Sony Walkman, a hip-flask of Pina Colada and a grin from here to Humberside. Listen – as long as you've got your health ...

PS She's home. One pound lighter with raised blood pressure, no doubt caused by over-excitement and the thought of coming back. Her new energy is terrifying. My cupboards have been totally reorganized. I can no longer find the cutlery drawer. Meatballs are simmering in the oven, iced buns are in an airtight tin and the new mother's help's been given a guided tour of the insides of every labour-saving machine in the house. I'm sitting quietly in my room listening to my heart pound – the child becoming farther from the mum ...

★

It was over a year later that Nigel Foster of J Walter Thompson told me that the next BT commercial would be set in Paris. Naturellement, I was thrilled and immediately invited my mother. Well! Some people take their lover to Paris ... I take my mother.

The film was shot half-way up the Eiffel Tower, just Zelma and me, a crew and several hundred English schoolkids shouting for Beattie, with the freezing French wind playing havoc with my padded underwear. The lingerie capital of the Western world and I'm in a vast sponge leotard which makes movement a miracle and peeing out of the question.

On the second day, when le temps fait beau, we set up camera in a park in the beautiful Place de Voges. This elegant square of arched houses which used to house Napoleon's horses now played host to Beattie and Harry, Bernadette and Claude, the writer/director, Richard Phillips, and sundry assorted technicians and crew. And, of course, to Zelma who, bless her, with Paris at her fingertips, chose to watch every foot of film that was tediously shot and reshot. Somewhere in the vaults of J Walter Thompson's cellar lie two minutes of film composed entirely of my mother sitting on a park bench in intense concentration, cleaning a spot from her mackintosh with a wetted hanky. It's the world's longest single take.

Finally, of course, she got into the commercial. Day Three and we're in a café in the Jewish quarter, the French and the English couples getting to know each other, and when Beattie leans forward to introduce herself, there in the background is Beattie's real mother, looking twenty years younger than her stage daughter and blithely trying to remember the director's instructions – 'For the twenty-second time, Zelma, *don't* look into the camera. Action.' And there she was. Immortalized at last on celluloid.

We spent the last day sightseeing in the magnificent Museum d'Orsay, cruising the Seine and spending our last francs on anything and everything. Paris is full of enchantment and one day, *one day*, I may just see it with my lover – let's face it, he's the only man who'd understand that his mother-in-law would be in the next-door room, if not sitting on the bed.

PS I phoned her after the commercial had been aired to see
if she'd seen it.

'Ye-es. It was on the other night. Isn't it a shame?'

'Isn't what a shame?' (I knew.)

'If your Harry had just leaned back a little bit you'd have
seen ever so much more of me than you did!'

Examination Unnerves

I think we're through the worst of the exams now. One more week and life should be back to normal, and those of you who've read the Lipman Diaries before will know how normal that is.

An excerpt from June 1988 read:

'The pre-match tension has been mounting for weeks, as both children approached their end-of-term exams. Whey-faced, they've haunted their rooms all evening long – emerging only for testing times. Testing for us, I mean.

'"Er, how does the act of fertilization take place?" I ask.

'"It doesn't start there – you have to start with Pollination."

'"Yes, but what if they phrase the question differently – you have to know the whole –" As I'm questioning and she's groping for words like stigma and stalk, I realize that I'm stalking her for what she *doesn't* know, not encouraging what she does.'

'Course, the difference these days is the fact that, as a mother, I'm testing *anything* except the consistency of a sponge cake. Both Jack and I agree that no one at home showed much interest in *our* educational progress, for better or worse. I mean, a good report meant the difference between a pleasant tea with your face in your *Bunty* and the same pleasant tea with the air throbbing with 'Just you wait till your father gets home' and smirks over the spaghetti hoops from the brilliant brother.

Occasionally, my academic prowess got a universal disclaimer as in: 'This is not a good report. Far too much time is being taken up showing-off and trying to create an impression. She has ability but she is wasting it in silliness.' To pre-empt the throbbing on such occasions, I tended to take the law into my own feet and stamp the whole bloody report into the nearest bike track – or worse.

Of course, PTA meetings didn't really exist on account the Ps and the Ts rarely Associated. We had a Founders' Day, but that was more on the lines of flowered hats, resonant versions of 'For Those in Peril on the Sea', and one piece of your neatest work on the Biology Room wall. Teachers tended to vanish into stationery cupboards, or spontaneously implode for all I know, at the approach of a Parent. Nowadays we queue up for hours for a little chat with Rog the Rugby and Del the Classics on the further adventures of Rosenthal Junior on the pitch or in Academia, clutching a reporter's notebook for fear we forget his negative qualities on the way home. I shudder to admit it, but we've even moved his Barmitzvah 'cos it clashes with his common entrance. Not perhaps a problem with which Moses' mother had to contend.

I mean, is it because we fear for their joblessness that we've become so obsessed with their education? I was a deeply mediocre student. So was Jack, he tells me, though I think the gentleman doth protest too much. It was only when the Sixth Form loomed large and the subjects grew more subjective that the Click happened. You know the Click. The same one that Tennessee Williams tells us you hear when you're good and drunk, or one of the two. The moment when you suddenly realize that it's You against You, not You against Miss Buss, Miss Beale and the Rest of the World.

From that day forth learning becomes a pain-free zone. If I've got a piece to write, a play to learn, I just go into that room with the L plate on it and do the necessaries. Easy. It only took forty-two years to perfect this skill. Unfortunately, nowadays my powers of retention are somewhat limited. In fact, between the time it takes to dial a phone call and the time the caller answers, I've generally forgotten whom I rang and I have to flail around saying things like 'Hi. It's me! Maureen. How's thing? And the family ...?'

But I digress. The fact that my timing was twenty years off doesn't mean the lesson wasn't valuable. And it shows how easy education should be. All you need to learn is how to learn. Oh – and one inspired, wonderful educator helps.

A leader. A Corn-is-Greenius. Personally, I've decided not to hold my breath till He/She comes along. Instead I'll keep saying: 'So how do you say "I will be leaving the table?"' And she will keep saying, 'We haven't done that tense of whatsit – er – thingy – sortir. No, I mean partir. No, don't tell me –' 'But you *must* have done the future!' 'Oh, you always think you know better than – ANYWAY, I KNOW *LE TABLE* !'

Now all we have to do is brace ourselves for the results. These come in dribs and drabs with varying degrees of defensiveness, ranging from one child who yells 'Eighty per cent for Latin! That's appalling! I'm going to bang my head on the door till I'm less of a pranny!' to the other who drawls 'I don't know why you're looking so miserable. Fifty-two percent is *good* – 's' great. Everyone got about that 'cept the goody-goodies! I thought you'd be *pleased*. Honestly!'

The most humiliating part of the whole business is my sheer ignorance of the subjects on which I'm testing them. Logarithms, fractions, matrices, cross-sections of plant-wort, Homer and his load of old belli – it's all Greek to me. It's like trying to recall the taste of gripe water. Been and gone, mate! And in what stead did it stand me, I wonder, as I skim through the batch of middle-brow sit-coms staring back at me from a bulging in-tray.

And it doesn't get any better. Excerpt from the diary June 1990:

'Right now in our house, it's GCSEs and Common Entrance. Every night that dawns, as my mother is wont to say, Amy and I sit facing each other across a groaning table whilst she draws endless doodles of herself with a giant nose, and I write letters to almost anyone.

'"What animal reproduces itself asexually?" said today's Biology paper. "A kangaroo," wrote Layla's daughter, Yvette. "What did *you* write, darling?" I ask Amy gingerly. "Nothing, but I was going to write 'lobster'," she mutters, eating hair at a rapid rate and thumbing morosely through Linda Goodman's *Love Signs*. "No point. Nothing I revised came up." "What about Plasma?" "Nope." "Respiration?" "Nope." "The components of soil?" Hadn't we spent most of last night building elaborate words out of the initials of its components, to make it memorable?

'SHE: "It's no good. I'll remember MOASM all right, but I won't know what the hell it stands for ..."

'ME: "Go to bed, darling. Have a nice hot bath and do the rest in bed and I'll bring you a –"

'SHE: (*tearfully*) "How can I? There's millions of checklists left and I haven't done the pancreas at all and it's History of Art in the morning!"

'ME: "Well, let me test you on it."

'SHE: "There's no point. I hate being tested. Besides, I don't care about Biology – it's History of Art as well and I've got to get an 'A' and I haven't touched Fauvism since Friday. I'm just useless. Why do people have to have exams anyway? I can't remember a thing! Melanie remembers *every single* date and I don't want to let everyone down and I'm so tired."

'ME: (*weakly*) "We've all been through it, darling."

'SHE: "Yes, I know, but it's different for me."

'In the end all I can do is all I can ever do. What I always do. I make her laugh. It's the only thing I'm good at. All through the next day I have a knot in my stomach from morning till the thinnest whitest face in town (other than her mother's) comes through the door.

'At 5.30 she rushes in and dumps herself in front of *Neighbours*.

'ME: "How did they go, darling?"

'SHE: "Shsh! Terrible. Shsh!".'

It'll be all right. It's May now and it's only four months till the results come through – I'll be fine. I mean *we'll* be fine. I'll take up a hobby. I'll volunteer for the peace corps or something. I'll learn to hang-glide. Something peaceful to take my mind off it all.

It doesn't stop does it? For years. Their thin pale faces and hunched shoulders. They'll come back from college or university the same. I know. And I'll be up in arms as usual, threatening to take the Board of Examiners to the International Court of Human Rights. This time one of the questions in her Biology GCSE was: 'What are the symptoms of gonorrhoea and how can the use of a condom help prevent its spread?'

'I don't believe it!' I shrieked from my safe little Nancy Drew world. 'What did you put?'

'Nothing,' she replied airily.

My face changed. 'What do you mean, nothing? You can't put nothing. You have to have a stab at it!'

'No point, I hadn't a clue.'

'Well, you must have known what a condom was.'

'Yes.'

'Well, then?'

'Well, then, what? What *is* gonorrhoea?'

You see what questions like this do to an average North London family? An entire lasagne dinner ruined by a description of gonorrhoea causes and effects. Thank you, GCSE Board, wherever you convene.

This would seem to be the ideal moment to mention the duck joke:

A duck checked into a hotel with his girlfriend. They were about to make love when she asked him if he had a condom.

'Er, no,' said the duck embarrassedly, 'I thought *you* ... I mean ...'

'Look here,' quacked the emancipated bird, 'this is 1990 – safe sex, remember? I'm not just any old duck you know ...'

'No, of course,' said the duck hastily. 'Er, what shall I do?'

The lady duck sighs heavily. 'Phone room service, of course.'

'Just like that? Er, yes, of course ...' He phones down, covered in all kinds of confusion and says, 'This is Mr Duck, in room 314 ... Is it possible to have a ... pot of tea sent up please ... and – er – a condom?'

'Certainly, Sir.' And in less time than it takes to boil a duck egg, there's a knock on the door and the waiter enters with a pot of tea and a condom on a silver tray.

'Will that be all, Sir?' says the waiter as the duck presses a tip into his hand.

'Yes, thank you,' replies the duck in his most dismissive tones.

'And shall I put it on your bill, Sir?' asks the waiter.

'What do you think I am?' hurls back the duck, 'a flipping pervert?'

Where was I? Oh yes, exams. . . .

The most vivid picture I have is of Adam, unable to swallow because of a sore throat, alone in a schoolroom about to commence his Common Entrance Greek exam. Just Adam and the invigilator – for fear he might copy from himself, presumably – an odd little oddyssey if ever I saw one. His headmaster had told the boys not to revise over the weekend before Common Entrance, but instead to have lots of physical exercise to tire them out. Adam and his friend Will took the advice to heart and spent Sunday afternoon on a two-hour hike in the pouring rain. 'It was great!' he beamed, hair clinging to his head like Robert Robinson's and wearing Will's mother's clothes. 'We had the BEST time!'

I had the best time, too. Lemsips/Zincolds/Hot Ribena and honey were poured down the boy most of the night, and as he staggered off in the morning, looking as though he'd been tumble dried and minus his mislaid glasses, he was decidedly unprepared for a day which would, at least, affect his entire future.

'Don't worry, love,' you lie, 'only another week and it's over and you'll never have to do it again.' No mention here of the inevitable fact that life, the rest of it, is one big exam. Will I get into college? Will I get a job? Will I meet my deadline? Will his parents like me? Will the bank give me a mortgage? Will my kid make the school team? Will I cope with his mother living with us? And that those two great invigilators who know it all, who sit in judgement, never quite give us the marks we think we deserve. I mean, of course, ourselves and our Maker.

Towards the end of term, there were a whole bunch of balloon debates.* Both of the kids seemed to fare less than well in these flights of fantasy, Adam being ditched from his

---

* Balloon debate – a type of debate where the speaker is given a famous character from History and must justify his reasons for being the last person in the balloon.

balloon in the last round in favour of Moses and Mr Chips (of *Goodbye* ... fame). This would have been totally acceptable had Adam not been debating under the name of God.

'It's a great title for your autobiography, Ad,' I told him, 'The Day God Came Second.'

Meanwhile his sister was faring even worse, under a less auspicious mantle, and hers was part of the GCSE oral exam:

'How did the balloon debate go, love?'

'Oh, it was appalling – I lost by a landslide. Even my best friend didn't vote for me.'

'No! How awful. Who did you choose to be?'

'Well that's the thing,' she somewhat sheepishly replied. 'I was the producer of *Neighbours* and Tasha was Nelson Mandela.'

Last week I stood in the hall of my son's new school with a crowd of other nervous new parents, passing my entrance exam into his next school. Trying to think of the right question to ask the maths master which would make me look like an intelligent, caring parent who wouldn't make too many waves, when all I really wanted to ask was 'Are there any other parents here from Muswell Hill who'd like to share a school run, and does anyone know the score from the England–Ireland quarter final?'

'Education,' said Pete Seeger, 'is when you read the fine print. Experience is what you get when you don't.' Wish *I'd* said that! (You will, Maureen, you will.)

Wanda the Honda's Sister Rhonda

As we have just passed the Chinese Year of the Snake, I've decided to shed a skin or two. There will – with only the merest hint of venom – be less slither, less circumventing and less likelihood of turning into an old boot.

I would begin by reading my car manual. I have a little Honda Prelude Automatic of whom I'm fond. She's a bit tide-marked on the outside and soil-strewn on the inside, but I wouldn't trade her for all the Burberrys in Japan. Having said that, I must admit that I'd rather read the complete works of Jimmy Tarbuck than the Honda manual. My mind turns to minced morsels at the mention of a spark-plug. However, the time has come. I knew that when my car refused to start one night outside the Fortune Theatre after two shows of *Re: Joyce*. (Apropos of which, a minicab driver who took me to the theatre one night glanced at my name in lights and said, 'Just you, is it? In the show? How long is it?' 'Two-and-a-half hours,' I told him airily. 'Jesus!' he barked. 'That must be bleedin' boring! Don't get me wrong – I don't mean for you, I mean for the audience.')

So, there I am, the new me, outside the theatre, 11 pm, broken down. The car, that is. Me – I'm decisive, resolute, butch as Croesus – and banging on the window of my pianist Denis King's car, begging him to help me find the bonnet. Without so much as a deleted expletive, he attached his jump-leads to my plus and minus – ooh, eroticar! – and gave directives to the wimp in the driver's seat. Incidentally, I found the way to open the bonnet. You press a little picture of a little bonnet on a little knob. A sort of Oriental minimalism. Be that as it may, as Den issued a command to me to rev up, I glanced at my automatic gear-shift and couldn't fail to notice that it was in 'R'. As in 'R' for 'Reverse'. Since the car only starts up in 'P' for 'Parked', this explained a lot. Like why the car wouldn't start.

'Try to accelerate,' yelled Den, looking tired but patient.

My decision was instantaneous. I slid the gear-lever into 'P'.

'Yes! It's started! Oh, thanks, Den. Marvellous. I don't know what I'd have done without you. See you tomorrow. Byeee!'

'I'll drive behind you to Camden Town,' he yelled.

'No! I mean – no – it's fine honestly . . .'

It was weeks before I could tell him the truth. 'You pillock,' he said, not unkindly.

Must buy some jump-leads of my own, I mused, passing a Car Accessories Shop. I was on my way to meet my chum, Julia McKenzie, between her matinée and my evening show. We had some big career crossroads to discuss, like where you can buy the wrinkle-cream I read about in *Vogue*, and we were going to do it over a nice, ageing tea.

I put on the felt reindeer antlers I'd got for Christmas. Yes, I did. Parked in the NCP and called for her in her dressing-room. Bless her, she laughed, probably to humour me. We had tea, sorted out each other's lives and I went back to my car which, unusually, was still there. Albeit with the lights full on and the batteries dead.

In the absence of Den, I stopped two or three cars, asked for jump-leads, used the odd car-phone to fail to get the RAC, and eventually threw myself at the clerk on the desk, who referred me to the nearest garage – the nearest, totally closed garage. Finally, I headed back to Julia's dressing-room, where I was delighted to see that I had been wearing large brown felt antlers through my attempts to be taken seriously. Do I hear a hiss coming from the direction of Chinatown?

One more attempt at maturity then I'll give up, I told myself. A weekend at a health farm, polish up the inner man and expose the outer woman, thwarts and all. I pack bathrobes, tracksuits and toothbrush – and books I've no intention of reading – fill up the Honda and set off on the A3. It was a journey of one hour and a quarter. Three hours later I arrive, grey with migraine, backache and a temper nicely exacerbated by 'Hello, hello, Mrs Jones never has that trouble' type British Telecom jokes at every service and police station from Guildford to Haslemere. The receptionist says, 'Your husband phoned, Mrs Rosenthal. You've left your luggage at home on the trampoline.' It's a good line but I can't laugh. Instead I burst into tears and have to be fed tea and digestives by Sister Dixon and put to bed with an aspirin and a copy of *Autocar*. You may smirk, but it's not easy having the mentality of a dizzy blonde and the looks of a stationary brunette. Roll on the Year of the Ass.

Back home, my Honda's been put on the social map, a gossip columnist who shall be nameless but who has a profile as high as an elephant's thigh has been to see *Re: Joyce*. So enamoured is he of the show that he hastens to his column to write full details, for a breathless public, of where I park my car. The stage door-keeper, he reveals, leaves two police bollards outside the theatre for me to park my, quote, 'Lip-mobile'. No, come on, the culture-loving public doesn't get nearly enough information about the Arts these days. Soon after, two burly fellows from Scotland Yard, no less – must have been a quiet day on the rape-and-pillage front – came and confiscated our bollards. I'd love them to do the same to the said columnist's, but would they ever find them?

So now it's round and round Covent Garden in search of a meter. Have you noticed the expressions on people's faces when you mouth at them 'Are you going?' as they stand beside their cars? Fear and petulance. It's as though you've said, 'Excuse me, can I sleep with your Borzoi?' Or 'Would you like hollandaise sauce on your cashmere?' Their look says, 'No, I'm bloody-well *not* going. It's taken me three hours to find this space – so go and suck a steam-iron!'

I parked finally in a space vacated by a space-wagon driven by a pony-tailed young man, who actually smiled and waved me in. It was Davy Jones, the pop-singer. The Year of the Monkee?

One night, around 5.30 pm and very low on petrol, I found a meter. Around 7.30 pm my dresser, Sally, casually remarked that she'd passed the car on her way in and noticed red and green lights shining inside. It was either Kryptonite, aliens, or I'd left the engine on. Wanna guess?

I nipped round to have a look. Yes, engine on, keys in the ignition, door unlocked, aerial up – the perfect way for a mature person to leave a car parked in Central London of an evening. I was about to wriggle on my belly across the face of the earth when I noticed something on the windscreen. It was a yellow tulip. With a note attached. It said 'Hello, Maureen, we love you' and it was signed by the waiters in Flounders Fish Restaurant. Sometimes there is pleasure, so suddenly, that it might almost be the Year of the Fish.

And now – a snake joke.

A rabbit is hopping through the forest when she comes upon a snake.

'Please help me,' she says. 'I'm blind and I can't find out what I am.'

'Well, small world,' says the snake. 'I'm blind too, and I can't find out what I am either. Tell you what, you wriggle over me and I'll tell you what you are.'

So, the rabbit wriggles over the snake and the snake says, 'Well, you're fluffy and small, with a puffball tail and long ears.'

'Oooh goody,' coos the rabbit. 'I'm a bunny! I'm a bunny! Thank you, thank you! Now you wriggle over me and I'll tell you what *you* are.'

So, the snake wriggles over the rabbit and the rabbit says, 'Well, you're slimy – and I think you're poisonous – and er – you've got no balls.'

'Oh shit!' hisses the snake. 'I'm an agent!'

And no one laughed louder when I told her that joke than a dear lady called Anne Hutton. Who just happens to be my agent.

The Cook, the Wife, Her Guests and Another

Even by my standards, it's been an interesting week. My arrival back from the States coincided with the departure of my husband to New York and my housekeeper to places unknown. So as of now I'm keeping my own house. It's very good for me. No, it is. Really.

On Monday I did three loads of washing. 'So what?' I hear you snort, reaching for your violin and smothering a yawn. Yes, I know you do that same onerous task every Monday of your lives – but do you do it as I did it, in a short velvet evening dress with floor-length taffeta sweep and enough make-up to bankrupt Helena Rubinstein? And are you, one hour and forty minutes later, up the Odeon, Leicester Square, attempting to curtsy in said too-short burgundy gown with Ariel Automatic under your fingernails in the presence of your ruling monarch?

Oh, you are? Well in that case – it's a bugger, isn't it? Just finding the words is hard enough when Her Majesty is looking a little cross and confused, as well she might since only one of the eight people lined up to meet her had anything to do with the première she was about to see. She asked each of us in turn if we were in the film.

'I say,' said my mother on the phone later – she'd caught it on the ten o'clock news – 'the Queen talked to you for ages – what did you say?'

'No, Ma'am,' I told her honestly.

The following day I cooked ahead (by which I mean I cooked for the next three days rather than the skull of a boar). Then I changed the sheets and towels, emptied the waste bins, swept the kitchen floor and tumble-dried yesterday's crumpled laundry by turning the broken 'on' dial with a pair of pliers.

On Wednesday I gave a dinner party for a visiting American colleague. By way of a change I happened upon a cookbook called *Caribbean Cookery* sent to me in my absence by one Judy Bastyra in return for a telephone interview I had apparently given to her. 'Chicken Fricassee' looked oven and idiot proof – I would buy the ingredients on my way home from my morning meeting at Central TV and cook two courses for ten people on my return. Abandon hope all ye who believe what ye have just read . . .

Instead . . .

Home from meeting at 2.10. Receive phone call from single-parent girlfriend in need of shoulder to drench till 3.00. Attempt Caribbean ingredients in M & S Muswell Hill on early-closing day in blizzard till 4.30. Soak fourteen pieces of chicken in suggested marinade which only stretches around three thighs, leaving other eleven high and dry. Recipe says, 'Reserve remaining marinade!' Stand rigid, staccato and immobile for many minutes in kitchen till entrance from school of son Adam.

HE: 'What's wrong, Mod?'

ME: (Barking) 'Boy in your school called Bastyra? Is there?'

HE: 'Er, yes. Why?'

ME: 'Phone number. His. Gimme. QUICK!'

HE: Complies, exits tapping head . . .

ME: (Pressing remaining marinade all over phone) 'Hello, Judy, I'm sorry to bother you – this is Maureen Lipman and I'm just cooking your Chicken Fricassee . . .

HE: (Returning with bulging black plastic sack) 'Sorry, Mod – but someone was sick in my satchel.'

ME: 'Ugh! It stinks!'

JUDY: 'Well, it shouldn't – was the chicken fresh?'

ME: 'No, no – it's the marinade – sorry. The marinade won't go round the chicken – there's not enough of it and . . . and . . .'

SHE: 'Oh, dear – are you sure you've used enough lime juice?'

ME: 'I'm covered in ruddy lime juice – but the chicken isn't and . . .'

SHE: What time are your guests . . .?'

ME: 'In two hours and I haven't started on the palm heart salad –'

SHE: 'Mmm – I suppose I'd better come over.'

ME: totally silent but if I'd had a rosary I'd have counted it.

At 5 o'clock she materialized bearing Caribbean hot sauce, and I got the feeling I'd known her for most of my grown-up life.

By 5.30 she'd re-marinated the marinade – and the chicken was fricasseeing merrily away. I retreated thankfully into my dumb brunette's role even to the point of murmuring 'Do I just cook the rice the normal way?'

'Oh, just leave it, I'll do it,' she said, chopping and basting and generally making life worth living. I could just hear my mother's voice, 'Honestly, if you fell in a bucket of you-know-what you'd come up smelling of freesias.'

Judy left at 7.20 through the back door and the guests arrived minutes later through the front one. The dinner was a triumph and I accepted the compliments with the sort of expression Princess Diana uses for groups of adoring Arab potentates.

At 2 am I stacked the dishwasher, cleared the debris and left a pile of wine glasses in the utility-room sink under a running tap. Then I went smugly to bed. It was only when I heard the sounds of the cat drowning that I ventured back into the utility room and stood immobile and rigid for the second time in one day, only this time, for variety, in six inches of water.

There were no old newspapers because of my housewifely efficiency. Ten towels and four rolls of kitchen paper hardly made a ripple in it and the squeegee mop just pushed it from one side of the room to another. Phone the author of *The Cruel Sea*, perhaps? No. Just go back to bed, close your eyes and the whole thing drifts away. Who says housewives don't need a fantasy life?

Tea Totally

'Put the kettle on, love. It'll all feel better after a nice cuppa tea . . .'

And, of course, it usually does. I don't know. Maybe it's not allowed – choosing a cuppa as your favourite tipple. Not for an article in the *Independent*? Not for all those Sainsbury's cork-sniffers with their own Vacu-Sacs, surely not?

Yet when the final 'Ivana and Donald' sounds and I'm standing in the sinners' queue, lacklustre for lack of liquid, I know that my final request will not be 'A pint of the Cristal Louis Roederer, please!' but 'A well-dunked bag, a thin china mug, half an inch of milk, hot water and plenty of it, and no sugs, thanks!!'

Should St Peter – or worse – start on the newly familiar routine of 'Earl Grey, Lapsang Souchong, Camomile and Kohlrabi or Valium and Spinach?' I shall evade the choice and plump for PG Tips out of loyalty to the chimps and the sheer boredom of pretending to enjoy drinks which do me good but taste like boiled underpants. Not that I'm a connoisseur of the boiled underpant.

My abstemiousness is due to what I like to term the three M's. That's Migraine, Myopia and My Age. A decade ago, when the children were under my feet and my feet were under the sideboard, the thought of the nightly G & T on the rocks was the only thing that got me through the daze. Once I ventured back into show business it was 'any glass of port after the storm, purely for medicinal purposes, of course' which occupied my mind for most of Act II.

Nowadays I have a Campari and soda on all occasions with 'very little ice, please' if I'm in America, where they don't understand that a mere photograph of an ice cube makes my gums jack-knife. Possibly the slightly medicinal flavour makes me feel that, rather like the daffodil and conifer teabags, the concoction is somehow doing me good.

Certainly the last time I sank my endangered ivories into a large Campari, I got merrier than a March hare. It was in an American diner where the TV set was blaring out some bovine quiz, and they posed the question: 'Which famous celebrity had a religion named after them?' And quick as a person plastered after one Campari and soda I quipped, 'Ethel Mormon.' This struck me as so unbearably funny that I laughed right through dinner, the journey home and, on and off, much of the night.

I haven't mentioned white wine, which I occasionally enjoy because I'm reminded of my mother's refusal of such a drink with the explanation: 'No, thank you, I don't drink wine. It makes my eyes go small.'

So, as the workman said as he strode through my front door one Tuesday, 'Mornin', Missus. Er – what letter would you say comes after S?'

ME: 'Er – T?'

HIM: 'Don't mind if I do. Two sugars, please.'

Barmitzvah Joy

Well, it's all over now Bar the shouting. The Barmitzvah, I
mean. It was no trouble. Looking back, it was a breeze,
really. Gale force 13. And like every major event in one's life
it passed by like a gale leaving nothing in its wake but ruffled
hair, a trance-like calm and a lot of bills for the repair work.

The boy himself was a triumph. I suppose the nearest
equivalent to a Barmitzvah in terms of emotional build up
would probably not even be one's wedding day, but one's
coronation. It seems like only yesterday, although he was six
at the time, when he crept, white-faced in his red Batman
pyjamas, into our bedroom and said in trembling tones, 'It's
only seven years to my BARMITZVAH and I don't know a word
of it yet!'

Well, he knew every word *backwards* on Saturday. He
could have sung it standing on his head – a feat which was
suggested several times during the day in reference to his
dad's TV play, *Barmitzvah Boy*, written, curiously enough,
thirteen years ago, and remembered with mixed emotions by
most of the people who attended the ceremony.

It was a tough act to follow. Not only for the boy. The
year had been spent finding the right location for the party.
As Jack said in his speech, 'Welcome to what was booked to
be breakfast at Claridge's, brunch at the Savoy, lunch at the
Grosvenor Rooms, Willesden, but is now, Maureen assured
me on the way here, almost certainly dinner at the Arts Club
in Dover Street.' I had, in fact, booked four other venues
before a friend stumbled upon this lovely old club in Mayfair,
with parlour and conservatory, stunning pictures, a cosy
dining-room and a familiar air of eccentricity about it. Rather
battered and leathery – not unlike your host and hostess –
what sold me completely was the bronze rhinoceros in the

lobby. My husband is a rhinophile. Another endangered species had found its natural habitat.

Over the months the tension grew. Appearing in *Re:Joyce,* a one-woman show, was time consuming enough. Appearing in a one-woman show whilst choosing tablecloth colourings and checking the consistency of leek tartlets is beyond this particular thespian. My then secretary Jo had built up an intimate phone relationship with Mr Gomes the – yes, you guessed it – *Irish* manager, and we decided to hammer problems out and prices down over lunch at the club. We'd got about as far as the Campari and soda when fire broke out in the kitchens. The dining-room was evacuated, and we lunched at Wheeler's – which almost became Location Number Five.

'We're having sea bass,' I told my mother back home.

'Sea bass?' she repeated, as though I'd said 'sea horse'. 'You can't give them that, it's not a Jewish fish!'

I pointed out that sea bass don't have trotters, don't crawl on their bellies on the floor of the earth and don't, to my knowledge, suffer from PMT.

Her response was typically predictable. 'Don't put it on the menu. If it's pink they might think it's salmon!'

I was due to close in *Re:Joyce* two weeks before Adam's opening. And it came to pass that both Jo, highly efficient secretary, and Yvonne, long-suffering mother's help, suddenly got offers they couldn't refuse and left two weeks before the event. It was pure coincidence and pure hell. The team was rudderless, the house was in chaos, my parents had been staying for four months, my father was in the house recovering from a stroke, and my mother was in the house giving *me* one.

On the last Monday the doorbell rang and the builders arrived. Irish and disarming, they laid dustsheets up the stairs, and removed the upstairs toilet. The following day, they returned and put in a new one. Then, as they were taking the wallpaper off the walls, Jack said, 'Why did they remove the toilet – it was the best toilet in the house?'

I looked at him askance and said, 'Do you mean *you* didn't ask them to?'

He hadn't. Actually they did a bloody good job. Whoever they were.

The invitations had all returned bringing joy and laughter. On the reply card we put: 'Please answer yes or no if you will be at the Kiddush' – this latter being a celebration with wine and food after the ceremony. One very dear, non-Jewish couple replied in the negative and when we asked if they were sure they didn't want to come, admitted they didn't think they could *do* it.

'Do what?'

'Well, *beat* the Kiddush.'

Poor souls obviously thought they were going to have to club a baby goat to death.

In the last week we did the table plan. Let me rephrase that. On Monday night we did the table plan. On Tuesday we redid the table plan. Then, slowly and inexorably, on the other remaining nights the table plan did for us. One night at 2 am we finally pushed the last place-card round the dining-table and said. 'We've done the bastard.' A hundred and forty-four people. A gross of guests. Ten people, all of whom vaguely spoke to one another, at the thirteen tables, and fourteen at the top. We gazed at one another, held hands, smiled a forgotten smile, and I said those three all-important words that mean so much to a married couple in a time of crisis: 'Bessie Edelson's missing.' An hour and a half and five tables reorganized later, we found her place-card underneath Helen Feldman's – almost where she ended up sitting.

The night before – some cancellations, some further reor-ganization – no word yet from my friends the flamenco dancers, who'd volunteered to liven up the cabaret. Mañ-ana – mañana – worried? Me? Noooo! What's Spanish for panic attack? Hispanic attack?

Meanwhile, the boy who's becoming a man tomorrow practises and practises, with drier and drier mouth, what is already practised till perfect. Underwater eyes, freshly cut hair, pale face grown up with grown-up worry. Only his dad knows how he feels – empathy being his trademark. Together they hear each other's Hebrew speeches and after-dinner speeches. Together they try on their prayer shawls, inquiring Talmudically over each fold and drape, Adam's a brand-new shawl, Jack proudly wearing Adam's old one. That night Adam does the Sabbath blessing and cuts the Chollah loaf. We're all a bit quiet now. The tension and nervous quibbling over – the calm before the dawn.

The day. Perfect. That's all I can tell you. I spent it as glazed as a carrot in a nouvelle cuisine restaurant. According to the *Mail on Sunday* I had 'Four hundred guests and Julia McKenzie'. According to the 144 people who were *really* there, we had a service in the West London Synagogue which took their breaths collectively away. Adam took half the service and sang his portion like the pro he is with fervour and modesty and pure clarity. Rabbi Hugo Gryn beamed with pride. I did my two words of Hebrew with only three mistakes, Jack and Amy were good and glorious, the choir took the roof away and the sharing of joy was everywhere. Relatives and friends convivial, speeches hilarious, and food, they tell me, divine. I choose to believe this in spite of Mother returning from a protracted table hop to say, 'No one's eating the sea bass at the far end.'

All over Bar the thank-you letters. And if anyone didn't like it – listen, we'll do it again next year – at Claridge's or the Savoy or the Grosvenor Rooms, Willesden – or probably the Arts Club. Possibly with salmon.

During the ceremony, like a drowning parent, most of Adam's life flashed before my eyes. I remembered his birth very clearly. It was on the same day that Selfridges delivered £800 worth of green- and white-flowered sofas to the house. I seem to have been present at both occasions. I'd bought the furniture in a pit of freak because the gynaecologist had told me that Adam was upside-down and I would need to have another Caesarian. On reflection I was relieved he was upside down thirteen years ago and not on this day, in a park somewhere in Willesden, like the lad in *Barmitzvah Boy*.

As a baby, he looked extraordinarily like Sir John Gielgud. Funny that. His face went sideways, not longways like the rest of us. People would pop into my hospital room and say, 'Gosh, you know who he reminds me of?' and I'd say, 'Yes. Sir John Gielgud' and they'd say, 'That's right. I knew it was one of them.' And I'd think, 'But all we *did* together was recite, "Shall I compare thee to a summer's day ..."'

He didn't talk much. He didn't need to. His sister was in charge of words. Adam just sat there thinking long and hard. Sometimes he reminded me of the story of the child who never spoke for his first five years. His parents took him to every specialist but they all declared that there was no physical reason why the child shouldn't speak.

One day at dinner the child said, 'This custard's got lumps in it.'

The whole family went into shock.

They screamed and laughed and stood and sat and raced to embrace him. 'You can speak! You can speak!' they cried.

Unfazed and somewhat disdainful, the child said, 'Of course I can speak.'

'So why did you never say anything before?'

The child thought, and replied: 'Because I never had anything to complain about before.'

And our lad hasn't stopped talking since.

Only his dad knows what he's thinking. To see them together is to be reminded of the two old men in the theatre box in *The Muppet Show*. Cricket and Latin, etymology and philology, Hebrew and cornflakes. They never stop discussing. When Ad showed a keen interest in astronomy his dad sent away for an eight-inch Newtonian reflector and stood with him for hours on frosty February nights in search of the universe through the flora and fauna of Muswell Hill. If the boy had said to *me*, 'Mod, I love the stars,' I'd probably have got him Des O'Connor's autograph. Incidentally, an eight-inch Newtonian reflector is eight inches *wide* not, as I thought, eight inches *long*. It came through the front door at 10 am and it was still coming through at noon. It also had to have an observatory built around it. With a sliding roof. It looks very nice in the garden and probably caused more trouble to build than the house did in 1910. In the end, no one was speaking to anyone, but the sight of the moon in the palm of one's hand is almost worth it. He's not in it *quite* as much as we expected, but we're optimistic that he'll take it up again once the cricket season is over and *Blackadder* stops being repeated.

Amy and I rather cherish our roles as the dumb brunettes

of the family. On a trip to Brent Cross for THE SUIT, Adam broke the strains of Streisand singing Sondheim with the outcome of his own particular strain of philosophical thought, to say: 'What would you say was a definition of the word courage?'.

His sister rolled her eyes roof-wards and groaned. 'Courage is going to Brent Cross on a wet Wednesday for a ruddy Barmitzvah suit.'

It was the same week that their father's new shirt had to be purchased. When I suggested stopping off at the suit shop to buy one he demurred. 'I can't do it *now*.' 'Why not?' I asked him. 'I've got the wrong shoes on,' he replied lamely. Absent-minded professors, the pair of them. Was it not Adam who, when I pointed Dustin Hoffman out to him and told him that Hoffman was in London playing Shylock, said, 'Really? D'you mean Shylock Holmes?'

His sister has a few words for the change in the boy becoming a man. 'One day he was listening to all my doll stories and doing what I told him, then suddenly he got very pale and thin and his legs grew and his pyjamas shrank and he stopped moving his mouth when he spoke, batted the air and made repetitive clicking noises. I sort of carried on talking and he stopped listening ...'

Mind you, Amy was in a fair state of tension herself. Two weeks before the big day was her biggest day yet. The day she starred as Anne 'with an E' in her school production of *Anne of Green Gables*.

It was the end of a two-year audition period in our house. The play had been on and off more times than Prince's clothes. The saga of whether to have real boys or girl-boys or teachers in short pants or total strangers who happened to be passing the school entrance, had been more tedious than the Channel Tunnel. The auditions were heart-stopping and the tension between them and the announcement of the casting made *A Chorus Line* look like half an hour in the Lisson Grove Job Centre.

Finally she landed the role, and Glory be to God, her best friend Melanie landed the role of Anne's best friend. Not one drop of help did she get from her show-biz parents, who were far too preoccupied with the shape of twenty-four table centre-pieces, and 'Do we invite the cousin from Belgium who's never seen Adam and doesn't speak to his parents?'

I only saw the dress rehearsal, as I was Rejoycing in the evenings. It was more temperamental than any show I've ever been involved with, and had all the hallmarks of success. Which it was. And she was. Was? She's now moved into the attic room, painted it green, dyed her hair red and is working on the freckles, with the aid of a soft brown crayon.

'Don't you miss a play *dreadfully* when it's over Mod?' She cries, and looks disbelieving and disparaging when I say 'Never: I like the memories, I like to look through the Barmitzvah photos and the Anne of Green Gables video and, when pushed, Grandma's scrapbooks, and to think: 'Thank God *that's* over – next?'

Almost a year later, I watch the Barmitzvah boy carving fastidious marks in the ground with his beloved Swiss Army Knife. The trouser-press was a godsend, particularly for my trousers, and all of the good and generous gifts have evolved into household necessities. Perhaps our favourite momento is the certificate given to him by ex-secretary Jo Kydd and her husband James. It is from the International Star Registry, Toronto, and it certifies the existence of a star in the firmament called 'The Adam Rosenthal Star'. So, aeons after my theatre greasepaint has sunk into the coal seams and Jack's plays have been recycled into kitchen rolls, there will still, thank the Lord, be a star in the family.

Now *that's* immortality.

2

Personal Column

Me, Myself and Eyes

It seems to me that I wore glasses before I wore zinc-and-castor-oil cream. Let's be honest, I was conceived in glasses. It was spectacular! This may well be a little rose-tinted, but that weighty, bulldog-clip-round-the-nose sensation appears to have been with me, and indeed to have shaped – not only me, but my nose – not only my nose, but my personality – for as long as I can recall.

Neither of my parents wore them. My mother didn't need them and was far too pretty to wear them even if she had needed them. My father preferred to screw up his eyes and lean forward should he need to see whether the pink or blue was about to be potted. His glasses were always 'in me other jacket pocket, behind the clock on the mantelpiece'. (There isn't a clock on the mantelpiece. Come to that, there isn't a bloody mantelpiece.) Elder brother Geoffrey (the Paragon), blond, brainy, sporting, the white sheep of the family, had, of course, the full 20/20. And no buck teeth. How he managed to *live* with all I had going against him was an East Yorkshire miracle.

I suppose I was ten when the school said I couldn't see. I invariably sat at the back of the class for reasons not unconnected with gang warfare, and if I needed to glance at the blackboard there was always someone to show me roughly where it was. But, no. A second opinion was sought and, short-sightedly, my parents agreed to put me in those gorgeous National Health jobs which are now sported by your average Yuppie but which then made you look second only in berkishness to the kid in the owl specs with elastoplast all over one lens. This was to correct a lazy eye. I certainly had one of those. It went with the rest of me. If the treatment really worked I should have been elastoplasted all over.

At first I only wore the bins for homework and blackboard but, as the years rolled myopically by, I came to rely on them more and more, too lazy to take them off. Ultimately I took to wearing them all the time, only whipping them off when approached by a boy I vaguely fancied, or at the door of a friend of my mother's with a boy *she* fancied for me inside.

My first boyfriend seemed to like me, specs and all. I couldn't believe it and, at the pictures, persisted in dragging them surreptitiously on and off whenever he took his eyes off the screen and looked at me. Mind you, he'd come home from university one time to see me in bed with 'flu, glasses and no front teeth, so I guess he was pretty immune to my charmlessness – or was too shortsighted himself to notice. Or maybe love really *is* blind.

During the Seventies, in my Lovin' Spoonful London Hippie period, I favoured tiny, blue-tinted, gold-rimmed Lennon specs like everyone else – and for the first time felt utterly at peace (man) with my bespectacled self. Meeting Jack in his butch horn-rims gave me a feeling of intense familiarity, and the first time we banged glasses together in mid-kiss I knew it was sight at first love.

Since then, whatever the frame, I've rarely had them off – to the extent that I began to hide, defiantly Su Pollard-like, behind them, never fighting being four-eyed except occasionally in the odd incongruous evening dress.

My first venture into contact lenses was a classic. I accustomed my pupils to the tiny hard lenses – building up their resistance fastidiously for an extra hour per day – then lost one down the sink and the other down the Holborn Public Baths. Back came the 'face-furniture' which required no solutions except that of remembering to wear them. But the problem remained of seeing and being seen. On stage, short sight is a positive advantage and many are the flowery eulogies some of our more sensitive critics have launched into in praise of this or that actress's misty gaze into the middle-distance, which could be more truthfully ascribed to her scarlet frames being confined to the dressing-room table, having failed to match her farthingale.

Many are the TV panel games and Awards Ceremonies

where actors are required to open envelopes and read the contents. At such occasions, actors' glasses are on and off more times than their love affairs – and millions thrill to the sound of '. . . And the winner is Dustman Hoffbin.'

During a run in a Neil Simon play, I struggled with soft lenses but they made me cry constantly – which was unfortunate, as Neil tends to expect laughs. Pink-eyed and lachrymose, I returned to the lens boutique in the Earls Court Road (on the cornea, actually) and complained bitterly that the lenses were a pair of over-priced disasters through which I could neither see nor play Neil Simon. Patiently, the practitioner examined them, me and us, and proclaimed that I would probably be able to see jolly well if I didn't have them inside out and in the wrong eyes.

'You must think I'm a very stupid person!' I said rhetorically.

'We're used to it, madam,' he sighed. 'The gentleman before you complained his lenses gave him double vision and headaches. Which they do if you wear your flatmate's instead of your own.'

Even as we speak, I'm wearing the new, soft 'Torric' lenses. These are specially constructed to cope with astigmatic people such as myself and have two tiny lines on their edges which mean 'This way up'. These lines are only visible if you're already wearing contact lenses! So you have to get a man in to line them up for you before you put them in. Once in, and pain subsiding, they very deliberately move around so that the two lines are elsewhere – and what you are reading looks like basic Sanskrit.

In America recently, I wore the lenses for a ladies' luncheon, then went straight to the theatre for the show, and did make-up, hair and costume in record time. As I took my place in the darkened centre stage for the opening of the first act, and the lights slowly came up, I saw a sight which I've never seen before, a sight which chilled me to the marrow and froze me to the spot. The audience. By now I was talking and singing on automatic pilot whilst my heart and brain were thudding with a heady mixture of adrenalin. I'll never know how I made it through to the interval, an hour later, but I do know that I wrenched those lenses out with such force that in the second act I was white-faced, red-eyed, and resembled one of the Brides of Dracula. It's not that I've anything against audiences, it's just that when they're a blur they're *so* friendly – just one big smiley mess. Sorry, but that's how I like you – warm, faceless, friendly and available – like a mother's breast.

Another innovation of lenses is seeing yourself without the cover of glasses from a three-foot distance for the first time since puberty. You simply freeze with the shock of the new. Or, in my case, the old. Mirrored lifts are the worst. No, I lie. Marks and Spencer's food halls are. Overhead fluorescent lights and mirrored columns prove beyond doubt that M & S have a deal with top Harley Street plastic surgeons – and 'Shall I take your bags, madam?' takes on an entirely different meaning.

It is You, isn't it?

I had a holiday recently in the Algarve. It was, in truth, the finest holiday I've ever spent on a building-site and I may never look a sardine in the gill again. But that's not the point.

The point is my face. My familiar, peaky little face. It's now what you might call 'on the circuit'. People see it and they have this immediate compulsion to come close and mull it over. It's too thin, it's too sharp, it's better than it looks on the telly, it reminds them of the wife, it gets right up their nose, etc. etc. Whatever it is, it's not my property any more and I can't put a 'Kindly Keep Off The Grass' notice on it. Sometimes I can handle it very well, other times I feel empathy with the gorilla-house on a wet Thursday in February.

At a one-donkey crossroads deep in the Algarve countryside, we stopped to take photographs. Outside the all-purpose store, bar and scrubbing-brush shop was a line of toothless old men on a bench. Whilst Jack sat with them and had a beer and a photo taken, I wandered into the gloom of the shop and rather studiously examined some Portuguese washing-up bowls. Into the shop came a young and very hot couple, leaving their bicycles outside. We exchanged a smile as they struggled to make their need for agua without gaz understood. 'Are you English?' I heard myself inquire. 'No, we're from New Zealand' came the reply. Then (and without surprise), 'And, you're Maureen Lipman, aren't you?' You could have knocked me down with a kiwi fruit.

It's when you see them coming towards you that your heart sinks. Not the nice ones, the kids or the ones who say 'Sorry to bother you but ...' After all, it goes with the job, doesn't it? I mean, 'Cripes, dear, if it was anonymity you'd wanted you should have gone into the family tailoring business,' I hear you say, with some justification. And why not? A lifetime of measuring men's inside legs and making weak jokes about dressing on the right side or the left – 'of the bedroom, I mean, sir! Haw, haw!' – would not have differed greatly from an average week in your average sit-com.

No, the ones who get me are the purposeful ones who are out to pull you down a peg or two when you were quite happy with the peg you were on. You can almost hear their conversation then they get back home ...

'Listen, you know me. I'm not backward in coming forward. I went straight up and I said, "Sign this. It's not for me, I can't stand you, it's for my mother-in-law, she liked your book. I don't know why! She's got no sense of humour!" '

One particular day I had a skinful of them. Amy and I went out for the day. At one point in an art gallery, I turned to see a formidable-looking woman dragging her recalcitrant husband and children in my direction. 'Come on, she won't mind, she's used to it,' she bellowed, blocking my exit. 'Sign this for the kids, will you?' A ticket-stub appeared beneath my chin. 'There, I told you she wouldn't mind!' I signed obediently, asking their names and writing one for each. 'Actually,' boomed their upwardly-registered mother, 'I'm always being ACCUSED of looking like you!' Amy and I exchanged speaking eyelids – it was the use of the word 'accused'. It could only mean trouble. 'I suppose it's *this*,' she went relentlessly on, 'I've been lumbered, too!' This was, of course, accompanied by violent jabbing of forefinger on aquiline bridge of nose. I smiled weakly. 'Oh, well, never mind, it hasn't affected your nature,' I said to her departing back. I looked round at Amy. Her eyes were filled with tears. 'Why do they always *say* these things, Mod?' she wailed, '*I* think you're beautiful!' It was quite a moment. I hugged her in front of the Matisses. 'Well, that's all that matters, then, kid,' I said, and we went off to Fortnum and Mason for a Peach Melba.

Later that day, and with a good half-inch of our respective hair on the floor of a Soho salon, we hit the black suede pump shop, where I was noiselessly relieved of a week's rehearsal pay on a pair of boots the same as the ones which fell apart in three months last time and a pair of the suede pumps ('EVERYBODY'S wearing them!') which, one week later, were flat and circular like dinghies. A couple of men were trying on shoes. One stood up to walk about in a left brogue and stopped in mid-tread. 'It's you, isn't it?,' he beamed, poking an elbow into his companion's anorak. 'Well, bloody hell! You look quite *normal* in real life. No, I didn't mean that, it's just that on the telly you look so ... so ...' Obviously, the appropriate adjective failed him because he burst into riotous laughter, abandoned the shoe and left.

Generally speaking, it's the voice. They look me full in the face and say, 'It's the voice I recognized, not you.' I wonder if Samantha Fox has the same problem? Someone once said he'd have known me anywhere by the voice but he'd have passed me by in the street on account I look *much* better in person than I do on the telly. They always mean that as a compliment, but it's a dubious one when you think about it: is it so very satisfactory to look MUCH better to one person than you do to twenty million?

One favourite came after a horrendous week of moon-lighting (working during the day on a comedy, *Exclusive Yarns*, in Southampton and whizzing back at night for the musical, *Wonderful Town*). At the end of the second show on the Saturday night, I virtually crawled out of the stage door and into a waiting cab. I collapsed into the front seat – I'm not a good backseat driver – and tried to harness my heart-beat. My eyelids fell. There was a twitch in my left cheek which I couldn't control. My body was leaden. Round about Camden, I was drifting into sleep when the driver slapped his thigh and said 'Well, I don't know, I *do* not know.' I opened one lip and managed to speak. 'Pardon?' I said. 'I'm saying,' said the jaunty fellow. 'My wife is going to be dead disappointed. Oh dear, oh dear, oh dear.' 'Why?' I asked politely, knowing the fault could only be mine. 'Well, when she finds out I had my favourite comedy lady in my cab and she weren't a bit funny – not one bit – well, what a shock she's going to get!' As you might imagine, I ignored him. For a full twelve seconds. Then I launched into the apology, the explanation and finally, by dint of superhuman endeav-our, the jokes.

Last Sunday I opened a tennis court. This required little other than turning up in Edgware wearing white on a somewhat blustery day. Naturally enough I had to play a couple of games for the long-suffering *Jewish Chronicle* photographer (who must have nightmares about having to snap me on his deathbed). I did this good-naturedly – and was as appalling as you might expect.

Afterwards, I signed tennis balls. Have you ever tried to sign a tennis ball? It's like icing grass. 'Can you write "Happy Birthday to Dominic, with love from Eliza, Lynne with an 'e' and Little Furry Niblick?"' Certainly madam – which kind of calligraphy do you favour?

I think my very *very* favourite though, was the woman who followed me falteringly around John Lewis's Lighting Department, stopping when I stopped, and making me very nervous indeed. Finally I turned and faced her. She stepped back timidly, proffered the obligatory cleaning ticket and stammered: 'I've been following you around ... I hope you don't ... would you sign this, please – you're a great fan of mine.'

I was. I *am*.

County Hotel, Westover Road, Bournemouth, Dorset   Telephone 22385

POST CARD

Photography by Morris Benjamin of Bournemouth

Photocolour

Ever Felt Red?

It was a red, circular skirt. Cut on the bias, my mother pointed out helpfully. In felt. All I knew was that I felt biased towards having it. Mother thought it was a liability, ie, it would have to be dry-cleaned, but I was twelve years old and had a Ph.D. in Advanced Whingeing. So finally, smugly, snugly it was mine.

Then came the search for the perfect sweater. In my mind's beady eye it was white with just a soupçon (had I known the word soupçon) of scarlet such as I'd once seen June Allyson sport in a skating sequence in some Saturday morning picture. Maybe if I got her outfit I'd get her husky voice to match?

After three successive Saturdays spent hissing in a changing room in C&A, I found it. It was white wool with a band of red figures waltzing round the welt. Gorgeous wasn't in it – but before you can say 'It'll show every mark' – *I* was.

That evening, while the rest of the family watched *Dixon of Dock Green*, I gathered together the total ensemble and placed it upon my person. Red skirt, white sweater, snowy socks, shoes Tuxon'd scufflessly white – not by me, needless to say. To top it all I added a red and white ribbon to the crest of my perm. To do my family credit, no one actually *said* I looked like an animated barber's pole.

The party was at the weekend. Saturday. In school. The teacher had been specific about dress: 'Don't wear your best clothes, girls, there'll be lots of running around and some floor-games!' Sod that for a lark, thought Lipman, who felt anxious to flash her felt at all costs. I climbed into it. Mentally I'd never been out of it. Peered into the mirror, pinched my cheeks, fiddled with my frizz, stuck out what should have been a chest, and, well pleased, sashayed, stiff with petticoats and pride, through the storm porch and out to the bus stop.

Strange to be in school at the weekend. Like some for-
bidden city. The cloakroom was all of a gossip with the
'ooh's' and 'aah's' of it. I bided my timing till the last, then,
Gypsy Rose Lee-like, flung off my good nap coat to reveal
all. It was worth it – a gobsmacked silence followed by the
'ooh's' and 'aah's' to end them all.

'What? This?' I demurred. 'Oh, I've had it for aaaages –
just never had the opportunity to wear it, so, y'know, I
thought I might as well . . . You coming up or what?'

Flanked by friends all a-flutter, we flowed into the
Assembly Hall, cleared of chairs for dancing and floor-games
purposes. The teacher in mufti (giggle, giggle, point, snigger)
called over the rabble: 'Girls, girls, pleeese, now can you all
make a circle and – QUIET, PLEASE – settle DOWN!' Here she
caught my eye, and then, swiftly, the rest of me. 'Ahem . . .
Could you all sit down' – here she definitely shot me a
disdainful and slightly triumphant look – on the FLOOR!' I
drew myself up to my full 4 feet 8 inches, flared my pupils
at the teacher, picked up my scarlet skirt, Vivien Leigh-style,
and, with a thud, parquet met felt and felt met parquet.
Frankly, my dear, I didn't *give* a damn!

It was halfway through Pass the Parcel that the penny
finally dropped. 'Nelly the Elephant' had just been chorus-
interruptus as she was saying goodbye to the thingy, and a
large girl in her mother's dirndl skirt from IIIB was attacking
the string round the paper with her teeth and pretending not
to hear that the music had started again, when I felt the red
drain out of my skirt and into my face.

'Don't wear your best clothes, there'll be floor-games'
doesn't mean don't wear your best clothes, there'll be floor-
games, you dull-brained twerp! It means don't wear your best
clothes, there'll be some girls who don't *have* best clothes, so
we don't want any showing off. Or up.

This thought, followed by an affirming glance round the
circle, was enough to ruin not only the rest of the party but
also the possibility of ever wearing my outfit care-lessly
again. It sat in my wardrobe malevolently for a while until,
out of sheer defiance, I grew two inches in as many months
and in most directions. Dry-eyed, I acquiesced when it finally

hit the bag of clothes for 'Poor Peggy, she's you-know-what-again, God help her', and I'm delighted to say I haven't given it a thought since. Not more than once a day, that is. For thirty years.

It was, I think, my first real understanding of what being spoiled meant, in more than one way, and it gave me a lifelong horror of over-dressing which, having just glanced through the photo-albums in search of an illustrative self-portrait, I seem to have conquered only too well.

Hair Piece

I awoke at 4.30 am with a pounding heart and the certain knowledge that my hair was orange. It was a mistake on my part to try to cover the grey with lowlights. A lowlight is fine for a casserole. They're less impressive as they smoulder, marmalade-like, over a pair of kohl-black eyebrows. It was the thought of facing myself in the morning light, followed by a swift but burnished appearance on a TV arts review programme later that day, that had caused me to wake up damp and thudding.

At 8.30 am I drove to my first appointment in Balderton Street, planning to buy a hat at Miss Selfridge afterwards, en route to the filming. While feeding the meter I had a sudden blank on whether my meter was in front or behind my car. I called on a conveniently passing traffic warden to help me out. She did, only partially concealing a smirk which signalled 'Well, *her* reputation comes before her!'

Sheepishly I fed the other meter, too, and slouched in to see my Alexander Technique teacher, who's helping me to stand up straight. Forty minutes later my neck was long, my hips were free, my knees were out, my back was wide and I'd learned how to sit down. It was a real breakthrough.

car *wasn't* and turned instantly into a small, twisted, carrot-topped fishwife. 'My car's been stolen,' I screamed at the same traffic warden. 'You remember me, I asked you about the meters ... well my car was just here on this corner and ...' I raced across the road, risking knees, neck and most other bent bits to grab her sleeve. 'Not this corner love.' She looked at me with pity and something like disbelief. 'Same corner, next street.' She pointed to where my car was, and always had been.

The filming was in Soho. I was reviewing a Steve (be still my heart) Martin film which had disappointed me. The producer put me, a sound man and a camera man into a London taxi (for street cred) and asked the driver to go round Piccadilly until I'd finished speaking. Needless to say, we never passed a hat shop. The taxi driver leaned through his window at one point and passed me a small scrap of paper. On one side was his name and number and status as an official London guide. On the other was an elderly Jewish joke, making much of the word 'Meshuggenah', or nutcase.

On the way to my next appointment with Denis King, a piano and some Joyce Grenfell songs, I stopped at a nearby theatre to smile winsomely at the box office boys in the hope that they'd recognize me, in spite of my Titian disguise, and sell me some tickets for their sell-out play. They didn't. My friend Simon Jones was over from the States and I'd promised him seats that night, and then forgotten all about it. After I had queued for forty-five minutes some returns returned and we were in. Triumph! When I reached Denis's, I'd almost forgotten about my brassy hair. He hadn't though. On the piano was a large tin of Duraglit.

No sooner was I home and motherly than it was time to dress up and head back to the theatre. I chose a discreet navy blue to cancel out the glow from above.

We drove calmly into town and parked easily on a single yellow. 'It's OK after 6.30 pm,' I confidently reassured Jack as he eased the side wheels of the car on to the pavement. 'It saves the £7 car park and the crush on the way out.' It was a balmy evening. In more than one sense.

Simon, his wife Nancy, Jack and I sat through the first act of the sold-out play. Then by comon consent we crab-walked through the foyer and out through the main doors, like kids escaping from double Greek which, in a way, we were. We were discussing whether the director had actually nailed the actors to the stage or not when we got back to where the car wasn't. Only this time it *really wasn't*.

'Er ... you haven't seen a blue Honda ... er, that was on this corner earlier, have you officer?' we asked levelly.

'It's in the police pound in Penton Street,' he replied even leveller and with considerably more alliteration.

'But officer,' (my scream was silent as an epidural), 'it was on a single yellow line.'

'Yes, madam, and the pavement.'

It was nine o'clock. We were sad, mad and starving. Which took priority? We opted for comfort and retired to our favourite chippie for lots of it. My friends, we were well into our starters when we realized the starters were now *hors d'œuvres*. I can hardly bring myself to tell you. The chippie had changed. It was no longer a chippie. It was a 'seafood pommefriterie'. With accordant prices. Walking out after the first act was becoming an addiction. Glumly we headed Islingtonwards for the ritual finger-wagging and fine.

Well, we were prepared for their sarcasm, we were prepared for their bill. What we weren't prepared for was their total closure. *Fermé. Fini. Fertig.* And other words beginning with F. Perfect. In the empty streets we finally flagged down a taxi, prostrated ourselves before him and persuaded him to drive to the hitherto uncharted climes of Muswell Hill.

Listen, we were really lucky getting home at all. What if other vicious criminals like us whose wheels had happened to be on a kerb after 6.30 pm had come from, say, Milton Keynes, to see the sell-out play? They would have had to add the price of a hotel room to their night out. So, £120 for the night, £57 to get the car out, £12 parking fine, £35 for fish and chips. £224 so far.

Take no notice of me. I'm just seeing red. Listen, it's a night out, isn't it?

I've discovered over the years that if my hair is all right, then generally speaking, so am I. I also notice as the years lurch by, and I wouldn't dream of telling anyone but you, that my mother was right. Not about everything, mind, but about a couple of things. Well – one. 'Sleeping with a bag on your head keeps your hair tidy!' I know, I know, it's against all the rules of nature, and we free spirits grew up in the Sixties letting our hair just *be*, didn't we?

No mention in the Leonard Cohen songbook, as far as I know, of *Suzanne* feeding him tea and oranges all the way

A book launch is a bit like an opening, so I wore my curtains and Ian McKellen made a curtain call.
(*Deborah Robson*)

Actress being recycled for charity.

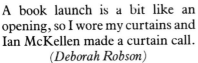

Comic strip. A young Lipman heaves a thigh of relief for Manchester United.

Men seldom go senseless for girls in soft lenses.

The papers called Frank Carson and I 'simply dashing' – I called us Tweed Undone and Twee Dundee.
(Syndication)

Who are all those weirdos with Mike Batt? British Telecom chief supporting the cream of RADA – and me.

He's done his portion – now he's ready to eat one! The Barmitzvah Boy and his family. (*Richard Shymansky*)

'Never mind the camera, your soup's getting cold.' Clockwise from hostess: Astrid Ronning, Denis King, Julia McKenzie, Jerry Harte, Anne Hutton (agent), Jonathan Lynn, Bill Freedman, friends Lesley Joseph and Louie Ramsay and producer Michael Codron. (*Richard Shymansky*)

Dad with Mum in the best of times.

Philip Sayer, to know him was to love him.

An old penny for your thoughts.
(Sophie Baker)

from China with a nylon bag on her head! But come the morning I don't suppose she sprayed it, gelled it and covered it in cans full of failed meringue, which made her hands curl. So presumably she didn't resemble an Elderly Finnish Troll either, like we do.

Around my bath sit biodegradable bottles of organic shampoo from pansies' brains or the like. Seaweed conditioner, mangelwurzel scalp massage, follicle repair builder and a perm and colour rejuvenator, which appears to have a Ph.D. In trichology. Another ology even.

Mother, on the other head, goes to Bernard of Anlaby Road once a fortnight, where she's ceremonially washed, lotioned, rollered, dried, combed-out and lacquered for roughly the price of my pansy-brain shampoo. Once home, rainhood under scarf, over head, she pins up the sides, grips the fringe, adds the elasticated bag for extra provocation and I swear, with my curly hand on a can of ozone-destroyer, that not one hair ventures out of its area for the full fourteen days.

I'm growing mine at the moment for a part I've been playing, which accounts for its condition. And mine. Two inches on my hair and I look as if I've had my face thinned and people start speaking in hushed voices in my presence. Cut off the two inches, or better still four, add forty quids' worth of 'body wave' and it's 'My word, you do look well. Have you been away?'

I've always fancied one of those glossy little cap hairdos – 'gamine', you know. Terrific if you've got a face like Bambi's mother and a figure like a beanpole. Less entrancing, I suppose, if you've got them the other way round.

My own daughter has an allergy to scissors. She's scissorphobic. Her fringe is so long, I sometimes mistake her for Rolf Harris. Not that I make a fuss about it. I don't. Mind my own business, that's my motto. Let her come to me *begging* for a haircut. 'Please, Mod – I can't see!' Let her implore. 'But, darling, why not part it and tie it in a knot under your chin?' I shall sweetly rejoinder. 'Headscarves are making a comeback this year, you know.'

Mind you, they do wash it themselves these days, the kids, I think. (Perhaps the brown line round the bath is just felt

tip and the hair in the plughole just cat.) At least the days of
Friday night being the night the neighbours report us to the
NSPCC for malicious blinding of offspring with intent are
over.

Yes, we *had* purchased the yellow polystyrene shampoo
guard from Mothercare – that had the same effect on them
as two crossed sticks had on Dracula.

'Just one more rinse, darling, and it's all done . . .'

'You always say that – then you – Waaaaagh! It's in my
eyeeee!'

'All better now, darling, – over in two shakes – come on,
close your . . .'

'My eyes! Waaagh! I hate you! I hate you! None of the
other mothers . . .' etc, etc.

And that was just the *first* shampoo!

Yes, at least it's clean now. Apart from Supernits, of
course. Is it me or does the school letter come crawling round
once a fortnight at your place? 'Look out! The nits are with
us again!'

'Should you find any of these intrepid little creatures in
your child's hair, it is more than likely that they are also in
yours.' (Oh, goody!) 'Simply soak your entire family and any
paying guests, pets and visiting gas meter readers in new
miracle "ZAPNIT" for fifteen hours and all traces of termite
will be terminated.'

What I most relish is the thought of me, eight hours
through the treatment, rushing blindly to a meeting at the
BBC, hair sodden, stinky and moving around of its own
accord: 'Sorry about this, it's been a bit of a lousy day. Er –
oh, you must be the Head of Lice Entertainment . . . Sorry,
I mean . . .'

Wearily, I take down my trusty toothcomb and lacerate
my children's tender scalps. 'Waaagh! Stop it! Gerroff, I
haven't gorrem!' So far, so clear. Actually my son's rather
disappointed, he was hoping to farm them and train them
into a novelty act.

Is your head itching now? Mine, too. Mine itches the very
moment I see the ruddy school letter.

Continuing the theme of mangled extremities, how are
your nails doing? You know, they're the spatula-shaped

chewy bits on the end of your fingers with bits of chipped magenta in the grooves and grey ends. I'm told that in the States, the state of your nails is regarded as an indication of the state of your psyche. I think it's interesting to have a split, grubby, overlooked psyche, don't you?

For Christmas, I had my mother's nails 'wrapped and extended'. She loved it. Kept waving her hands around like a Jewish air hostess. She's furious now, though. Having spent £2.50 on a pair of extra-strength rubber gloves, 80p on cuticle remover and £1.20 on ridge-filler, the bloody nails have all broken off again – ridges, cuticles et al. It seems that I'm responsible. It's sad because I shall cherish the memory of her gazing at the palms of her newly extended hands and saying 'Fancy. It's the first time in all my life I've been able to see the back of my nails from the palms of my hands.'

I'm going to cut the kids' toenails tonight. I'm allowed to do it once the nails have begun to grow round and underneath their toes. It's a doddle. I just stuff the offensive foot in a waste bin, peer short-sightedly into the darkness until my glasses fall off, squeeze the scissors and await the sickening sound of two months' growth of calcium piercing my ear, my nostril and my bra. I shall then use a little bit of language that'll make their hair curl up and dye.

Transen-dentals

I went to the dentist for the annual scale and polish. You know, the one where you sit there and lie through your teeth about spending every waking hour flossing and probing and massaging and never go out of an evening without your single-headed brush, and the Aussie hygienist who looks like Brooke Shields on a good day takes one prod at your gum and it spouts blood like Moby Dick on a bad day and the game's up there and then. The one where you end up buying, out of guilt, an electric toothbrush costing £89 which tickles your gums to the point where you giggle helplessly in your bathroom, alone, and the family get over-concerned and leave jars of Passiflora in obvious places.

Well, this time I did well – almost got a badge to stick on my lapel saying 'I was a brave girl at Martyn the dentist's today'. Almost. I didn't have a Valium injection and I didn't have laughing gas (who needs that when you've got an entertaining toothbrush?), and I didn't cry or faint or bite the hygienist or do any of the things normally associated with one of my trips to the dentist. Either I'm growing up or my gums are maturing. One dentist I know, is so used to dealing with hypersensitive children that he says – and I mean to *me* – 'Now, pop this in *like a lollipop*', but I don't mind that either because, about twenty years after everyone else, I've discovered the benefits of meditation.

Oh, I know I'm always on about some alternative or other. You've no doubt yawned frequently to the sound in print of me extolling osteopathy, Alexander Technique, Royal Jelly, Republican Jelly, Bach flower remedies, Bach-again flower remedies, Reflexology and any other 'ology' that fails to carry the approval of your average GP. But what I say is – if you didn't want the benefit of my second-hand wisdom, you shouldn't have put down that Dr Ruth book, which taught you how to make love with one foot on the shag-pile and the other in Sainsbury's, in favour of this one. The point remains that twice a day for twenty minutes in your own time and in the location of your choice you can refresh the parts that Dr Ruth can only fantasize about.

Years ago in Manchester, my husband was taught to medi-tate by a Yiddishe guru in Didsbury. I'm serious. He found it incredibly rewarding and had a couple of momentous experiences of such excitement that he tried to recreate the excitement instead of going back to what caused it (the old Orgasmic-Goal orientation – see Dr Ruth, pages 12 to 461), so he gave up for a few years. But not before he taught me 'the way' and even gave me – probably when short of a birthday present, his 'mantra' – his personal word by which to meditate (sssh, don't tell the guru, he'd turn in his cave – you're not suppose to reveal your mantra to *anyone*. Even if you're living, eating and sleeping with them. In whatever position. See Dr Ruth – what page? The well thumbed one!)

Well, I was interested, which won't surprise you, and tried it on and off, mostly off, for the moments of stress over the momentously stressful years. Then, on a weekend's trip to Grayshotts Health Farm to recharge the batteries and the credit cards, I attended a lecture on meditation given by a simply marvellous, crumply GP with about as much airy-fairy, guru-y wispiness as, say, Denis Healey, and I was moved to find out more. He claimed that it didn't matter what mantra you said, or indeed if you didn't have one, as long as you cleared out your mind. In fact, he passed round a hat filled with old, used mantras and I've used the one I picked ever since. One lady, he claimed, almost lost her marbles when the word she picked out of the hat was the same as the one she'd been handed 27,000 feet up a Himalayan mountain in her backpack and bivouac, far-out, cool-man days. Listen. These things happen. Nothing mystical about it . . . So why are my neck hairs rising just writing about it?

The doctor's mild and unsensational belief was that fifteen minutes twice a day, on bus or train, in the roaring traffic's boom, or the silence of your lonely room, can utterly change your life. And if that doesn't sound better than a Paul Daniels tape, I'll eat my copy of *Nobody Does It Better* by Carly Simons.

Back in the stress where I live, I imparted the info to my trusty co-star and pianist, Denis King, expecting his habitual response to such suggestions: 'Bollocks!' Instead, uncharacteristically, he went and signed up with the Maharishi, paid out £146, and has never regretted it for a single minute, although in fairness it has to be said that his wife *has*. The sign on his door saying 'Do not disturb – meditating' is like a red flag to a Young Conservative to her and to their three-year-old son. Be that as it may, fired by his enthusiasm to my enthusiasm – I've started doing it again. Meditating, I hasten to add, before you ask me 'In bed, on a chair or on the shag-pile?'

Funnily enough, I do it in a chair. Hands on knees and lights out with a mind buzzing like a bee and the strong conviction that I should be sorting out something more tangible than my mind. It was at its very best in between shows of *Re:Joyce!* Two-and-a-half hours on stage, alone, but for my mystical meditator Denis, followed by another two-and-a-half hours is not your average form of relaxation. If you think it was hard for me, think what it was like for Gary, the sound technician, who had to sit out front in a box, wired up and WATCH the whole thing seven times a week and twice on Saturdays. He began to wilt after four weeks. After ten he was hardly able to look me in the ear. I resolved to tell him my mantra.

So here I am extolling the worth of twenty minutes' silent meditation as a means of renewing and refreshing your channels. I mean, I'm well aware you don't have to face single-handed and prattling, blowing your own cor-anglais and generally acting up before a captive crowd of thousands. But you could use it to combat office harassment (do I hear you say 'Chance would be a fine thing?'). Or the girl with the nail polish and cuticle remover on the five-items-only check-out at Tesco's, or the doctor's waiting-room at 9.35 am when the surgery says SHUT and your child has a conker in his windpipe. The unbelievable thing is that it's easy. And it works. Two things which are not always synonymous.

There is a school of designer Buddhism around at the

moment whose disciples chant regularly whenever and wherever they need to. I was once handed a business-card by a rather large, florid trumpet-player which read 'Nam Myo Renga Kyo' or something similarly memorable. 'Just say it,' he said, 'it really works.' It rang a bell. I realized that the odd muffled mumbling from the direction of my co-star before our first entrance was the sentence on the business-card. They were *all* at it! At the time I scoffed. And no one scoffs louder than I scoff, but now I'm prepared to eat my business-card and say 'Whatever gets you through the night, chuck . . .'

Alternatively, phone Dr Ruth – appointments only – wear a frogman suit, a lace pinafore, and carry a riding crop and a packet of plastic floss-threaders – and take the bit between your teeth – mmmmm!

Is There an Alternative to Alternatives?

It was Denis's idea that Jack and I should have a medical.

'I have one every year,' he said, implying, 'Doesn't every-one?' in his tone.

His wife rolled her eyes rather and murmured, 'And I get to hear about it every day,' as her husband hastened away to show us his computer print-out from the medical labora-tory.

I was impressed – 'Cytology', 'Albumin Globulin and Total Biliruben' (sounded like a Kosher delicatessen) – MCV/MCH/HCT – I was hooked as only a true hypo-chondriac can be. 'How do you know what it all means?' I queried.

'Well, you don't, really – but if anything was fatal they'd probably tell you.'

After a few more days of subtle hints – 'If you're a smoker, with young children, over a certain age, in a high-stress job, it's *lethal* not to have a medical' – 'Oh all right! All right! You on commission or what?' – I booked us in, though Jack was against it: 'I had one for insurance six years ago. I'm fine.'

The offices were frighteningly smart, more like an adver-tising agency than a doctor's. Black leather and chrome, pools of light and velvet pile carpet. ''S the only pile that'll ever dare come in here,' I whispered to Jack. Not a trace of the files and advertising matter and bits of old stethoscope and fading eye-charts that clutter our family doctor's surgery. No Sandra in reception shouting 'Right, Maureen, he'll see you now I like the commercial 'ow's Adam's verruca doin'?' Just a slip of a doe-eyed girl at a black ash table and not another patient in sight – was it a front? Might we both end up balloon-dancing in Hong Kong?

The young doctor looked like a young doctor in, say, *Young Doctors*, lean and fit in a striped shirt and tie, yuppie-style, with dark curly hair and a tan. We sat in adjacent chairs opposite him and he asked, 'Why are you here?' Quick as a flash and game for a good laugh, I said, 'Because Denis sent us' exactly at the same time as Jack said, 'Because Maureen wanted to have a good cry . . .'

(Actually Jack's little quip was true. I always cry at the doctor's, have done for years. Also frequently at the dentist, the children's headmasters, and the music from *The Way We Were*. Nevertheless, it was unnecessary of him to say it – I've spoken to an analyst about it and I'll probably grow out of it, when I'm bigger. So there!)

The doctor picked up his silver pen and hovered it over a blank sheet. 'Well, we'll do Maureen first as she has to rush off. Are you quite fit generally?'

'Oh yes.' Jack glanced at the hypochondriac. I glanced back. 'Well, considering I'm working as hard as I am with all the stress involved, I think I'm probably very fit.'

'No chronic problems?'

'No – not really.'

Jack leaned over and bellowed conspiratorially, 'Tell him about the migraines.' This in front of someone I am trying to *impress* with my good health, my vivacious vitality, my lack of need to be there.

'Oh' – grudgingly – 'well, yes. I get migraines. Sometimes.' A ten-minute discussion ensued with much writing of joined-up words and drawing of arrows.

Then: 'Anything else?'

'No, not really.'

'Tell him about the pneumonia.' Again he's here, the man on my right who didn't want to be there.

I told him. About the pneumonia. And the bad shoulder. And the sudden pain in my chest when I'm on my trampoline. And the floaters in my right eye. And the PMT. And the fibroid and the caesarians. And the cramp and the croup and the bag under one eye. Finally when he ran completely out of paper and was writing on his cuff, I stopped.

There was a silence in the room as we all simultaneously racked our brains for a missing disease. Then the doctor suggested he and I went into the next room for an examination of the condemned woman.

It's odd how you can chat so animatedly whilst someone you've only just met is poking your most intimate spots, isn't it? At one of my less intimate spots, my right ear, he stopped sharp.

'What's this 'ere?'

I laughed politely. It seemed like a routine doctor's gag.

'No, really,' he said earnestly, torch in ear. 'What's this piece of metal in your ear?'

'Oh, that,' I remembered, 'that's just my acupuncture needle. For stress.'

I could see he was troubled by the need to start a new piece of paper when we got back to the surgery.

'Does it work?'

'Of course it works!' I yelled. 'You don't think I'm normally as effing calm and relaxed as this, do you?'

'Are you on any medication at all?' he asked as we returned to the surgery.

'Yes. I take Concorde every evening before the show.'

His pencil stopped again. 'You take Concorde every evening before –'

'It's Regina royal jelly and ginseng combined. Gives you an energy boost. Oh, and it probably makes you a bit – you know . . .'

'A bit what?'

'Well, a bit – you know . . .'

Jack was studying a potted fern with enormous interest.

'It's a bit of an aphrodisiac apparently,' I explained – 'which is tremendously useful when you've just done a two-and-a-half hour show, driven 45 minutes home, eaten a baked potato the size of a human foot, scrubbed off two layers of greasepaint, nose shading, violet eyeshadow and seemingly permanent mascara, brushed one and a half cans of lacquer off the split ends, flossed the gums, massaged the bridgework, popped the ear plugs over the acupuncture needle, put the airplane mask over the anti-ageing eye cream and – pièce de lack of résistance – applied the 'Tonic Bust' to prevent anything descending further south during the night.

The doctor re-focused his eyes and returned to his paperwork. 'Well – er from yes – er, on that subject – I think you should probably have a mammography.'

'Oh yippee!' I groaned. 'A mammography – every woman's idea of a real good time.' For the uninitiated, you place your breast on a breast-high slab of ice-cold metal and then watch in deep disbelief as a second slab of ice-cold metal descends onto the breast, elongating it into a sort of Bourbon biscuit shape. Then they photograph it. This is neither comfortable nor attractive and leaves you wondering whether the radiographer will ever eat another Bourbon biscuit, let alone dunk one.

I swallowed noisily. 'Fine,' I said.

He continued with the feed-line for the punchline of the decade. 'It's best to have one yearly, after forty, and quite frankly – your breasts are a bit of a nightmare to a doctor.'

There was only the merest hiatus before the breasts-in-question's husband said, 'What would they be to an accountant?'

There are several reasons why I love the man. This had to be one of them.

Seriously though, the medical worked wonders. No, there's nothing like a good laugh to make you feel better about yourself. Expensive? Noooo! 'Just send the bill to Denis, will you?'

Incidentally, I've just had *another* medical, this time for insurance, and I seem to be perfectly fine, except for one thing, I've grown. Half an inch. I speak as a forty-three-year-old. Does this mean that someone could say 'At last Maureen Lipman is growing in stature?'

Unnecessary doctor joke:

> Doctor: 'I have some good news and some bad news. Which would you like first?'
> Patient: 'The bad news.'
> Doctor: 'OK. The bad news is that you have six months to live.'
> Patient: 'Oh my God! What's the good news?'
> Doctor: 'The good news is – you see that nurse over there? The blonde with the enormous breasts?'

Patient: 'Yes.'
Doctor: 'Well, we "did it" at lunchtime.'

To add insult to injury:

Doctor: 'I'm afraid I have bad news for you Mr Bristow.
You have GLSH.'
Mr B: 'What in hell's name is that?'
Doctor: 'I'm afraid it's Gonorrhoea, Leprosy, Syphilis
and Herpes.'
Mr B: 'Oh hell's teeth! – What can you do for me?'
Doctor: 'Well, we put you in a private room and feed
you nothing but veal escalopes and pancakes.'
Mr B: 'And will that help my condition?'
Doctor: 'No. But it's all we can get under the door.'

Finally and in total conclusion I must tell you what happened
when we took Adam to a specialist to find out if he had a
particular familial complaint. The specialist was caring and
considerate towards Adam and explained very carefully the
nature of the symptoms and the tests they would be doing.
Adam listened intently. Finally the doctor completed his
explanation and said 'Now, Adam, are there any questions
you would like to ask *me*?'

There was a twenty-second pause then Adam said: 'Yes.
Do you believe that man can levitate?'

Let's Piste Again

What I know about 'la piste' could be engraved on the side of a nose shield. Just the one trip. Austria, it was, before we were parents. With another couple who were also first-time skiers. Thirteen years later that other couple have just booked their fifteenth skiing holiday. We, on the other hand, are just getting over the first one.

It started on the aeroplane on the way out. Jack happened to glance at his hand. 'What's this on my thumb,' he mused. I joined him in gazing at the large red lump forming just below the joint and we mused together. 'It's a lump,' I diagnosed. He agreed. 'Does it hurt?' 'Only when you press it.' I pressed it. It did. I thumbed through the aeroplane magazine looking for articles on pre-ski protuberances – curiously there were none, and we decided to ignore it in the hope that it would go down roughly when the plane did.

Once in our picturesque ski village, our friends were anxious to hire the gear and get straightaway into the serious business of descending headfirst down something snow-capped. We queued up for our boots, our poles, our skis and met our instructor, Hans, and the rest of the eager beavers in our party.

The first thing that struck me was the weight of everything. Not just the skiing equipment but the sweater leaning on the anorak, the goggles leaning on the nose and the woolly hat leaning on your ears. Admittedly I'm not really the right shape for it all. If you can imagine a benevolent and myopic stork in goggles and woolly hat, then you've just about got the picture. As for Jack – two words say it all. Eric Morecambe. Plus what had now turned out to be a ganglion. Apparently you are supposed to beat a ganglion on the head with a heavy book and it will subside. But what book? And

how do you hit the base of a thumb without dislocating
what's meant to be grasping a ski-pole for the next week?

As we togged up and down the Seefeld baby slopes learning
how to sno-plough and how to get up when you failed to
sno-plough, it became apparent that this was, with or without
ganglion, perhaps not going to be Jack's Number One sport.
Each time he set off, it was obvious to those of us who loved
him that he was wildly out of control and a danger to those
who came before and after him. He also managed to look as
though he were in shock, in pain and in hysterics at one and
the same time. At the end of the day our friends and I had
mastered 'bend ze knees' and 'turn in ze feet' and had turned
a healthy shade of scarlet around the nasal slopes. Jack was
by now mumbling as he hauled his way up the slope to face
further pain and humiliation.

'Christ! This is bloody hard work – if I'd wanted a holiday
like this I could have gone down the mines for a fortnight.'

I mumbled back reassuring words about sun and invig-
orating air as I sweated in line behind him, and ignored his
face and his thumb in the exhilaration of that first controllable
lurch into the unknown. It's like feeling the car move to your
bidding on that first driving lesson – thrilling, potentially
dangerous and powerful. I'm convinced politics come under
the same heading but I'm not too sure about thumbs.

After a day or two of piste-aching Jack threw in the towel
and headed off to join the cross-country skiers. Somehow,
in his absence the fun went out of it and I decided to slope
off and join him on the flat. I giant-stepped for a mile or two
until I came upon a picture that is for ever engraved on the
goggles of my mind.

Ahead of me was an elliptical circle of maybe twenty
people, the combined ages of whom must have seventy score
and ten. Most of them were windcheatered, leather-skinned,
leder-hosened Austrians of indeterminable sex, on very short
skis, who made Jack clutching his poles in throbbing hands
look curiously like an evacuated child.

'And a-von and a-two and a-von and a-two and leeft ze
back foot high and a-von and a-two,' said the ancient instructor as the geriatric circle slow-motion goose-stepped its way
round and round the circle like an animated (but not very)

roundabout. I began to laugh, at first to myself and then uncontrollably for Britain and the Home Counties. I wheezed and spluttered and whooped and finally overdid it totally and ended up by subsiding with my chin in a snow-drift in an attitude of Muslim prayer.

After that Jack gave up the skiing altogether and I took it very steady. The competitiveness in the group reminded me of the casting board at drama school. 'How high are you going tomorrow? How's your turning? Hans reckons I'll be on the big slopes by Thursday' etc. The shmoozing (old Yiddish word meaning to suck up to) of Hans which went on in our party was stomach-turning. Tall, blond and muscular, he was without doubt one peach of a downhill racer, but he was also unsophisticated – he was a baker during off-piste season – and clearly bewildered by much of the attention he was getting après ski.

'Your country very beautiful Hans.'

'Oh ja – beautiful, ja.'

'England very dirty and depressing.'

'Ja?'

'Oh, ja – air very polluted and people sad – ' (Great grimace for illustration.) 'Here your people very happy and friendly all time.' (Don't mention Hitler, I restrain myself.)

'Oh, ja – maybe only sometime.'

'You must see our terrible country?'

'No, I very much like see Carnaby Street Liverpool.' (This cat would kill for just one *glimpse* of our terrible country.)

'Oh, no, you wouldn't – Austria has much beauty – big cakes – big lakes – England none of these things. Have more Gluhwein, Hans.'

'Oh, danke.'

'Your nightclubs better than ours – your sweaters better than ours – your Gluhwein better than ours!' Big cheers all round – Hans is our hero.

The night before our departure I watched this pageant of mock humility rise in a crescendo of thanks, tips, tears and promises of sometime next year. Scraps of paper were passed relentlessly from the skiers to Hans – 'Any time you're in Swindon – *anytime*. You'll be more than welcome – ugly and

depressing though it is – we'll show you a good time – we
mean that, Hans – we really do.'

'Now, Hans, that's my office number and these two are
our home numbers – now, Pat and I really mean this –
anytime you're in Doncaster or even in Leeds – we'll pick
you up. Bye bye. Thanks. See you next year.'

Slipping back to rescue the camera case, Jack was charmed
and moved to see Hans quietly remove all the addresses from
his anorak pocket and throw them casually on the fire at the
same time as he ordered an English beer.

We came home, those of us who'd skied and those who
hadn't, with a warm glow inside and outside of our skins.
There was a true feeling of achievement attached to our little
'I skied down a mountain' certificate, and a bit of weight had
definitely dropped from the thighs on to the slopes. I've been
meaning to go again with the children. My son would adore
it – my comfort-loving daughter would work hard to achieve
a ganglion before leaving and sit contentedly by a log fire for
the duration with a good book and a hot Ribena. And why
not? Different slopes for different folks.

Spoilsport

I was watching the Sumo wrestling on Channel 4 the other night and it occurred to me that perhaps, at last, I'd found my sport. Over 300 lbs of oscillating blubber held modestly together by a taffeta jock-strap which serves to keep one cheek from slapping the other – the whole lot topped by a hairstyle which looks like a Sainsbury's Catherine Wheel. This was Sally, the ginormous Hawaiian. And as I watched him hurl handfuls of salt round the ring as a prelude to hurling handfuls of Japanese wrestler around the heads of the spectators, I could feel my heart begin to beat behind my nightie and the partisan words begin to form on my open lips: 'Tear 'is 'ead off, Sall! Kick 'im in the kimono! Get stuck in, Sall! Chew 'is thumb!'

Suddenly it put me in mind of *The Gloria Hunniford Show*. Before I answer the question springing to *your* open lips, I have to tell you that my mother has just rung. The conversation went as follows:

'I say, what do you think about Fergie going skiing when she's pregnant?'

'I'm outraged, Mother.'

'Really? Everyone is *here*. There's a lot of controversy. Don't you think it's ridiculous?'

'Mother, for all I care, she can abseil off the top of Harrods if that's her pleasure. The girl likes to ski – it's her sport.'

Mother didn't, couldn't, will never understand why a sport should take precedence over sensible activities like, say, a nice coffee morning, or an afternoon in the House of Fraser or a kaluki evening (that's a nice card game, not to be confused with an unendurable evening of Japanese theatricals).

In many ways, it must be said, I share her views. Not for me the pursuit of excellence on the playing fields of England.

Or anywhere. I was the one at school with the four-year period. 'Please, Miss, can I be excused hockey/netball/gym – I'm U-N-W-E-L-L.' Of course, they didn't fall for my cursed excuse, so I then tried going into sharp reverse to avoid the dreaded twice-weekly occurrence. 'Oh, Miss, Miss!' – clutching stomach, rolling eyes and hyper-ventilating – 'Please don't stop me playing hockey! My temperature isn't that bad – it's only 109°! I don't want to let the side down – don't send me to the Sick Room! I'm fine, HONESTLY! It's NOTHING!'

Every skill I ever learned in the Art of Coarse Acting I learned in that sweaty cloakroom before Double Hockey. I must say my daughter seems to have inherited them. Effort-lessly, she contrives to have a violin class which clashes head-on with hockey. I'm all for missing hockey – how could I not be when my class coined a special place in the team-list for me: 'Lipman IVb. Position: Left Outside'? I just wish her violin-playing showed any sign of improving through this extra-mural enthusiasm. I've a feeling she talks all through the class – probably about hockey.

My son, however, is a sports fanatic if ever there was one. His feet just naturally kick things. Or he pots things or he over-arm bowls at things. Just like his dad – who, one memorable Sports Day at *his* school, broke the *world* record for the 100 yards sprint. For ten minutes the school erupted with the dazzling success of it. Until some spoilsport thought to measure the 100-yard track – and found it was just over 70 yards.

My career as the world's fastest cyclist was ended sharply by my protruding teeth. It was just a fantasy I nurtured for a few years as I puffed and panted my way through the ten-foots and alleyways of downtown Hull. My cycling was so fast, it seemed, that I was almost invisible to the naked eye. Was it a bird? Was it a plane? No, it was Fly-Mo, the fastest thing on two mudguards. The dream ended one day when I hit a hole whilst flashing at the speed of light down Chan-terlands Avenue. Bike and biker parted company and, some slow-motion seconds later, my two front teeth touched down on the tarmac. Over the years I reckon Raleigh Cycles and a highly developed sense of drama have cost me about £7,000 in porcelain and untold damages in gum-erosion.

So. I'm a rotten sport. Mind you, I swim like a fish – a cooked one. No, I mean it. My dad used to take me to the baths every Tuesday night. I can still smell the changing rooms. The water was as full of peril as an early Spielberg film. Hulking great men would leap off the edge, in fives, and land on me. My perm would stink under my swimming hat. My bathing costume was going to roll down and reveal what breast stroke really meant. I would spend a miserable hour hopping from one foot to the other just out of the babies' end with my eyes scrunched shut and my mouth in a knot. Finally, with 'Don't walk on the wet edge, you'll get a ver-ruca' ringing in my ears, and 'Make sure your hair is BONE dry before you go out into the cold' ringing in my brain, we would lay siege to the fish-and-chip shop which was my main reason for going in the first place.

Anyroad up, *The Gloria Hunniford Show* sent Nigel Havers and me to Croydon to review the wrestling. I could have thought of a marginally more interesting way for us to spend the evening together, but it would have been harder to review. Expecting yawning boredom, I found it riveting. The audience, not the wrestling. It really is true. Perfectly normal women in bouclé hats and Windsmoor jackets turn into tribal warlocks at the flash of a pair of trunks pressing a man's upper arm into a figure eight. 'Finish-'im-off-rip-'is-guts-out-fump-'im-in-the-belly-ya-big-ugly-bag-of-chisels-yer-tattoo'd-dick'ead! Ruin 'im! Grab 'is goolies!' – and that's only the printable part.

Nigel, the old Charmer, and I were half-nelson'd with mirth. Later that week on *The Gloria Hunniford Show* we tried to explain what we'd seen – and found ourselves, without prior consultation, wrestling each other to the ground and rolling all over each other.

Like I said, when you find your sport you should stick with it.

Last year I was invited to Wimbledon on the big day by ticket-holding members of the media. I was terribly excited. I love to *watch* tennis. My playing greatly resembles my swimming – steady, sturdy and tremendously boring, with just the one stroke. The acquisition of a new Wilson racquet fooled me into thinking I could teach Adam how to play. He overtook me after three tantrum-filled games (mine, not his).

The day was balmy and strawberry-filled. The Wimbledon Courts seem small and friendly when you're actually *in* them, and the finals, though tense tennis were terrific tennis. Steffi smashing hell out of Martina and Becker demolishing Edberg.

In between the ladies and the gents (matches I mean) we were ushered to private rooms, where, beneath striped awnings, we were right royally entertained to a distinguished tea. Playwrights rubbed padded shoulders with heads of commerce and newspaper barons passed clotted cream to the wives of the men who produce documentaries on waste in the Third World.

At one point, Paul Fox the managing director of BBC TV threw forth into the welter of conversation what I took to be the following line: 'Well, what do we all think of yesterday's historic meeting, eh? Mandela and Botham – whoever thought that day would ever come?'

I stopped silly-mid-scone, eyes flying saucer-wide and leaped in as only I could. 'Are you serious? Did they really? I can't believe it! Honestly? Why?'

Mr Fox seemed pleasantly surprised to have so pleasantly surprised me. 'Why, yes. Didn't you know? Incredible. What do you suppose they talked about?'

'Heaven only knows,' I replied, amazed. 'I didn't even know Mandela *liked* cricket.'

Funny how a thread of dialogue at one table can silence a roomful of people, isn't it? You had to be there, really, to fully appreciate it.

Afterwards, having made desperately light of the gaffe, I defensively hissed to Jack: 'Well, it's not pronounced Botha is it? It's Buoerta.' How was I to know that old Ian hadn't trekked across South Africa with a couple of elephants and demanded 'an audience with Nelson or I'll smash you with a stump'.

Funny. This year's invitation hasn't arrived yet. Probably got lost in the post. Still, I expect *Grandstand* and *Question Time* are even now fighting it out over who gets me first. At any rate, I reckon I'm in with a sporting chance.

P.S. I've just been informed it's arrived. The Invitation. Halleluja. My chance of a comeback. From the Ashes.

Well, I went. I saw Graff beaten by Garrison and Sabatini slaughtered by Navratilova. When I saw them, I mean I vaguely saw them. Without close-ups and action replays, I'm afraid it seemed an awfully slow game and I started counting the number of people in the crowd wearing red, and longing for the little athletic wagtail who kept hopping onto the electronic line bleeper to hop back again.

The first game was good, but it came down to one player, Garrison, who was desperate to win, and one player, Graff, who just kind of didn't want to lose. Much.

Such a serious business. So joyless. The night before we had watched the World Cup game between England and West Germany, and had been elated with joy and pride. We were six in all, including my friend Lizzy, who is wont to stand up, Grenfell-like, and yell, 'Oh, for heaven's sake lob it over, you pathetic little person!' When we drew level the six of us did a protracted and violent Mexican wave, screaming at the tops of our lungs and behaving like the thugs we are. As of today Clint is coming down from my kitchen wall and Gazza Gascoigne is going up.

What's more, I've started golf lessons. For the second of the TV series, *About Face*. So far I've had four lessons and I'm quietly obsessed. My teacher, Peter Brown, made the mistake of praising my swing and now I swing in the kitchen whilst stacking the dishwasher, and just before bedtime in the bedroom whilst Jack's out brushing his teeth. I swing where I used to flamenco. Of course, once holes and walking come into the scenario I shall get frustrated and ball blind, but as of this moment I'm a thug, a fanatic and possibly the Oldest Swinger in town.

A Dish Called Fonda

A man goes into a shop and says, 'Can I have *Death Wish II*, please?'

'You what? This is a fish and chip shop. We don't sell videos,' says the assistant.

The next day, he comes back.

'Can I have *When Harry Met Sally*, please?'

To which the assistant replies, 'Look, I told you, this is a fish and chip shop. We don't do videos! On your way, and stop wasting my time!'

The following day he returns.

'Can I have a bag of chips, please?'

'Yes, you can. I should think so too!' She gives him the chips and he says, 'Oh, and *A Fish Called Wanda*.'

My mother is wont to say, 'Ooh, I love a good film,' and although her idea of a good film generally involves Barbara Stanwyck losing life, love and dignity in a plain brown felt hat, and mine involves Daniel Day Lewis in a Czecho-slovakian accent, moody lighting and no clothes, I sort of agree with her.

My daughter's idea of a good film is one where she starts crying round about the end of the queue for tickets. We have wept more over our sodden copy of *The Way We Were* than Streisand must have done on Robert Redford's last day of filming. *Terms of Endearment* had her wobbly-eyed and puffy-lipped for days, particularly when I pointed out to her that it was Shirley MacLaine's performance which won the Oscar, not Debra Winger, for whom Oscars should have been invented. She fixed me with a look of vengeance and demanded the home phone number of the President of the Academy of Motion Pictures. Jack recently told us the plot

of a 1951 Jane Wyman movie called *The Blue Veil* and we
both broke down sobbing at the same point of the story and
sobbed for minutes. And he told us separately!

Why does the cinema feel like a treat and the theatre, so
often, like a penance? Why do I settle so gratefully into my
faded plush seat, shedding my faded plush shoes, oblivious
to smoke, sweethearts and surroundings, expecting nothing
but my money's worth and more. Trailers, commercials,
even turgid travelogues whet my appetite exactly as intended,
and the sight of the MGM lion, the Pearly Dean Gates or
even the Pathe cockerel gives the quiet hum of anticipation
one usually associates with meditating monks.

Too many years ago to be worth mentioning, I had a
boyfriend who failed to understand the religious nature of
my viewing, any more than I understood his motivation in
inviting me to view along side of him. This was less to do
with Olivier's plunging rousingly into 'Once more into the
breach, dear friends' than with his own attempts to plunge
'Once more into the bra straps, dear friend'.

Poor boy. After fifteen minutes of 'Ssh – gerroff' and 'WILL
YOU STOPPIT!' he was reduced to a petulant stare and a
resentful stroking of the space between my thumb and forefinger, which drove me batty. Why couldn't the boy just keep
still and watch the bloody film? Of course, I didn't know
then that he was responding, in the standard fashion, to the
powerful combination of a girl (any girl), the darkness, and
a roomful of adults all looking the other way. It took me a
lot more years, and even more boyfriends, to cotton on, by
which time most of the occupants of the back rows had been
married to each other for years and were on their second spin
dryer.

Often in American movies, the sentimentality, the insistence on 'dotting the eyes' and manipulating the emotions,
makes me puff up with venom like a cobra. But I never walk
out. I sat through *Beaches*, *Steel Magnolias* and *The War of
the Roses*, in abject contempt until the bitter end. This from
one who has majored in sneaking out of bad acting in theatres
all over the world. (Can't do it anymore, of course. Inevitably, months later, some actor will hiss, 'Heard you were in
for the *first half* the other night,' prompting instant fab-

rication of husband having a miscarriage and mad cow disease in row F). Why then do I remain seated for Sally Field, in soft focus, gulping back emotion, Sigourney Weaver groping for emotion – any emotion – and Kathleen Turner proving once again that she can't open a fridge door without flexing a buttock.

On the other hand, I sat in my New York hotel room for a good five hours' Bloomingdale-spending time watching *Sex Lies and Videotape*, *The Fabulous Baker Boys* and *Sea of Love* without so much as moving to the fridge to flex a buttock muscle of my own.

Actually, it felt no more of a wasted morning than wandering round the Guggenheim would have done, and I still managed an afternoon's lingerie shopping. Imagine seeing three *PLAYS* in a morning, then having the energy for Bloomingdales!

Let's face it, the theatre demands more of one. And 'one' wasn't schooled for it. Regular Saturday mornings of Roy Rogers and Trigger followed by Mandy Miller in *Dance Little Lady* bred a habit I can't break without the help of the Betty Ford Clinic. Our annual visit to the New Theatre, Hull, to see Ronnie Hilton in *Goldilocks and the Three Bears* somehow didn't breed the same addiction.

By the time I'd learned to appreciate the Stage, I was already *on* it. Learning its tricks. Now, I could count on the thumbs of my right hand the times I've forgotten myself in a theatre. Or ceased to be subjective and judgemental and just simply as my mother would say, 'Be taken completely out of myself.'

Quite recently Jack, my mother and I went to see a film called *Enemies: A Love Story*, a story of three Holocaust survivors set in 1940s New York. ('What's it called again?' said Ma, doubtfully, '*Enemas: A Love Story*?') The cinema was the Screen on the Hill in Hampstead, one of the new and welcome brand of cinema which dispenses coffee and snacks as well as the usual array of warm Maltesers and plaque-inducing popcorn. Thrilled with the sight of the hot coffee, Mother took a paper cup and gingerly walked towards the darkened screening room. 'Oops,' we heard. 'Oh damn! A bit of coffee's gone on the sleeve of my anorak. I'll have to dab it off in the Ladies.' So saying, she thrust the coffee into Jack's hand and made for the light reading 'Ladies', rubbing and muttering as she went.

The film began. No sign of Zelma. The film continued. Still no sign of Zelma. The film began to develop its theme of sex as a means of blocking out the past. Fifteen minutes on, the screen began to vibrate with full frontal, graphic scenes of the passionate coupling of Lena Olins and Ron Silver. As the gasping reached a climactic point, the door of the Ladies slowly opened and into the aisle stepped Mom in her freshly scrubbed anorak. She gave a brief glance at the screen, dropped her jaw by at least a metre, and walked backwards, first into the back wall, and then slowly and hypnotically down our aisle, past our row – in spite of our waving and hissing cries of 'Mummm!' – then backwards again, eyes never leaving the screen, and past us in the other direction.

Jack finally got her and led her back to the seat, where she folded her anorak carefully, eyes still glued to the screen. Then as the scene switched to a New York supermarket and 'normal' life ensued, she turned to us and said, 'Ugh! Isn't it disgusting.' (It was a statement, not a question.) 'Why they have to put things like that in a film I *don't* know. Ugh!' As Jackie Mason says, 'Every Hollywood producer talks about one thing. The sex scene. Where do we put the sex scene? It's the most important scene in the movie because everybody has sex in life and the movie represents life so you have to show the sex scene. And I want to say "Everybody in the world has sex. Everybody in the world also has soup. How come I never hear you talk about where to put the SOUP SCENE? There's a helluva lot more people out there having soup than having sex – so where's the SOUP SCENE?"' And Jackie Mason never makes a joke without making a serious sociological point.

One night I promised myself a hot water bottle, a basket of marzipan fruits and a video. It had been a hard day. I'd 'sat-in' for Anne Robinson on her morning radio show and the experience had winded me badly. I'd walked into Broadcasting House with a smile on my chops and gas in my Reeboks. I'd practically come out on a stretcher. Nervous?

I made Frankie Howerd look fluent. My mind blanked on alternate minutes, my heartbangs sounded like the 4.30 at Epsom, and my mouth felt like cat-litter. By the time Don Black, lyricist of *Tell Me On A Sunday* and *Aspects of Love*, and one of the funniest men in the Western Bloc, came in to the studio to be interviewed I was a frothing heap.

'Come on, darlin',' he said incredulously. 'You're doing great – what's to be nervous about, sitting in an underground room with nobody listening to you, eh?'

It was the multifarious nature of the job which got to me. Letters to be read out were spread all over the desk, along with newspaper clippings and research notes on my two guests. Every time a record drew to a close my heart started up again, my mind went blank about what came next, and my glasses slid down my perspiring nose. No first night in America, no guest appearance on *Wogan*, no live appearance on the Royal Variety Show has ever made me quite so pathologically crazed as that little radio show. Curiously enough, once Don was on, he took over so naturally and hilariously that I forgot to be frightened, had a thoroughly rumbustious time and breezed through the remainder of the show.

The funniest moment came after I'd read out a letter about a young couple who were getting married at St Luke's Parish Church in Charlton, let's say at 2 o'clock on the whatsit of May. It wished the young couple well and sent love and congratulations from her family and friends. 'And here for you, Trudy and Brian, is the "Hawaiian Wedding Song".'

Five minutes later the phone rang in the control room and producer Geoff Mullins's eyes rounded beautifully. In the next record gap he came trundling into the studio to tell me that the phone call was from the bride's stepmother. She was in a fairly emotional state, in that she'd known nothing *about* the wedding, wondered why she hadn't been told, and demanded the time and location of the ceremony.

I kept thinking about that reception as I drove blissfully home. Shades of the christening party in *Sleeping Beauty*.

The following week was a doddle. Not a nerve in my body, perfectly prepared, calm as a courgette. I didn't even touch the tube of Rescue Remedy on the desk before me. Denis Norden was as delightful and urbane a guest as Don Black had been, but this time I could actually hear and respond to what he was saying. I'll tell you something, though, people are divided into two categories – Hosts and Guests. I've known for years that I'm as good a guest at a dinner party as I am a lousy host. Not for nothing have the return invitations dwindled a bit over the years. And media hosting is no different. You pop on to *The Michael Aspel Show* as a guest, crack a few jokes in a borrowed gown, plug your latest book/show/film/affair, mop up more than your rightful share of Sancerre in the Hostility Room, and go home in a studio limo.

Never a thought for your poor host/hostess. A week of planning, programming, reading up on your research, wondering whether the major American movie star will show up and if so, will she be on her knees in the make-up room snorting Yardley's Luminescence powder up what's left of her nose? Will the public mind if she doesn't appear and John Inman goes on instead? Will Ruby Wax lyrical about her smear test and will Oliver Reed flash his wedding tackle? Also, what do I wear and will they say my legs are not even as good as Terry's let alone Sue Lawley's? Worst of all, what if my mind goes completely blank with panic and I can't even remember who *I* am, never mind who's coming on next and what the hell *this* one is talking about now?

All these fears and many more went through my mind when the producers of *Wogan* rang to say 'Howzabout taking over Terry's spot while he's away on his hols?' I was in Connecticut when the call came.

'Erm. It's very nice of you to ask me – erm – but I've got a lot to do when I get back to England – erm – I'd like to have a lie down ... and there'll be piles of washing ... and I haven't got a hairdresser ...'

'Please don't say no,' said the producer, who produces nothing if not charm in abundance, especially over three thousand miles when you're hungry for a closed vowel sound. 'Think about it and let us know when you get back – we won't pressure you, but I know you'd have nothing to do but relax and be your wondrous self.'

Already I'm mentally in my wardrobe discounting everything I own. Then he tells me about the clothes allowance, and then I know why Sue looks so dishy three times a week, and then I start to salivate because you get to *keep* them! (I'm always, in my innermost being, the starving actor – you know, the one who shouts 'Quick, auditions at the National for chorus and scene shifting.'

'But why are you taking "spear-carrying" work when you're used to playing a part?'

'Times are tough, old boy – and there's a "practical" cake in Act III!') So I put it out of my mind until I got home. Then I found a hairdresser and finished off all the washing. Then the phone rang.

This time a salary was mentioned along with 'Come on, you can do it, you know you can. Pick any guest you like – Robert Redford may be in town ...' That did it – Redford opposite me, with my track record of talking to the stars! You know, the one where I retreat into a broad North Country accent which makes Su Pollard sound like a stockbroker, and start straining sycophantically and laughing before they've finished the punchline ... No, No, a thousand times No! Redford and Mo? The way we weren't. I'd die, honestly, I'd just look into the space between his eyes and I'd say something deep and intellectual like 'So – er – did you do it with Barbra Streisand? I mean the film, not – no, come back – '

My mother couldn't believe I'd turned down the highest single accolade known to show business aside from *This Is Your Life* (which I've also managed to avoid by dint of a pact with the reclusive man with whom I share my digs). This just, according to her, to rile her, personally. She was gasted beyond her flabbers.

'They can't believe it in Hull when I told them you won't do *Wogan*,' she phoned in. 'They all think you're mad. Jean said you'd do it marvellously. Everybody said. And the money and all your clothes – can't you change your mind? Ring them up and say "I hope you don't mind me messing you about like this but I've been thinking over your kind offer, and I realize I could fit it in after all because of a sudden change of circumstances at home and my mother's coming down to help me out – oh, and if there's a spare ticket – "'

'Mother,' I interjected, 'it will kill me. How dead do you

want your daughter? I'm not a chat show host. I'm an actress, or I used to be. Why do I have to give myself galloping shingles and chronic insomnia just so as the critic of the *Evening Standard* can say, "Maureen Lipman is to the world of chat show hosts what Frank Bruno is to the world of petit-point"?'

After the phone went down I sat in the garden like a very old terracotta gargoyle. Number one husband saw my fainted state and raced to Film Knights for the antidote – Leslie Neilson in *The Naked Gun*. It's a spoof cop movie from the team who brought you *Airplane*, and if you've never seen it then don't sit here reading this élitist drivel – race, hop, limbo or mince to your nearest 'Videorama' and prepare to BARK with laughter, split your stays, and have the parts refreshed that other sagas cannot reach. As Zelma is wont to say, 'You can't beat a good laugh.'

Before leaving the subject of old terracotta gargoyles, have you noticed the spread of middle-aged crumpet in the movies today? Burly Bob Hoskins, Crumpled Caine, Weedy Woody, Hero De Niro, Rugg'd Reynolds, Nice Newman and Crinkly Clint. Sex-symbols, stars, centre-folds and dishes-of-the-month to women north and south of The Wirral, including the Cinque Ports. And don't give me that 'Yes, but it's their *talent* that comes across' routine, because your idea of coming across must be very different from mine.

But where are their female counterparts? I'm thinking of Ellen Burstyn of *Alice Doesn't Live Here Any More*, Louise Fletcher of *One Flew Over the Cuckoo's Nest* and Cloris Leachman of almost anything. One or two films, then it's 'Movie of the Week' or, at worst, *Falcon Crest*. And I'm deliberately not bringing Joan Collins into this argument because I'm talking profundity not hormones.

Of course, it's easier for fellas to look sexy longer. They learn from birth to expect no help from artifice. Unlike myself and many of my sisters, to whom life without Erace and Ultra-Glow would mean the difference between a career as a working mother and a career as a recluse in a brown-paper bag, men learn to accept themselves as they are.

True, a haircut, a smattering of designer stubble, the odd earring and a spot of UVA can make a difference, but basically it's the inner man who's on display. Which is why most women, when asked what they first look for in a man, reply 'Wit and humour'. Ask a man why he first looks at Page 3 and he's hardly likely to say 'Witty titties'.

Whilst working on the drama series *A Little Princess* with a dozen twelve- to fourteen-year-old girls, I noted that although they were all sweet kids most of them wouldn't be seen dead without their eyeliner. Why do we make our daughters so appearance-conscious? At thirteen we were branded either jail-bait or 'Still, I expect she's clever with her hands' – and we spend the next thirty years living up to it or living it down.

I suppose accepting yourself as you are is very sexy. Being pleased with yourself, of course, is not. After all, how can you make another person happy if your prime concern is your rating from one to ten?

So, take our celluloid heroes. (Thank you, I'll have them wrapped and delivered on separate days, please). One thing's for sure: 'Toy Boys' they ain't, unless you're talking vintage Dinky. These faces all look lived-in, world-weary even. Why does that attract us? My husband, when I met him, looked intensely lived-in, and after seventeen years of me, 'squatted-in' would be more the term for it. I fancied he looked more than a bit like Yves Montand, and told my friend so – long distance from Manchester. 'He's got these interesting lines around his face and great, sad eyes.' She promptly spread it around London that Lipman had fallen for a wrinkled depressive called Eve.

Meanwhile, we can still thrill to the sight of Paul Newman looking better year by year. Is the secret in the salad-dressing? At least a film a year. Less work, though, for the lovely Joanne Woodward. Why? Sean Connery grows lustier as he grows crustier, and his acting grows the more his hair stays on the pillow. Nicholson and Hoffman, Duvall and De Niro, Paul Hogan – I'm still leaving the house for them.

In fact, Paul Hogan doesn't know what I've gone through for him. One February Sunday, on just about the coldest night I've ever known, four of us queued up outside a cinema in Golders Green for over an hour to see *Crocodile Dundee*. It was my one night off of the week, and a lot of thought went into how I spent it. I tackled the manager, standing warmly in the foyer, as to why he wanted people to die of hypothermia in his precincts, but apparently he didn't make the rules. Finally we were allowed to shuffle in, pair by pair, with the other animals, paid our money at the one-person-only box-office, and spent the remains on hot snacks from the kiosk to bring the blood back to our frozen digits.

Once inside, we sat through a fascinating short on turtle-trapping in the Galapagos Islands or some such thing, and twenty minutes of mouth-watering trailers and commercials. Finally, as *Crocodile Dundee* snapped into being, the sound-track wound down, the film distorted, flashed up the odd clapperboard number and packed in.

The manager, warmer than ever now, bustled down the aisle and made a short but moving speech about power-cuts and projectors, then asked us to bear with him. We gave him a Bronx cheer and a brief round of applause, ate and chatted our way through two more boxes of popcorn, until, finally, fifty minutes later, we were told the only remaining power was in his elbow and would we like our money back?

This was a difficult decision. Yes, we would like our money back. What we didn't relish was queuing up again in the gloom of the stairwell to get it. That ten pounds is, somewhat fittingly, still in Golders Green.

I finally saw *Dundee* on my forty-first birthday and I pledged the ten quid to his lovely leathery face and his matchless, understated performance.

I'm glad I saw it before I saw New York. It prepared me better than anything I'd read or seen for the crisp exterior and soft centre of the Big Apple. It was the corniest, happiest, most affectionate movie I'd seen in years.

So where – back to my original question – where are the leathery ladies? I guess they're all on Broadway, kicking up their infallible legs or reminiscing on camera about their days at RKO. On the scrap heap, girls, after fifty, unless you alter and stretch so much that the staples keep hitting the continuity girl. I guess neither men nor women want to look at cellulite on celluloid. Silicone, they don't mind. How can we ever look up to Jane Fonda again? Flawless females and craggy, baggy blokes. Haven't we come on!

My top ten films: *Cinema Paradiso, The Graduate, The Producers, Being There, My Life as a Dog, The Unbearable Lightness of Being, Les Enfants du Paradis, Day for Night, La Cage aux Folles, Nashville* ... *Duel, Born Yesterday* – I know, I KNOW – *The Front Page* (version one), *Forty-Second Street, Cabaret, The Philadelphia Story, Calamity Jane, The Sunshine Boys, Camille Claudel, One Upon a Time in America, Crossing Delancy, Close Encounters of the Third Kind, Reds, ET, Brief Encounter* ... I know! *Julietta of the Spirits, Pierrot la Fou, Cousin Cousine, Prizzi's Honour, Klute* ...

Charity Begins in a Home

That's it. I've had it. I'm as sick as a bit player in a Ben Elton script. I'm choked up to here (gestures just below eyes) with them all. If I get one more letter, one more wheedling phone call, one more black-mailing, whinging final demand I shall – I shall utter a twelve sentence expletive and tell the poor, beleaguered sod exactly where to stuff his appeal form.

In short, I am feeling uncharitable. One week it was out 1.30 pm till midnight raising money to fight the effects of the Clause 28/9 Bill. A brutish and dishonourable ban. And one which, don't get me wrong, I was honoured to stand against. But for so long?

Any member of my profession (the second oldest) will tell you that not a Sunday goes by without a request for you to present your battered old body at a similarly battered venue for the benefit of Dyslexic Seals, Anorexic Pastry Chefs or Friends of the Ozone Layer.

Even the Telethon. Twenty-two million pounds. It was touching and exciting to be there at the end singing 'It's a lovely day tomorrow' with Cilla and Su and Cannon and Wisdom and Norden and Ball, and God could only bless the GB Public for their incredible largess.

But therein lies the rub, or vice versa. Because somewhere in my mind, a mind which boggles with the last-minute sketches and songs and sudden announcements and warm wine and stale sandwiches and endless pacings round the corners of empty dressing-rooms – a still small voice is saying, 'Why? Why are we, the so-called celebrities and you, the Golden-Hearted GBP, coughing up week in week out of our time and our money to pay for what we were brought up to believe our taxes paid for? Namely our old, our sick, our disabled and our victimized! People who for one reason or another cannot fight for themselves.'

Charity has become big business. 'Greed is good,' said Gordon Gekko in that chilling film *Wall Street*. 'There is nothing basically wrong with making money,' breathed his British counterpart, our PM, in her infamous Sermon on the Loch.

Thus the rich and famous and the mega-rich and those who are famous for being mega-rich are liberated from guilt and encouraged to contribute. To distribute. To sponsor and to offer largess in a patronizing way (in both senses).

I mean, take my mail this week – *please* take my mail this week. I'm going to sound like an arrogant sort of a swine here but – publish and be panned! Leukaemia, MS, Homeless, Starving, Single Parented, Down's Syndrome, Help the Aged – every one of them a deserving cause, deserving of my attendance, my money, my commitment, my clothes. My God! Yes, Him, too. Do you have any idea of the number of Jewish organizations there are in my neck of the woods and how many of their organizers have my phone number on the kitchen wall? Last week I even had a letter from Yugoslavia asking for a donation towards Disabled Esperantists! I mean, how many Esperantists can there be? Let alone ones who have problems getting about?

Then there's the friends. The ones you can't refuse. And the friends of friends you can't refuse. 'I hope you don't mind my ringing you at home, I got your number from Alice, in the wet fish shop – she said you wouldn't mind. Now. We're holding an arm-wrestling and spinach-risotto evening at the Cock and Pullet in Poplar and we'd very much like you to do a twenty-five minute cabaret and cut the first slice of a twelve-metre onion quiche, baked by MOLES, you know, Mothers of Optometrists Lesbians, Esperantists and Social Security Clerks.'

Every day's post brings another batch of unturndownable requests. And it's not just Cancer and Heart Disease and Child Abuse and the Homeless and the Disabled – all of them in the utmost need of support. It's the others. It's Seals and Dogs and Whales and Ozone Layers and laid-off trawler men and victims of rain-forest abuse.

And inevitably: 'I know you must be asked this all the time

but this one is really different – you'll love it – it's a ball to raise money for . . .'

'When is it Rick?' I asked my old friend, Ricci Burns.

'You'll love it,' he reiterated. 'Great people, darling, you'll love it.'

'RICK, when is it?'

'Er, the 19th. We'll pick you up . . .'

'Rick I have to go to Hull, it's a family memorial, I can't miss it. I'm sorry.'

'We'll drive you there – you gotta be there, they want you – we'll take you to Hull in a chauffeured car. You'll love it. You gotta do it.'

'Rick – *I can't.*'

'You can. You gotta – you'll love it. Say yes. We'll drive you.'

'We-e-e-ll – ' The fatal pause, and my fate was sealed and British Rail had lost a customer. My last words before sentence were, 'What's the charity?'

'It's to raise money for Dressage at the Olympics – you'll love it.'

'Ricci. What did you say? Did you say Dressage? Ricci, that's bleeding horses – I've never even seen a horse, dear, except with a policeman underneath or on *My Friend Flicka*, and I don't care WHAT they wear at the wretched Olympics.'

Mentally, I'm on the other line. 'Hello Mum – it's me. Er – I can't come on the Saturday night – I've promised Ricci I'll be at a charity for – er – er – for Dressings for – er – wounded people in remote areas of er – Olympia.'

Fade out, fade in: 'Ring Ring Ring Ring'. 'Helloooo – I'm sorry to ring you at home but I represent the High Hills Park Golf Course and Leisurama Centre and we'd like you to open our new Theme Park and Sub-Aqua Scuba Centre. It will only take a few hours of your time. There'll be a fork supper to follow and we would adore a short speech, say twenty minutes on a theme of your choice relating to 'Me and the Great Outdoors'. Now, we have spoken to your secretary who has told us your usual fee and we would be happy to donate that amount to your favourite charity!' All in one breath I SWEAR and what's left of yours!

Meanwhile, in your spare time you can write out recipes

for a new-angle celebrity cookbook, some of the proceeds of
which go to a cause so worthy it makes your eyelids retract.
Whilst drawing a cartoon, fishing out a school report, and
recollecting your memories of 'My First Goldfish' and 'Why
I Like Soil'. Now, it's no use saying to me, as an editor did
recently, 'But Maureen, you sound so ... angry', because I
can't help it when I'm having a bitch. It doesn't mean I
won't do them all! 'Course I will. I'll draw. I'll bake. I'll cut
ribbons. I'll judge marmosets if you catch me nicely in a
weak moment on the end of a moribund week. But just don't
expect me not to whinge about it.

There's nothing intrinsically funny, is there, about a man
saying to an actress, 'I've been meaning to ask you – would
you be available in November to do a Rotary Club dinner?'
Nothing at all. The humour, I think, came from the fact that
at the time of asking I was lying with my head near the
ground and my feet near the ceiling and the man in question
had most of his right hand in my mouth, his other hand
on a high-power drill and his knee wedged round his own
spittoon. I mean, how can a girl say no?

What these marauding fund-raisers don't understand is
that there's only three of me, and two of those are wives and
working mothers. What they *have* grasped is that the other
is a dubiously soft touch who knows she's been lucky so far
and feels guilt-ridden enough to want to put something back
into the public melting pot which has been kind enough to
approve of her. This knowledge ensures they start every
letter with 'I know you must be swamped by requests to
open bizzarres [sic] like these but – ' and 'Your secretary
assures us that you are unable to speak at our annual dinner in
John O'Groats but – ' and that's about as far as understanding
goes.

Of course, if they get me on the phone, I'm lost. Layla,
our loving secretary, has at last learned that when she's
adamantly refusing some tenacious committee member and
I say, 'Here, give me the phone. I'll deal with it!', her next
move is to open the diary, because as sure as Tesco's eggs
are free-range my next sentence will be: 'Now look, as my
secretary has told you just the six times, I am totally booked
for 1990 and I can't possibly ... oh dear ... I *am* sorry ... I

didn't know about your son's leg ... yes, it must be ... and your husband's lost his what ...? Oh, how careless ... I'm afraid I ... but ... oh, I see ... no, I didn't realize your job is on the line if I don't ... Right then, yes, I expect I can fit you – sure, July 17th will be just perfect – I'll just cancel my holiday and postpone the opening ... no, I'll just write it in, no, no thank you. I'll see *you* on the 17th – bye-eee. Layla, get up – stop laughing, it's not remotely funny.' Layla has now taken to curling up in the cubby hole of the desk to answer these calls. That way I can have no possible access to the receiver.

Another hazard of the job is when you say, 'You will understand, won't you, that if I say "yes" to the Pontefract Panda Protection Barbeque in October 1992, there is an outside chance that I'll be filming in Bogotá on that day and won't be able to – ?' The reply comes zooming down the phone: 'Of course, dear, we'll understand – don't think another thought about it – we're just looking forward to seeing you, and we'll be in touch nearer the time, dear ...' Fade out, fade in: two years later the job in Bogotá comes up – actually the last occasion it was Australia for British Telecom – and the dreaded cancellation call has to be made. 'So I'm terribly sorry, but I won't be able to c – ' I break off on hearing a low moan then an uninterrupted wailing noise, followed by the gnashing of elderly dentures, the grinding of elderly cheek muscles, the solid thud of arthritic knees hitting tufted twistpile, some steady gasping and choking noises, then worst of all, the terrible silence of a condemned committee member.

ME: 'Hello – hello – are you all right? I'm sorry – it's awful, I know, but I've only just heard and – Hello – is anybody there ...?'

SHE: (*fingers twisted around phonecard, phonecard twisted round neck, then suddenly, piercingly*) 'You can't do this to me! Who do you think you are? The tables are taken – the floral arrangements are ordered – there's four hundred kosher poussins sitting in the freezer – you can't – it'll kill me – I'm not a young woman!'

ME: 'But, I always said it was a possibility – I did warn

you – I couldn't be more sorry but what can I do ...?'

SHE: 'What can you do? (*Decibel level 2000*) DON'T GO!! That's what you can do. Don't damnwell go, pardon me, is what you do. If you have any value for human life – it's been in *The Jewish Chronicle* for God's sake – have you no heart?'

Before they all consult their lawyers, I should point out that the above conversation is a slight exaggeration. But only slight.

On the sweet subject of Telethons – or Telecoms, as most people call them, to me at any rate – these monstrous TV raffles which raise millions each year to take the place of decent health care for people who've paid their National Insurance for decades, are big business. Big show business too. Last night I returned from a stint on the 1990 ITV Telethon, with steam issuing from my every pore. For months its organizers had been pestering me to turn up. They started ringing and writing from March offering tit-bits such as: 'Would you do a U-turn in a rally car dressed as Margaret T?'

'Er – no.'

'Would you do a marathon of keeping your feet off the ground for as long as possible with Les Dawson?'

'Er – no.'

And the pièce de résistance in desperation in late May:

'Do you Lambada at all?'

ME (*somewhat drily*): 'No, I do not.'

During this ceaseless pursuit of the right métier for my particular brand of foolishness, I had already pitched up for a Telethon trailer to flamenco dance for the cause. It was to be filmed in a Spanish club off Oxford Street, and I promised my flamenco friend Nuria, who taught me all I knew for my part in the *About Face* playlet, *Señor Duende*, that I would don a leotard and flounce for her.

On the night I turned up in my red leotard and dippy skirt with a heavier than usual coat of paint on, to find, to my horror, that Cleo Roccas of Kenny Everett fame and a young lady much featured on Page 3, called Gilly, I think, were already up on the stage, surrounded by a sixty-strong swarm of Street of Shame photographers, all climbing up each other's anoraks and screaming 'Lean forward, Cleo – a bit further, give us a smile, lick your lips, Gilly – lovely, lovely – hitch that skirt up a bit ...'

Into this Masterclass of mindlessness steps Maureen, on whom 'lean forward, lovely' is slightly wasted. I could lean forward till my head was between my metatarsals and they'd still need a zoom lens to catch even a hint of Page 3. Page $2\frac{1}{2}$, maybe. The classifieds? I've seldom been more embarrassed. I stuck it till my teeth began to scream and then I ducked out of the line-up and no one noticed I'd gone.

When the film finally ran out of their cameras, an ambisexual person in headphones said, 'Can you give us a funny line to get people to watch Telethon, Maureen?' and 'Action!' And like a well-trained dog I stuck an arm in the air and said, 'I'm putting my foot down for the Telethon, how about you?' Honestly. And without a scriptwriter, too.

So. Fade out, fade in. A couple of months pass. Still the phone calls persist. 'You will be there, won't you? Can we send a car for you? Someone will ring to confirm. If we can ask you to man the telephones for us and take part in a studio discussion, perhaps ...'

I agree to do so. There is a charity called AMNASS in which I'm involved. It's for sufferers of amnesia and their carers, and it's run by Deborah Wearing whose husband, Clive, was the subject of a film by Jonathan Miller called *Prisoner of Memory*. Clive Wearing has no short-term memory, the result of a virus which attacked his brain, and he needs twenty-four-hour care and attention. It's a nightmarish complaint, as he looks perfectly well and can still play/compose the complicated music by which he made his living. However, if he's left alone for a minute it feels like an hour to him, he cannot remember what has just been said to him, therefore he will repeat himself endlessly, and he has no frame of references to enable him to take part in any kind of conversation. He's been in St Mary's Hospital, Paddington, for five years because there is simply nowhere else for him to go. He's not mentally ill. If he were, there would be many places for him to go. He needs therapy and some rehabilitation to enable him to cope with the constant uncertainty of his life and the violent frustration his condition causes him. There are no such places. Not one. In the length and breadth of England.

Deborah works from a tiny office, alone except for one part-time secretary, and I wanted very much to talk about this tiny charity and her hopes for its growth. Obviously it affected me personally because my father's condition was similar for the last fourteen years of his life. We agreed that Deborah would cover the administrative side of the discussion, the need to raise funds for rehabilitation, for residential care and for support for the carers (whose life is as devastated by the loss of the person they previously knew as it is by the burden of twenty-four-hour dependency.) A short film would be shown of a man who'd lost his memory through a cerebral stroke at the age of twenty-three, and was learning to programme his life so he could live alone, and then I would speak about the day-to-day struggle of living with someone who is in no-man's world without reference and without time.

Come the day I arrived at Docklands TV at 5.30 pm and went to man the phones till Deborah arrived. This entailed taking down details of every pledge – which is fine, except that most pledges were for £2.50 and were donated on Access or Visa.

'So that's 4032601209 – oh, sorry – 902, er – 31206 – oh, sorry – 306 – er – . Where were we? Let's start again – and the expiry date is – yes, certainly I'll wait while you get your other bag – Hello, yes – oh, it was the wrong card, was it? Let's start again, shall we?'

Finally, long after her 'spot' had been and gone, Deborah arrived, hot and flustered having been shunted down the Thames from London Weekend on a boat with a troupe of belly dancers all making last minute adjustments to their costumes, or lack of them. In vain she had remonstrated with the powers that be that she had to be on the air in the Docklands by six, and when she finally pitched up, I had been put back on the phones for another session of 'And your address is – can you spell that please?' Finally they placed us in front of the studio audience to begin the discussion, and

I quickly inquired from Judith Chalmers – working by now on some reserve energy tank:

'How long do we have to discuss AMNASS?' 'Er – ' She consulted her clipboard. 'Er, you have, er . . . you have forty-five seconds exactly.'

My face must have registered something because she took a step backwards.

'Do you mean each or together?' I murmured darkly.

'Together. Isn't it awful?' she whimpered.

And we were on!

Afterwards, too late, I realized how I should have used my twenty-two seconds. Simply to say 'I was going to speak to you about a wonderfully deserving and little-known charity but the producers have only given me twenty-two seconds because they're cutting straight to a sponsored lard-slice in Abergavenny, so I won't.' As it was I just sat there fuming with frustration, gabbled one senseless sentence and went swiftly to where charity is supposed to begin, muttering 'Never again' all the way, but omitting to add 'till the next time'.

The next day the TV critic of the *Express* noted that the Telethon had been full of publicity-grabbing TV stars jostling to exploit the programme for their own careers.

There are times when one would almost relish amnesia. No. Forget I said that.

St Peter said, 'Charity shall cover a multitude of sins' and Francis Bacon said, 'In charity there is no excess.' But then in their day, I think I'm right in saying, there was no major Telethon. On either channel.

While we're talking of things charitable, I was listening to a phone-in about animal rights liberationists, in the wake of the last bombing. A lady phoned in saying she'd been sitting in a café when some animal rights campaigners carrying collection tins arrived and ordered a meal. Apparently their bill came to £17.50. Without pausing for breath they emptied their collection tins on the table and paid the bill with the contents. I guess they were animals and they had their rights.

*

One more thing, and then I'm through. It was Amy's six-teenth birthday and ten girls had to be picked up from town, lunched, let loose on Hampstead, given dinner, board and breakfast the following morning. All of this would have been enjoyable – or at least bearable – without miserable old mother me having the meanest migraine in living memory. It manifested itself in the small hours at such an advanced stage that no cure save amputation of the head could bring relief.

Suffice to say the day and night passed in a deeply unpleasant fashion and the following morning brought no respite. At 12.15 I was due at a function to pose for a photo-call to launch a twenty-four-hour helpline for a worthy and deserving charity. It was an hour-and-a-half's drive away. In desperation I phoned all over London to track down the PR firm who organized the lunch. When they phoned me back I told them I was ill, made profuse apologies and asked if one of the other celebrities could open the helpline. The reply was a flabbergasted burble followed by a desperate plea to get there at any cost: 'The press are expecting – I mean, the TV cameras and everything – please, look, we'll give you a room to lie down in, *anything,* if you could just – '

'But what about the other celebrity guests – couldn't they? ...'

'There aren't any, look, I mean, honestly ... you'd be doing us such a – you see, the Duchess of York's got your name in her speech and we don't want to ... I mean, you're one of the guests of honour and ...'

'I'll *be* there, I'll *be* there, I'm leaving now, all right, bye. Ja-ack!'

Two more Migraleves later we left, drove tentatively through the driving rain to the appointed restaurant, past the police cordons and into the reserve car park. Once in the marquee I spotted good old Barry Norman, dear Michael Denison and others. 'Psst – Jack,' I hissed as he joined me damply in the breeze-filled tent. 'Look who's over there. And there! Talk about being indispensable.'

'I know, love,' he murmured wryly, 'and they're on the top table with Her Royal Highness. We're on Table No 5 with no one we know.'

'Nice one,' I said darkly.

As it happened my 'tablees' were fine and fun-filled and the only remaining knee jerk came after the Duchess had made an excellent speech and I was called up before 150 people for the photo call, which turned out to be a speech. An impromptu speech, to say the very least.

'I don't know how you do it,' said Jack, as I moved somewhat magisterially back to my seat.

'It's easy. I just lost five years of my life and most of my hair follicles,' I breathed. 'Come on, love. Let's get the hell out. There's probably a knees-up afterwards to which we're not invited.'

It goes without saying that when a charity do is well organized and welcoming, it can be the greatest joy and can give you a good deal more than you'd ever anticipated. Joyce Grenfell was right, as ever, when she said there is no giving without receiving, that they are both part of the same circle which makes up a whole spiritual act. It's just that, sometimes, you can't help but feel that what they want you to give is blood.

One Sunday morning, that was precisely what they did want. I'd arranged, then immediately forgotten (not entirely out of lack of self-interest do I support AMNASS), for a young doctor and a film crew to come to my house to film myself and Jack being blood tested for a little-known disease called Tay-Sachs, in order to encourage people to be tested to see whether they were carriers. One small snag. I'd er – omitted to tell Jack of the arrangement. He arrived home from picking up the Sunday morning bagels and the lad from Sunday school, to find his study full of arc lamps and white coats, and to have his sleeve wrenched unceremoniously up and a needle shoved in his vein. He was quite surprised for a minute, but didn't put up too much of a fuss. Not on nationwide television anyway.

We were both tested and forgot about the whole thing till a few weeks later. Jack received his all-clear and I received my: 'one or two discrepancies – we'd like to re-test you as soon as possible' and instantly made my will!

Words cannot describe my panic. Suffice to say that the young medic concerned must have wished he'd picked on any person in the history of Equity rather than your hyper-ventilating authoress. I plagued him till he finally arrived in the gloom of night with his needle and re-did the test virtually on the tube on the way home. It's OK. I was fine. 100% OK. And my heart returned to a human being's heart beat rate in – oh, just a few days, give or take a month or two.

My friend Julia McKenzie is wont to say 'You said you could do it when you wrote in,' but these days she's more into saying: 'When will you learn to say *no*?' And last night it was: 'Look, write a "Sorry I can't" letter and I'll have it photocopied and send it out to every number in the Yellow Pages.'

It'll End in Tears

The radio play came my way during rehearsals of my one-person show. It was a one-person radio play. (One could be forgiven for thinking one couldn't get anyone else to work with one, but one would be wrong-ish.) It was called *The Child Behind the Eyes,* by Nava Semel. It was the ruminations of the mother of a Down's Syndrome child the morning of his first day at school. I read it in one twenty-minute sitting, howled like a baby for ten more minutes, then phoned the producer and practically begged her to give me the job.

The night before the recording I read through the play again – this time in a more technical and objective manner to prepare myself for my performance. The technical and objective manner lasted for about nine pages, then the eyes watered up again, the voice started strangulating, dirty great blobs welled up over my vision and I got seriously worried about my ability to perform this piece in a grown-up manner.

The next day dawned as next days tend to do. The corridors of the BBC are long and pea-green (the 1984 setting of Orwell's book, reputedly), and I followed a uniformed attendant through and round them for the obligatory ten miles before happening upon Studio B10. Janet Whittaker, the producer, her assistant and the engineer greeted me and we all had a cup of hot beige stuff masquerading as tea, before the first read-through of the script.

'I'll just read it for timing, shall I? I won't act it yet, eh?' I asked Janet with studied casualness. She agreed but thought she'd record it anyway, just in case. The last thing I remember before the green light for 'Go' came on was that I hadn't brought any Kleenex with me.

I was fine for the first few pages. Then the voice started to wobble a bit. I soldiered on. Obviously I could tell I was getting pathetic, but surely I sounded completely under control as far as the director's box was concerned? Finally, the engineer's dispassionate voice came through. Perhaps, he suggested, we might take a pause here, as the sound of my tears hitting the green-felt table sounded exactly like the BBC Effects Department's tape of galloping horses.

By lunchtime we had two complete runs of the play in the can. I'd gone through three packets of tissues from the canteen, and a flunkey had been dispatched to Underwoods to buy me a large box of Men's Size. Meanwhile, the BBC photographer had arrived to photograph me for the *Radio Times*. My face resembled the back of one of those baboons who let it all hang out at mating time. Red, lumpy and raw in the middle, and smudged and furry round the orifices. The camera hasn't yet been invented which could have captured the magic of my mush that morning. Bless him, he went away with the promise of a full sitting when I'd got my face back from the cleaners.

I mean, if there's one thing I'm really excellent at, it's crying. No, don't knock it, it's a skilled art being lachrymose. Next to me, Richard Attenborough looks about as emotional as Anthony Blunt. *Anne of Green Gables*? I can scarcely write the four words without going to pieces, and watching it actually makes me lose weight. *The Phantom of the Opera*? I saw it twice, the second time to see what I'd missed through racked sobs the first time. Afterwards, I crawled backstage to visit Michael Crawford, forgetting that I'd been wearing Clinique's face-bronzer for that glowing, outdoor, tanned look we all know and simulate. Michael must have wondered why I'd come to visit him disguised as a zebra. Only after leaving did I glimpse myself in the mirror. The mascara, coupled with the face-gleamer, all running in a southerly direction gave me the interesting look of a woman behind bars. Waterproof mascara makes no difference. Steam setting the powder base makes no difference either. My only hope, should I ever see the show again, would be to cling-film the whole face and fasten it below the chin with a Twist 'n Seal.

The annoying, the infuriating, the debilitating side of being a weeper is one's inability to control it. No point thinking of hilarious moments from life's rich tapestry of jokes, Morecambe- , Groucho- , Woody-style: 'You mean you haven't had sex for two hundred years? Two hundred and four, if you count my marriage ...' Nothing stops the flow. *Nothing.* Look up at the light, blink rapidly, breathe deeply from the diaphragm – yes, I do all of those things. *Then* I cry. At the doctor's I generally last four minutes before collapsing whilst trying to describe the muscle pain which *he* knows is a muscle pain but which *I* know he's only saying is a muscle pain to disguise the seriousness of his true diagnosis.

Oh, I wish I had a two-pound coin for every toilet I've burst into, hissing at myself: 'Stoppit will you for Godsake you're forty years old will you stoppit STOPPIT GROW UP YOU BERK I am not crying I am NOT GOING to give them the satisfaction – waaaagh!!'

Worst of all is crying in an argument. Are girls encouraged to whinge and cry instead of getting angry? Is that it? Is anger supposed to be unfeminine? It's fine to assert yourself, to demand, to challenge, to clear the air – even to abuse – you can still win your argument doing any of these. Just don't break down and weep because, sister, you're lost. You may win the battle but you've lost the war. I wish I had a *three*-pound coin for the number of masculine hands that have patted my weedy little female head in mid-shudder, in accompaniment to the words 'Aw, come on love, it's all right, baby, just leave this one to me, darling, trust me, would I do anything that wasn't in your best interest, would I? There now, let's dry those big brown eyes, we just want you to be happy and not to *think* so much. ....' Game, set, match and same old balls.

Just to cheer you up, I shall tell you about my journey home from the BBC. 'I'll take a bus,' I thought fondly, 'one of those new little fat C2 buses I've sat behind for so many hours, wishing them in hell. I'll take one to Kentish Town, and change to one that goes past my house. It'll be fun.' It was. The bus was cosy and, as I stood dangling from a strap with the other excess passengers, someone asked the driver if Hampstead Road was still closed off to traffic going north. The driver – a sandy young Irishman (I mention this as it *was* St Patrick's Day) – replied brightly, 'Oi don't know 'bout dat – but dere's trouble ahead 'cos dere's some fellow tryin' to jump off a building round the corner.' There was a low murmur of consternation round the bus and, encouraged by it, he went on, 'Yes, it just takes one little ting loik dat and it snarls up the traffic for da whole day!' (I took out my biro and started taking notes.)

At the diversion, the policeman sent him round the block. He was instantly lost. Obviously these privately owned buses hold no truck with The Knowledge, because our lad didn't know his St Pancreas from his Bell-Bow. From this point on he might have been in Oz for all he knew. People began throwing suggestions at him, some kindly, some less so, as the same shops came zinging past for the third and fourth times. He hailed another C2 with relief: 'Do you know wheer you're goin'?' 'Follow me!' called back the lady driver, and immediately vanished for ever.

Someone told him how to get back to the Euston Road. 'Now wheer's dat?' Our driver had never heard of the Euston Road. It wasn't part of his brief. It's only the busiest and best-known road in London linking Kings Cross, Euston, Baker Street etc, so why should he have? He was unconcerned about this, or indeed anything, and once having finally crossed the said Euston Road, sunnily began to take requests. 'Anybody here want Albany Street?' Somebody did. So he turned round and went back to it. Someone pointed out that perhaps we should go on to Camden Town or we'd end up back in the diversion. 'Oh, don't worry 'bout dat,' he chirped, 'I've got all the toim in da world. I'm on till twelve tonoight!'

It was war and, appropriately, all the passengers began chatting together almost as if this wasn't England. So much so, that I missed my stop when it finally came round and I ended up stranded in a place called Parliament Hill Fields, where you can't get a bus or a tube anywhere except back to the BBC. All in all it took two-and-a-half hours to get home. I could have gone to Birmingham in that time. That really would have brought tears to my eyes.

Incidentally, I've cracked it now, the lachrymosity factor. The method's worked twice for me, so it may be the definitive cure or just a pathetic coincidence. Here's what I did: just at the moment the tears were about to gush out over the waterproof liner, taking the soft lenses in a Niagara-like descent towards the jawbone, I looked at a poster or a newspaper and thought about what the words *meant*. Pictured them. 'Pritt Stick' or 'museum', 'sausage', 'poll tax' – I don't know why it worked, but it did. The acid test, of course, was to sit through *Driving Miss Daisy* without shedding a tear. It worked well enough until Jessica Tandy grasped Morgan Freeman's hand and said, 'Do you know, Hope, you're my best friend.' Oops – er – 'Friend' I thought – er – friend as in childhood friend, someone to – er – lean on friend, tell all your troubles to friend, share your lunches with, your lunches with – waaagh! Waaagh!' – Jack leaned forward and passed me his handkerchief. I drowned it.

Listen, if you can think of a cure, let me know. I'm willing to pay through the nose – eyes – and all available ducts.

Love in the Time of Colic

Virginia Woolf was asked once why she stayed married for so many years to Leonard, a man most of her colleagues found to be her intellectual inferior. Her definitive reply was 'Because when he comes into a room I never know what he is going to say.'

I don't know about you, but that comment, which was surely not a carefully considered one, rings truer than any homily on the state of matrimony I've heard on *Oprah* or seen embroidered on a sampler.

When I knew from nothing about affairs of the heart or the mortgage, I played a short season at the Edinburgh Festival. Aged nineteen, never kissed back and greener than Kermit, I was sipping Crème de Menthe in the basement of a jazz club, when an elderly roué (as in twenty-two) from the Oxford Union made a pronouncement which made my spine stiffen. 'Love,' he pronounced, with the world-weary wisdom of a man who wore dark glasses after sundown and owned at least three psychedelic ties, 'love is farting in bed with someone who doesn't mind.'

I was horrified. Mortified and every other 'fied' including 'petri'. '*How* can you say that?' I piped with all the passion of a Cartland virgin (which indeed I was, mentally if not technically). 'You've obviously NEVER been in love or you'd never think of it so vulgarly! Some love *you're* talking about. I'm sure Elizabeth Taylor and Richard Burton would have a slightly different story to tell – huh! Or Shakespeare – no mention of farting in *Romeo and Juliet* that *I* noticed. How disgusting. How *pathetic*.' Exit trainee thespian to toilet for good cry for no obvious reason.

I'm not saying, twenty-five years later, that big Dave's metaphor was quite as incisive as Virginia Woolf's, I'm just saying that I know now why he wasn't entirely wrong.

I guess people fall in love with other people for all sorts of odd reasons, most of which are chronicled once monthly in the glossed-over pages of *Hello!* against a background of stately piles and Smallbone finishes. But no one ever mentions two things which seem to me of prime importance in the whole relationship saga. One is that the process of *falling* in love is as different from the process of *loving* as it is from any other experience in life. And for very good if slightly mean-spirited reasons.

I mean, could one do the Tesco superstore, pick up the bedding begonias and the kids from their respective nurseries, shell peas for the boss's wife and remove the rotary drier from its rotospike so as not to offend the neighbours who've stuck a Sky dish up against your patio view, whilst obsessed by lust? I'm asking ... could you do any one of those things as well as eat, sleep, do it a lot, *and* phone your mother, if you were permanently in the chemical state induced by falling in love?

To put it another way: when the cat is on heat (which she hasn't been since the vet gave her the unkindest cut of all), nevertheless when she *was,* she had very little time for chasing moths hanging unsubtly round the fridge or cuddling up for a neck scratch. She was out cruising for a bruising from morning till night, and when she was apprehended soliciting for trade up the high street and gated for the evening, she spent it flat up against the back room window, flashing her underparts at any passing Harry, Dick or certainly Tom, and making the most loud and ear-curdling noises by way of enticement.

You take my meaning? Combine this imbalance with a tendency to introduce the loved one's name into every topic of conversation (They're selling cabbages for £1.25 at Austins' – 'Oh, really? Funny that, when *Jack* was a student in Sheffield he worked in a fruit store and THEY sold cabbages. Gosh! Funny that, Jack was only mentioning ...') Or the need to race to the phone like a lunatic every time it rings (for someone else) and to blame your mother because you were at the pub when he *did* phone. Add to that a predilection to falling off buses because you think you see Him on every corner, in every crowd, at every window, and the inevitability of actually seeing Him in the off-licence when you weren't expecting to, and feeling your entire stomach lurch forward involuntarily like waking from a dream of falling. All this with a thudding heart, hot flushes and the school run? Please – forget it.

Whatever the rapture of first love and the obsessiveness of courtship (sweet old fashioned word) and marriage, it is a class act which can retain that rapture through the rigours of parenthood, child care and mortgage repayment. Obsession is easily diverted, and an all-consuming passion for your lover can shift almost transparently to one for your child, making your partner vaguely uneasy and prone to a curious sense of loss.

This is a mine-field which few of us admit to being trapped by. Honestly, though, who out there hasn't at several junctions been reduced by sleeplessness, exhaustion and sheer frustration into staring over the heads of your babies at the man who fathered them, and thinking what in hell's name am I doing with this person? And it's no use giving out with the 'Try a little tenderness' technique, you know, 'Let Granny take the little fellow for the afternoon – draw the shades, chill the wine, slip into a backless silk negligee, and remind yourselves how much fun it was making the little fellow in the first place.' Great advice. Particularly when Granny lives in Nairobi, the shades are spattered with Milpar, you haven't bought a bottle of wine since you opened your Mothercare account, the backless negligee is fine so long as you don't roll over and reveal the stretch marks on what used to be your breasts, and you feel about as compelled to have sex as you feel compelled to have gangrene.

The theory is that it passes. You know, the – er – revulsion thing. It certainly does. After – oooh – a mere nine or ten years, when quite suddenly you become consumed with lust and frighten your by now placid partner into a state of wary suspicion. It's at this stage that one or other of the partners may start to get an eye so roving as to become a nose and take up with the first cloth-eared bimbo who gazes up or down and says, 'I can't believe you're over forty – that's sooo sexy.'

Of course, the cloth-eared bimbo sometimes graduates into becoming the Second Mrs/Mr Tanqueray and becomes the person about whom your children start saying, 'Sophie makes these *wicked* cakes – they just melt in your mouth and *she* doesn't mind what time we go to bed and she and daddy are always giggling and cuddling up and when can we go there again?' Where does that leave you? It's all very well for our rejuvenated Lothario. For a while. Except, more often than not, the Second Mrs Tanqueray reveals herself to be a carbon-copy of the first one in almost every way but one and *that's* only until the new Tanqueray brood arrives, whereupon Lothario takes to ringing up the first Mrs T to say 'Where did we go wrong?'

Do I sound cynical? If so, I'm sorry. I don't mean to, it's just the way my pen slants. I also don't mean to be sexist because the same scenario works when the sexes are reversed. And I certainly don't mean to be marriagist or altar-ist or whatever else the expression isn't. I'm all for it. And even if I wasn't, would that stop lovesick mortals from shelling out for orange-blossom, hiring a vicar and promising to love, honour and mumble at least once in their lives? It's no secret that swans mate for life. It's no secret either that they are one of the most nasty, bad-tempered species on God's earth. Elephants, on the other hand, kick out the fellas as soon as they've done the necessaries, kick out the boy children as soon as they've started to shave, and live in a contented matriarchal world afraid of no man but the ivory poacher.

Within a week of meeting Jack, I knew I was going to marry him. It only took him another four years to feel the same way. When we met I felt the most enormous sense of 'coming home'. Almost of familiarity. It could have been just relief that someone would have me. Over the years my thoughts as well as my eyes have roved and as Jimmy Carter once said 'Ah have lusted in mah heart,' but as the car leaves the party and we've waved our goodbyes to the other guests, it's a rare night indeed that I haven't looked over and thought 'Thank God I'm going home with *him*.' I like to think Virginia would have approved of that.

Such Sweet Sorrow

I've been very concerned with mortality of late. My head's buzzing with it so you might as well share my tinnitus. First of all, my dearest man friend died of cancer, aged forty-two. His name was Philip Sayer and he was the actor who starred in *Floodtide* and *Bluebell* and other series and plays you may have seen. I met him on my first day at the London Academy of Music and Dramatic Art in 1965. He was a Welshman and a fine actor, capable of greatness. But, to me and to hundreds of others he was a unique, dashing, elegant, outrageous, witty, beautiful friend – and to share his last weeks, even from a distance, was an inspiration.

He died on the opening night of my one-woman show *Re:Joyce*. The end of the show was a slow fade as Joyce dances into a kind of immortality after her death from cancer in 1969. Fortunately I wasn't told about Philip till the curtain came down and it's impossible to convey how lost I felt. A committee of his closest friends planned a memorial celebration for him – and the meetings were interesting, to say the least.

Grief brings out the best and the worst in all of us, I've discovered. When my husband's mother, Lakey, died, an extraordinary scene of pillage went on in her little Blackpool bungalow after Jack had uttered the fateful sentence to visiting friends and relatives 'Take whatever you want.' I seem to remember one of them, one whom my mother-in-law had never much cared for, loaded down on her way to the front door with ornaments and household bric-à-brac from stomach to chin. By the door was a ghastly troll's face, in yellow glass, much adored by Lakey and much feared by anyone else who had the misfortune to let their gaze fall upon it. As the pillager passed by its glassy protuberance, she hesitated, swallowed her natural nausea and reached for it – thereby precipitating everything else she was balancing on to the tesselated tiles and into oblivion. Jack glanced heaven-ward and whispered 'Well done, Ma!' We finally departed from the house as the pillager's husband was scrabbling through the kitchen drawers in search of a rubber band he knew he'd once seen in there somewhere . . .

Just before my sister-in-law died, Jack and the kids went to see her. And the kids, then aged eleven and thirteen, sat by her side for four hours holding her hand and telling her she was going to get better. They hadn't known her well at all, but for some inexplicable reason they seemed to take charge of the situation and to deal with it in a totally intuitive way. Jack said to me later, 'If you ever feel like banging their heads together in the not-too-distant future, you should remember this day and be proud.' Needless to say, we didn't remember it for long.

At the funeral near Belfast, Jack was startled by a tap on the shoulder in the church and a man's voice hissing, 'Do ye want a lift to the cemetery?' As his hip was in bad shape at the time, Jack hesitated and asked, 'How far is it?' and received the whispered reply, 'Only three hundred yards.' 'Oh, no thank you then,' he whispered back, 'I'll walk.' 'Yess, yess!' insisted the man. 'But do ye want a lift?' Wary of causing further commotion, Jack said OK and found to his astonishment at the end of the service that the question had not been 'Do ye want a lift?' at all – not at all, at all as they say in the Emerald Isle – but 'Do ye want *to* lift?', and as he staggered along on his then-arthritic hip bearing the coffin with five other pall-bearers, he kind of wished he'd stuck to 'No thank you, I'll walk.'

There comes a time, of course, when your life seems to revolve around very little but hospital wards, white coats, foul-smelling flower-water and comatose doctors. My father had a stroke whilst staying chez Rosenthal, and my most vivid memory of the day we followed the ambulance to the hospital was of the junior doctor in charge trying, and failing, to clean her own glasses. She had been on duty since Friday morning. It was then late Monday. All the clichés are true. Nurses really *are* angels. Patient, kind, understanding, miracle-making angels. A Government which rewards its caring professions with nothing but penury and workhouse hours deserves, I'm afraid, its own sickness.

'I'll never moan about hard work again, Jacko,' I lied as I set off to make a packed audience laugh like drains, with a face the colour of one and stomach that sounded like one. On two occasions we were called into the hospital in the wee small hours, expecting the end – but the dear old rogue had nine lives and, at seventy-nine, he seemed to be negotiating for another two. We were by then in our fourth month of living with my mother in the house and, although the cooking was vastly improved, I seemed to have bitten through my cheeks, eleven of my ten fingers and was starting to bite through Jack's.

The memorial celebration for Philip took place at the Aldwych Theatre – and it was triumphant. A magnificent send-off, starting with 'Jesus Dropped the Charges' sung with soul by a superb black singer, and ending with 'Say A Little Prayer For Me' sung by six hundred people. In between we had excerpts from *Under Milk Wood* and *The Rocky Horror Show*, and the Class of '65 from the London Academy, including your sad scribe, sang 'Les Trois Cloches' (well, I sang the 'Boms' and the 'Aahs' and introduced us as 'The class of '65 culled from the five corners of the earth and the dregs of Equity'). And – yes – I got through my 'appreciation' of Philip without crying *once*, and with recourse to only one swig from the Rescue Remedy, with nothing more than red, puffy eyes, a bursting heart and a thumping head for the next twenty-four hours.

Best of all, the warring factions of the committee somehow came together on the night. It was clear that everyone had felt equally proprietorial about Philip. Each person had thought that he or she knew him best and each person had felt he had the right to more sadness than the others. And the pitched battles about white or black pianos, sad poems or funny poems, red evening dresses or gold, white flowers or no flowers, were all part of the childlike behaviour caused by the burden of adult grief. On the night we were all united by one single feeling. Love.

Joyce Grenfell wrote:

> If I should die before the rest of you
> Break not a flower nor inscribe a stone
> Nor when I'm gone, speak in a Sunday voice.
> But be the usual selves that I have known
> Weep if you must
> Parting is hell
> But life goes on –
> So sing as well.

And, oh boyo – did we ever! It was only when telling someone about the finale, weeks later, that I realized the unconscious pun of '*Sayer* Little Prayer' and he washed over me all over again. We were all unconsciously singing Philip's name.

During the many weeks of my father's hospitalization, I often came close to accepting that he was on his way. In fact, months earlier, before there was any real cause for concern over his health rate at all, I had a sudden flash forward. It was a bright spring morning and Dad had put a chair out in the middle of the lawn and was sitting, eyes closed, head uncomfortably angled, taking in the sparse sunlight. My mother and I were in the kitchen when I saw him and involuntarily said, 'My God, he looks as though he's ...' It was too late not to finish the sentence and she already knew what the sentence meant anyway ... 'not long for this world – on his way out – dying' ... words which were impossible to say.

Dad had been ill for fourteen years, on and off. The dashing, temperamental, beautifully groomed businessman with the sharp, irreverent wit and the sudden mood changes from light to stormy had disappeared one fateful day when he went into hospital for a routine prostate operation. We will never know what happened during that operation because, like most English people, we suffer from excessive politeness with figures of authority and we don't question or harass them when their explanations seem superficial.

That Dad had had a minor stroke, was that superficial explanation. There was no physical manifestation of this, he just couldn't remember anything. His immediate memory had vanished. The shock sent tremors through the family which are still reverberating today. He could remember the distant past and his family and friends, but ask him where he'd just been, what he'd had for lunch and which room he'd just come out of, and he was stumped. Perhaps that doesn't sound like too big a problem, but when your memory goes, all your conversation goes with it. Your frames of reference, your certainty. You begin to repeat yourself. You lose your confidence because you never know whether you've just asked that question or whether you are simply talking out-of-date rubbish. Also, you can't be left alone because every minute seems like an hour.

The only thing he could talk about with any certainty was his condition and how it made him feel. He was an emotional man at the best of times and a proud one, and the one often cancelled out the other. Sometimes it made for unbearably funny moments.

One day both parents accompanied me to a fund-raising luncheon at the Savoy, an afternoon rehearsal, tea at the house of an old friend in Twickenham by the river, the recording of a TV show in which I appeared in front of a live audience, and supper in a lovely restaurant with the cast.

Back home dad was looking very morose. 'Are you exhausted, Dad?' I asked him.

'No-oo, love, not really,' he murmured. 'I think I'm more *bored* than tired really.'

Apart from Mum, Jack was the person he depended upon the most.

'Coming for a ride out to pick up the kids?' Jack would say.

'Righto,' Dad would say, leaping to his feet with the zest of a thirty-year-old. 'Will I need my coat?' Pristine to the last, he would wear a tie and a suit, whether just pacing the house or going for an evening out. Then, in the car, the two of them would sing nonsensical songs, made up from Yiddish slang, at the tops of their voices and talk gibberish – childish, therapeutic, playful gibberish.

Once, at Lisson Grove, their car drew up alongside a rather battered Ford Cortina.

'Don't I know that fella?' said Dad, who because of his memory loss thought he'd already seen every film or play he watched, had read every book he attempted, and knew every story he heard.

'No, Moishe. You don't know him, you just think you do,' said Jack with all the patience he could muster.

'Well, he looks just like whatsisname . . . and so does she, look – give a look, go on.'

Jack sighed and glanced sideways, briefly, into the Cortina where Prince Charles and Princess Diana stared ahead obliviously, on their way to who knows where. Before he could speak, the lights changed and out of innate respect Jack remained stationary, waiting for his once and future King to go first. The Cortina blasted his horn and waved him on and that was that. Dad was thrilled rotten, not by seeing the Royal couple but by getting one up on his son-in-law.

Dad and I clashed more than I'd like to think about. We were too alike. Stubborn, proud, and often stiff-necked and argumentative. When he was ill, though, I could handle him. I didn't panic like Mum did and I think I calmed him. He had an attack, a stroke, or a black-out whilst staying with us. Mum was staying in Geneva with my brother for a week. She needed that break. Her life was structured totally around caring for Dad – if she was out of his sight he panicked. Often he tried to stop her leaving the house. Being a gregarious person, she found this hard to bear. There was no help from the social services, no kind of day care or replacement care available in or around Hull. Fourteen years. She was fifty-three when Dad first became ill.

When this attack came, Jack called an ambulance, but by the time they arrived Dad had come round and was violently opposed to going into hospital. Hospitals frightened him, and no wonder. He fought their attempts to carry him out with the strength of one possessed. He was seventy-eight and it took four ambulance workers and Jack to finally get him in the ambulance.

I was at Wembley, filming for BT when it happened. They released me for the day and I sat in a cab desperately trying to keep calm whilst my mind raced through the practicalities of getting Mum back – cancelling the filming, getting the

kids looked after for a while if . . . God forbid. The journey
was long. Very.

At the hospital, Dad was propped up on a narrow bed in
casualty. 'Hello, love,' he said. He looked terrible, grey and
haggard. 'Where's your mam?'

I told him. Then the nurse said, 'I'm going to take your
temperature now, Mr Lipman.'

'With a figure like yours you can take anything you like,
love,' said Dad jauntily. The nurse and I laughed, but from
different emotions. He looked over at me. 'Where's your
mam, love?'

I told him.

We went with him to the ward. They thought it best if he
stayed in overnight. I wrote him a long note explaining where
he was, what had happened and where Mum was. Then we
went home and waited for her return.

She panicked immediately, as we'd known she would. She
should never have gone, it was her fault, if only she'd come
back a day earlier, how would she manage if . . .? We tried to
calm her as we set off back to the hospital.

We found him confused but in better health. They still
felt it best to keep him there. He had my note, but he kept
putting it in safe places then forgetting where he'd put it.

'It's out of date now,' said Mum. 'I'll write him a new
one.' She did this quickly as visiting time was over and the
staff were anxious for us to leave. Afterwards I slipped back
to make sure he had the note by his side. He had. It read:
'Dear Moishe, Your teeth are at Maureen's. I'm back. Love
Zelma.'

Confused? You won't be . . .

Next day, he was home and as far as he was concerned it
had never happened.

For the next two years his health remained stable although
the hospital had told us he might have more mini-strokes.
Over the phone he was the same old Dad.

'Hello, Mammele, how are you?'

'We're all fine, Dad. How are you?'

'All right, love, how's Jack?'

'Oh, we're all fine, thanks. What are you d . . .'

'And the *kinder* – how are they?'

'Yes, fine, we're all fine.'

'Well, it's lovely to talk to you. I'll put your Mam on.'

We spent Christmas 1989 at the Feathers Hotel in Woodstock. There were twelve of us and we had magnificent food and attention. Dad, though, was never very happy away from home and his own surroundings and was uncomfortable about celebrating Christmas anyway. I had bought him a musical tie which woke him up from an afternoon nap when he rolled on to it. Puzzled and furious, he frisked the entire room in search of the culprit and practically committed a felony on the tie when he found it.

Sitting at the table one evening next to Astrid's mum, Peg, from Massachusetts, he opened up, as one sometimes can, to an interested stranger and spoke for hours about the old days and about his condition and his feelings. I was yards away down the other end of the table, yearning to hear WHAT ON EARTH he was saying and suffering pangs of guilt that I spent so little time encouraging him to unburden himself to me.

His last illness was the most violent, and his doctors were astounded that he survived it. He was, unbelievably enough, staying with us again. I'd sent Mum to the acupuncturist to try and give her some energy, and Jack and I were in the house when we heard a terrible thud. Dad had fallen and cracked his head on the fireplace. He was unconscious and bleeding. It was the most frightening moment of my life and I was icy calm. This time the hospital kept him in for several weeks and his condition deteriorated until the Sunday morning the phone rang at 6.30 am and the words 'We think you should come to the hospital as soon as you can.' He wasn't Dad any more. He was tiny, bird-like, and full of tubes and needles and very far away from us.

Life became, as life sometimes does, a desert around an arid oasis. In our case the oasis was the Whittington Hospital in Highgate. Every day the same visits, every visit different from the last. Every question a maybe. 'Would he wake up?' 'Would he breathe on his own?' 'Would he regain the swallowing reflex? The use of his arm? Walk again? Speak again? Go home again?' Each day two steps forward, one stumble sideways. Nurses you care for, sisters who never tire, doctors who are so tired they can hardly focus, consultants who hand out hope, pharmacists who hand out dope. Hospital tea, hospital phones, hospital Kit-Kat dispensers, corridors, lifts, bedpans, other patients' progress, other patients' parents, and suddenly, one day, you turn a corner and he's sitting up. Sitting up grumbling. 'Where were you? What have you brought me – when am I coming out?' Whispering voice, atrophied muscles, bowed head, lifeless hand and fighting spirit. He's not going. He's not ready. He'll go when he's ready. Not yet. Good old Dad!

Eight weeks later Dad went home to Hull, took one look at the nice convalescent home we'd booked for him and said, 'I'm buggered if I'm staying in here. Take me home, Zel.' Slowly, slowly, he regained his powers of speech, movement, began to shave and dress himself and gently throw his increasing weight about. Mother cared for him with a gentleness born out of genuine relief at still having him to care for.

He died just after his eightieth birthday. After a night out, and a cake with candles. A chest infection turned into pneumonia. He fought a last furious fight and finally gave in. I was in New Haven, Connecticut, unable to get home. Jack took Amy and Adam to Hull for the funeral where Amy sobbed her heart out and Adam, less than three months after his Barmitzvah, threw a clod of earth on to his grandad's coffin as his first act of manhood. Not a day goes by that Dad's face expressions, his bizarre Yiddish phrases, his looks and his own kind of loving don't pass through our collective consciousness. And that's immortality, Moishe.

3

All Work and Some Plays

Careering Down the Line

Since I last put indelible to vellum, three projects have woven their way through my life, interconnecting and overlapping. They are *Re:Joyce*, British Telecom and *About Face*. And between them they make up a total of thirty-eight different characters. Only one of them is famous, however, and award-winning. And she (my doppelgänger) is the easiest. Here to stay for at least for another year and to haunt me for the next fifteen.

I'd often thought of doing a TV commercial. It is no longer the kiss of death to an actor (watch this space), and it's one of the few ways we have of paying the school fees on a regular basis. There was an abortive attempt at a 'Maureen Lipman says write to me about your washing problems' which made me squirm with embarrassment to the extent that I've blocked out the name of the liquid detergent concerned. No wisk of wemembering it, either.

But when the Telecom commercial arose, it was with very little reluctance that I went along, with most of the other ethnic actresses in England, to audition for the role of the Jewish momma, then masquerading under the name of Dora.

Richard Phillips is the Mary Shelley who created the monster, and I have no doubts in saying that he is as mad as a snake and supremely gifted in his chosen field. Shaven-headed, Raybanned and with a wardrobe which makes Georgio Armani look as though he spends far too much time in C & A, he's known in the agency as The Birdman of Alcatraz on the grounds that he never finishes a sentence. But, oh boy, does he start some. A typical exchange would go:

RICHARD: (*bursting into room*) 'Hello – sorry – all right?

Er – ' (*he begins pacing then stops, freeze-framed, body facing one direction, head angled strangely and facing the other. He may be wearing psychedelic Bermudas, a toning but different psychedelic silk T-shirt, a straw panama, severely fashionable horn-rims, and unusually busy sneakers. He continues*)

'What I'm gonna do is . . .' (*he raises one finger then looks at it suspiciously, as though it may attack him or at worst disagree with him*) 'What I'm gonna – what I'm planning – all things being – (*thirty-second meaningful pause*) 'I mean, anything could happen, right? What do you think? Eh?' (*He takes off his hat, raises his eyes to look where it was, smooths down his smooth egg of a head, places hat on table and resumes pacing.*)

'I'm gonna start, right? In the kitchen, right? Er – and there are two ways I might do it, right?' (*Artist's heart now sinks at thought of fifteen-hour day on account of two ideas leading to twenty permutations of two-line scene: 'But Richard –'* 'Yes, I know, but the thing is – er – let me put this another way' (*so far he hasn't put it* anyway) – 'Look –' (*He freezes mid-pace, cocks his head as though listening to an external sound – which indeed he is – draws a deep breath through his nose, rolls up his eyes, turns down the corners of his mouth, then, forgetting to expel air because a new thought has struck him, he gasps:*) 'I'll tell you what, right? This is what I'm gonna do – lemme ask you something, right?' (*Forty-second challenging pause.*) 'I'm gonna ask you something, right? I mean. I think this is brilliant, I want to float this past you, OK? Just say what you think, OK?' (*He resumes pacing, then, spinning on his heels to avoid the wall, he veers round, stares you straight in the face, hands flared, fingers spread frozen in time and space, chin tucked in on itself like a gossiping neighbour, takes another deep breath through the nose, opens his mouth, swivels his eyes to left and right and walks clean out of the room. As he leaves, via the door which leads into the wardrobe department instead of the corridor, you hear him saying to two puzzled coat hangers:*) 'Hang on. Sorry. Hi! Er – I'll be back in – '

Thereafter the truly experienced Phillips-watcher will know that he is to be found in the corner of the studio conducting a vehement argument with himself on the subject of whatever he just didn't tell you, and will shortly be sending an assistant back to pick up his hat.

It is a phantasmagorical performance, perfected over many years in advertising in which the prime requisite – apart from, or in spite of, talent – is to get yourself noticed, talked about and sought after. At first it amused me; after my first year it drove me to distraction; in my second year I learned to take a novel with me to work and, with a bit of luck, get through it in a two-day shoot. In Australia I learned to love the dynamism of his presence. No gathering of the clan was really gathered properly until Richard arrived, sartorially plumed and bearing the news from Aix to Brent.

In my third year I learned to adore the man; he can virtually do what he likes and I'll still adore him. He is a collector's item as full of hot air as he is of magical ideas. He's Professor Brainstawm in Bermudas and I'm delighted to play the housekeeper, Mrs Flittersnoop, to his crackpot inventor. And, of course, my whingeing deadpan counterfoils his explosive energy, and we indulge in some devilish flights of fantasy around the thoughts of Chairperson Beattie.

Back in 1988 though, none of the above was known to this actress, who fancied herself as a serious artist who'd been through the portals of the National and the RSC, albeit coming quickly out the other side, and whose biggest ambition was a) to perfect a stage yawn, b) to trim her inner thighs, and c) to fry a perfect fishball.

After the initial meeting, I felt that 'they' – that's the advertising company, personified by Richard – felt that I was their man. A lot of discussion went on between J Walter Thompson and my agent's assistant, who told me the idea was to vary the commercials considerably so as not to bore the general public. No warning bells chimed in this mere mortal mind.

Then word came that they wanted me to do a test! This seemed a bit of a cheek as we had read the scripts together, discussed the lady in painfully familiar detail, and all our opinions had tallied. Obviously, they were *so sure* that I was the right person for the job, that they needed a second opinion. I said no to the test. They assured me it was for make-up and wardrobe only. I said yes to the test. Story of my life, shaking my head and saying yes. Costumed in an elegant silk blouse, Corocraft jewellery, and bouffant and bewinged steel-grey wig, I sailed forth into a studio full of camera crew, agency men and sundry traders who basically sat there blinking expectantly in my direction.

I cleared my throat. Well, if I hadn't who would? Then I launched into a sort of 'Clap-hands here comes Sophie Tucker crossed with a couple of Golden Girls and a dash of every mother of every girl I ever grew up with', live from Carnegie Deli. It was the ultimate audition. Sweat poured through the starched severity of my wig and the small studio took on the character of a Comedy Store try-out for a middle-aged alternative comic.

My only props were an empty cup and saucer, a telephone and a lifetime of past experience. Looking back at the tape of the test, I can see my nervousness. I was unsure whether to make her Northern, like my own mother, which works wonderfully well with Zelma-like lines, eg. 'If you were me, would you wear the blue dress with the beading that everyone's seen me in, or the new one I've kept hanging up for two years?' or 'Shan't I buy the beef, then? You want me to get lamb chops, do you? Righto then. Aren't lamb chops beef, though?' This made for a softer, more innocent and ingenuous 'Dora', but perhaps what was needed was a slightly sharper, more bristly Dora with a hidden vulner-ability, which came more naturally when I gave her a North London accent...

To warm myself up I did a few tried and tested jokes, 'You don't have a vase?' being my oldest and most standard one. It broke up the crew and left the cameraman shaking under-neath his camera. I felt better, and tried 'Minnie on safari with the gorilla'. Better still, but perhaps I should be acting not entertaining. I picked up the phone.

'Hello, operator, I'm trying to get through to the Kosher butcher – it's on the blink and I've people coming for dinner Friday – Oh, thank you, dear. Hello – Hello, CLIVE, how are you? Yes! fine thank you, dear, and yours? Lovely, now listen, I want a nice piece of brisket for the weekend, very little fat, how's the baby? Aaah, Aaah. Is she? Already! Bless her, and some liver, thinly sliced. Calves'! What do you mean what kind! How's your sister-in-law since the ... oh, I am sorry – all out – well, a lot of people manage with just the one.... Have you got any frying sausages in? Twenty-four in four separate bags for the freezer – listen, there's someone at the door – can you deliver? Morning or afternoon. Yes, all day and if I'm not you can leave them with her next door – her bark's worse than her bite.'

It was all over bar the peeling off of clothes and the mopping up of mascara. It was perfect. They wanted it just like that. I shouldn't change a hair. Then they changed the wig, the make-up, the wardrobe and the voice. Other than that they loved it. I should have known.

We began filming with Richard Phillips on the sidelines (by which I mean on the floor, through the windows, in the lounge and peering at the man peering through the lens), Nigel (Grubby) Foster and Michael Hall representing J Walter Thompson, the Agency. Grubby was and is the most unlikely man ever to be a hit in the world of advertising. Bearded, chubby and deceptively jovial, he fields problems in Ronald Reagan-like fashion (and I mean that in a Dame Edna-like caring way). He laughs, disappears and the problem goes away. I don't know quite how he does it. I've never seen him in a flap, or anything less than pleasant whether dealing with an actor who's completely shaved his head only a few days before shooting a strict continuity commercial, or calming down the 'real' Rene Goodman who has rung the *Sun* to complain that the latest BT commercial takes her name in vain, and people keep asking if she's getting divorced.

On location in Australia, he was nothing if not the life and soul of the party. In my most cherished memory of him, he is standing on his chair, at a table for twenty-eight in The Last Great Australian Fish Restaurant, bopping and twisting and bellowing his way through 'I Can't Get No Satisfaction', with his walkabout phone precariously jammed in the back pocket of a pair of apparently descending blue jeans.

Wait – an even more cherished memory of him is on the set at Wembley Studios after a particularly gruelling day shooting the 'Call to Confirm' commercial. This featured Miriam Margolyes and Bernard Bresslaw as our friends

Harry and Dolly who unexpectedly arrive for dinner, giving
Beattie nervous dyspepsia and terminal embarrassment.

At the end of the day Miriam and Bernard's section was
completed and they were sent home. In fact, Miriam went
from the studios to the airport and back to America where
she now 'largely', and I mean that in yet another caring way,
works.

Sudden panic on set. We've missed out a shot of Bernard
which has to be done over Miriam's shoulder – which is now
30,000 feet over the Atlantic Ocean with the rest of her.

The solution is not immediately obvious. Miriam is not an
easy shape to duplicate. Cinderella's shoe is a morceau de
gâteau. If you get the height right then the width seems
preposterous. There was only one person in a studio of over
eighty people who could fill out her dress. All eyes turned to
Grubby. All Grubby's eyes turned to heaven.

I think, the moment when I saw him, bearded and rotund,
in a plain Paisley sheath, grey socks and sneakers, was the
moment when I seriously feared for my health. I lay on the
floor shouting with laughter for at least twenty minutes.

Director Tony Smith had just completed the prize-
winning TV series *Tutti Frutti*, but these were to be some
of his first commercials.

You know, there is a similarity between a good director
and a good hairdresser. The moment a good hairdresser puts
his hands through your hair you relax. You stop worrying.
You put your hair and your immediate future in his hands.
Conversely a limp hand in the wash basin and the inevitable
question: 'Have you had your holidays yet?' will guarantee
you a despair which can't be dispelled until your head is
safely home and inside a bucket of water.

Tony is an actor's director. He directed each 60-second
commercial like a play. A dramatic play. He kept the performances 'under the top'. I had suggested Geoffrey Chiswick to play my husband Harry. We'd worked together on a
BBC play called *Shiftwork* and he had a slightly wry, sullen
world-weariness about him which reminded me of so many
downtrodden husbands. It's not an easy quality to portray
without resorting to wimpishness. You know the joke? A
Jewish actor rings his mother and says: 'Momma, Momma,

I got the part! I'm playing the husband.' Mother responds: 'Really? You couldn't get a speaking part?'

The other piece of extra-curricular casting I did was of the young boy playing the grandson – 'voice like an angel' – Oliver. It was Yom Kippur, and in one of the breaks in the day-long service, I spied a young dark-haired lad shinning up and down a pillar and asked him if he liked acting.

'Well...' he replied, 'I was a sheep once in the Christmas play, but I never got any of the good lines.' I hijacked his mother and the next day he was hired.

As Richard and I chronicled in our 'book of the ads' *You Got an Ology?*, in the first two-week shoot we made ten commercials. We worked at an unheard-of pace. We shot the son who never calls, then when he does call Beattie complains he never visits; the Mrs Jones commercial, done in almost one or two takes; the 'Happy Birthday' song; an answering machine, starring only my voice and my son Melvyn (it was actually my favourite and was never shown); and the one which launched a cache of catch phrases – the 'Ology' commercial, coincidentally starring Jacob Krichefsky, son of Bernard and Judith, my Muswell Hill neighbours.

One evening we filmed at six o'clock a commercial which I'd been handed in script form at five o'clock the same evening. It was a monologue called 'Good News', in which Beattie enthused down the phone at great length to a young man who'd apparently done her the most enormous good turn. 'Oh, Clive. Thank you. That is such good news. I can't thank you enough. I'm so grateful. Oooh, you are good. If you knew what this meant to me...' etc. It was shot entirely through a mirror past which Beattie paced, stopping only to pat her near-perfect hair. The punch-line to her terminally puzzled husband was: 'It's all right. He's had a cancellation for a perm – he's fitting me in.'

Sounds simple enough. It was the most technically complex piece of acting I've ever had to do. The complication was in saying the newly minted lines at the right side of the mirror whilst arriving at the same place each time. King Lear would have been a doddle! It was, needless to say, never shown.

The last shoot was the phone card ad, with Zia Mohyeddin,

shot in Battersea the day after the first Great Hurricane. One hurricane was much the same as another to me after the two weeks I'd just had, and I slept right through it. At 7.00 am the next morning I drove across London in shock and second gear. Roads made impassable by great shattered trees, Regent's Park a cemetery, Hyde Park, Battersea Park – it looked like the *War of the Worlds*. We shot in intermittent black rain and brilliant sunlight with a canopy over the lens – finally abandoned it, and went home early.

Suddenly it was all over bar the doubting. *That* followed. The market research people moved in and pronounced their findings. Their unimaginably awful findings. It seemed that nobody liked *anything*. In the researchers' view, if the character was to have any kind of success she should reflect a more contemporary lifestyle. She should be a tracksuit granny who jogged and did aerobics and presumably finished up having two ribs extracted to make her waist look smaller. The campaign was as dead as a dodo.

Except that I have a daughter who doesn't believe in the extinction of the dodo. She claims there are two left. Lilac ones. They live behind the *Neighbours* studio apparently, and sometimes visit Harley Street for a check-up. The dodo lives – and so, thanks to somebody high up at Telecom Tower and to Richard Phillips, would our 'antiquated' ads. Old-fashioned they may have been but they proved a point, which today's deregulated TV stations would do well to heed, that what the public actually want to see is characterization, plot, and relationships. Like – well, like a play.

Almost immediately the national press began taking up the campaign. Anne Robinson, of the *Mirror*, was the first to write about it. It was the 'Ology' line that hooked her and other papers followed her line. Right down the line. *The Times*, the *Financial Times*, the *Sun* (twenty things you didn't know about your favourite Jewish Momma – twenty things which, needless to say, I had never discussed with the *Sun*.

About this time, JWT announced they wanted four more ads, and another three more after that. Of the ten we'd made, about seven ran. On one, we had the wrong logo, on another the wrong *phone*, and the answering machine ad featured built-in obsolescence. Apparently there was a shortage of available answering machines . . . !

'How many more do I have to do?' I asked my agent's assistant. 'The more I do, the more they seem to want.'

His reply poleaxed me. 'Well, they are actually entitled to do up to twenty-five commercials a year.'

'I beg your pardon?'

'Yes. It was always in your contract. Remember? They wanted to do lots of different ads so that they can vary them and the public won't get bored.'

'I'm sorry, it must be this line.' I gave a mirthless laugh. 'I thought for one moment you said twenty-five a year.'

'Twenty-five, yes, that's right. It was in your contract.'

In my first year as Beattie I made eighteen commercials. And changed my agent.

Shopping for a new one was interesting. I hadn't been on the open market for so long. Single and over forty, or as they say in the world of women executives, SINBAD (Single Income, Neurotic, Bankable and Desperate). One agent I met with admitted that I was known in the business as a 'bit of a cheap turn'. I was thrilled. It's not often a girl in my position gets to feel promiscuous. A bit player in the Cynthia Payne story.

It's all right now. I've settled down. 'Love's more com-f'table the second time around,' the song says. My new agent, Anne Hutton, who coincidentally was Joyce Grenfell's agent, is a good partner and we intend to be very very happy together.

During the second shoot, Dora finally metamorphosed into Beattie. I'm partial to a nice pun, and BT's image began to soar in direct ratio to the growing number of commercials on the air. With the awards season upon them, J Walter Thompson were being showered with strange-looking trophies in perspex and metal alloy, and were forced to get a little man in to build them more shelves. Even *I* was pelted with a couple of little pointed things from the *TV Times* and was heard to admit that 'awards are like haemorrhoids – sooner or later every bum gets one'.

Moreover, my forays outdoors became adventures into

loonyland: for instance, asking directions from a garage attendant: 'Lost, are you, Beattie? 'Ere, boys – what do you think of young Melvyn, letting his mum out on the roads without a minder? Bring the old girl a chair will you, lads?' Suffice to say, I was in street clothing at the time, looking, I'd thought, the right if not the accurate side of forty, and Linal Haft, who plays my son, is three years older than I am.

And the time when I did my citizen's good deed and spotted a wobbly wheel on the car in front. I pulled out precariously alongside of him, signalled wildly and, when he pulled down his window, informed him of the danger. As we pulled up at the lights, he leaped out, kicked the wheel cap back into place, grinned and said, 'Thanks, it happens about every two years or so,' got back in his car, then signalled equally wildly for me to wind down *my* window. I complied and he bellowed 'Five months, I've been waiting for my telephone. I've called British Telecom every day for five months and what have I got? One line, that's all I'm asking for. What do they expect me to do, eh?' His car was stuffed full of large pink teddy bears. I contemplated telling him where to stuff his stuffed stuff – but drove off instead.

And on the Jimmy Young Show, as the news of Telecom's unannounced increase in charges was discussed: 'Well,' said Jimmy, brightly, 'let's take some calls on this issue and the first one is Mrs so-and-so from whatnot . . .' and, yes you've guessed it, what did Mrs so-and-so from whatnot have to say? 'Well I think it's disgusting that "that Maureen Lipman" didn't tell us about it.' Frothing at the mouth, I raced into the house, dialled the BBC, and got straight through. To the David Jacobs show, of course, who were mystified.

And in the *Financial Times* 'Lipman boosts BT's yearly profits'. And the *Punch* cartoon depicting BRITISH LIPMAN on the side of a Telecom van, and the newspaper hoarding which stopped my daughter and me in our tracks after a visit to the acupuncturist in Baker Street. LIPMAN SET TO TAKE OVER THE WORLD. Quite honestly, as I wrote at the time, 'if my waters could have broken, they would have broken'.

As it happened, it merely meant that the monster had

sprouted two heads. J Walter Thompson had beaten their rivals to win the BT *International* account. It was the culmination of two years of mounting media attention for Beattie. My one telephone never stopped: 'How many phones do you have? Where are they? How often do you use them? What models are they?'

A double page spread appeared in the *Mail*, featuring Beattie's real mother, Zelma, in her house in Hull, and revealing that she prefers to use Mercury as it's cheaper. Flushed with fame, Mother ceremoniously opened a new telephone shop in the city centre. Was there no end to this flagrant Beattification?

The International campaign took us to Australia, and sister Rose arose from Sydney Harbour to offend and irritate her sibling phonemate. In visor and sunshades I swatted antipodean flies, my cheeks padded with sponges and my eyes squinting through blue contact lenses, and the whole world thought it was a backdrop. Australia blinded us with torrential rain and howling gales and somehow two commercials were shot under sizzling arc-lamps, and wildly flapping plastic sheeting. By now Richard Phillips was wearing his directorial hat, and he's worn it ever since, both down and out in London and in Paris. Last year when *You Got An Ology?* was published, Richard and I graced a couple of books signings at which the chief draw was a constantly playing video of all thirty-three adverts. Who needs *When Harry Met Sally* when you can have *When Harry Met Beattie* ... 'Harry, I don't understand why the girl was making those funny grunting noises in the restaurant. Was it the food or was she supposed to be a tennis player?' No less a person than Gloria Estefan rang my startled publisher before leaving London, to order the *Ology* book, because she was crazy for the commercials. I was pleased. I'd just bought her record 'It Cuts Both Ways'. It does.

The other plus is the bright red phone box at the foot of my garden. It's a gift from BT if not from Tardis. It took six men, a lorry with a hydraulic lift, one hundred and fifty feet of tracks, a tray on wheels and four hours to get it there. Assembled for the event were myself, my secretary, my domestic help, my mother, my kids, two photographers, and a press rep from BT bearing an assortment of foliage for the photocall.

The main road was blocked for twenty-five minutes whilst the three-quarter-ton monster was winched out on to the tracks, and cars soon began diverting themselves through the portals of the nearby Methodist Church.

During the course of the four hours, twenty-four cups of coffee were consumed and any amount of light snacks. Astrid arrived in shorts, and took the kiosk-pushers' minds off their work for a while. 'What is that huge red thing doing outside your garage?' she inquired.

Jack arrived home from a meeting. 'Hello, love. There's a big red thing lying on its side in the driveway . . .'

My old friend Lesley (*Birds of a Feather*) Joseph showed up with her children. 'I do not believe what is on your LAWN!'

And my mate Lizzy showed up with a migraine and a helluva problem over her son's school. She stayed long enough to tell me the story and never once remarked on the Ealing comedy taking place outside the window.

At 4 o'clock I posed in a flower-decked kiosk wearing Amy's brand-new Marks and Spencer's floral cotton and an awful lot of Elizabeth Arden's Flawless Finish. It was the hottest day of the year, the sun baked the glass, the glass baked me, and the result looked not unlike Dirk Bogarde at the end of *Death in Venice*.

There have been other pluses too, I must confess. Like the new telephone system, which Beryl and June of Crouch End BT kindly installed in our house after a spate of anonymous and asthmatic perverts got wind of our number. Suddenly we found ourselves the proud owners of three switchboards, two lines, thirteen phones and a miraculous fax ('Oooh, you must have to roll them up ever so small') machine. On behalf of my sixteen-year-old daughter, and the rest of us who occasionally wrestle the receiver from her, I should like to say thank you.

It seems that even the 081/071 switch-over went seamlessly well owing to Richard and his expert ease as writer/director. On May 6 Mother and I went the full complement of floors up to the very top of Telecom Tower, there to shake hands with Sir Dickie and to share a shuddering scaffolding (I almost said erection – but I didn't) with Michael Aspel, one of my all-time four minutes' warning men. (See page 193.)

Searchlights combed the skies as I switched London over to the new system and said, 'Ladies and gentlemen, this is the second biggest turn-on I've had all week – the first was undoubtedly my precarious position up here with Mr Aspel.'

The last couple of ads were the 'Sounds like a Gorilla' scenario set in London and Florida, and a virtual all-nighter of a shoot which produced 'Anniversary'. Almost every Jewish actor in London was assembled in Beattie's living-room – it was my mother's idea of Paradise. The gossip level was 23 on the Richter scale, the air jammed with jokes. Now, fingers on the buzzers and no conferring: what did the caterers serve for lunch? Yes, you guessed it. In one. Baked potatoes, green beans and a nicely basted pork roast. No, fair do's, it takes a lot of forethought to come up with that one.

Pause here for gorilla joke:

A man is walking down Oxford Street with a gorilla on each arm. A friend sees him and expresses amazement.

'Yeah,' the man tells him, 'a friend of mine in Kenya sent them over to me. I don't know what to do with them.'

The friend says: 'Well, if I were you I'd take them straight to the zoo.'

'Good idea!' says the man, 'I think I will!'

Two weeks later, the same friend is walking down Oxford Street when he sees the same man with the same two gorillas.

'Crikey!' he said, 'I thought you were going to take those two to the zoo.'

'I did,' says the man, 'they loved it. So today I'm taking them to a matinée.'

The final BT chapter is yet to be conceived. How much longer can I continue to be the thinking man's Busby? Well, the answer is that my contract expires after six more commercials. I don't know what Beattie's demise will be. Maybe she should be flattened by a telephone kiosk on a wavering winch. Maybe her daughter-in-law should slip a little hemlock into her shmaltz herring. Maybe she should fall asleep and wake up as Maureen Lipman, saying 'It was all a terrible nightmare. I thought I was a sixty-five-year-old woman with grey hair and a crepe neck.'

In the meantime, I've come to terms with her. We've reached a watershed in Beattie-tudes. I'm over my paranoia that she's taken over my life. I've accepted that if I open in a play in Lourdes about the life and times of Mother Teresa, the press will write: 'Yiddishe Momma in NUN-sense'. The fact is, she's funny. Beattie makes us laugh not because she's a Yiddishe momma but because she's a mother. All our mothers, be they Irish, Italian or Basque Separatist. Did you ever meet a mother who's complained that her child phoned her too often? Me neither. And if my next fifteen years are spent pounding the pavement in search of a job without a handset in it – too bad. We'll just have to call in the receivers.

Re:Joyce: Chapter Wan

Why Joyce Grenfell? Why me?

My answer is never the same. Because she made me laugh. Because I liked her. Because reading her writings startled me out of my narrow conception of her talent. Because I wanted a new public to be equally startled. Because it seemed like an opportune idea at the time. And because in many ways I identified with her.

Not superficially, though. On the surface, we couldn't be more different. She was born, if not with a silver spoon in her mouth, then certainly not one with any chicken soup on it. Her mother was a flighty, dainty and delicious Southern belle from Virginia, one of eleven sisters including the legendary Nancy Astor. Her father, Paul Phipps, was an architect, also of American parentage, who influenced his daughter's love of music and the arts and her abiding faith in the Church of Christian Science. Nannies, boarding schools, 'bright young things', coming-out parties, tennis parties, house-parties for Noël and Gertie, Mrs Patrick Campbell, George Bernard Shaw, Darling Binnie and Boo...

'When I was a girl there was always Time,
There was always time to spare.
There was always time to sit in the sun
And we were never done
With lazing and flirting
And doing our embroidery
And keeping up our memory books
And brushing our hair
And writing little notes
And going on picnics
And dancing, dancing, dancing ...'

All a pretty far cry from 30 Northfield Road, Hull, where a nanny was a goat, a boarding school a threat, and a bright young thing something who'd probably just passed their eleven plus. Where Mother fried the fish, lit the Friday night candles and laid out the clothes in the order my brother and I would put them on. Where my nearest brush with show business was when my father, a tailor, made Ronnie Hilton's jacket for Buttons in *Cinderella* at the Hull New Theatre.

Not that Joyce's parents were rich. By Astor standards they were penniless, but they lived a society life which enabled Joyce to have a bird's-eye view of that society. She became a people watcher, and what she observed, she remembered and recycled. In a small way, perhaps, from the inside of an ethnic minority, I was doing the same.

'I never heard what the teachers said,' she wrote, 'because I was always too busy watching how they said it.' To perpetuate a cliché, that could have been me talking.

Certainly, when I watched her in the St Trinian's films, I knew I was watching someone who not only knew all of the people I knew, but could do a wicked job of 'taking them off'!

Joyce went on the stage in 1939 – by accident rather than design – and during the next forty years she became both an international entertainer and a national treasure. She received the OBE for her work in hospitals and camps during the war. She visited fourteen countries, going to places which often no one else would visit. On one occasion her piano was dragged up a hillside to the door of an isolation hut, where she sang for five rather surprised soldiers. 'You don't mind smallpox, do you?' beamed the matron.

She played her one-woman show on Broadway, across America, and was called back four times, by popular demand, to Australia. When she retired from the stage she took her greatest pleasure in her marriage, in travel, in bird-watching, in music, in her vast correspondence, and in the success of her two autobiographies.

I on the other hand went on the stage entirely by design and it was no accident that after twenty-odd years, I found myself thinking more and more of my childhood heroine. Five years ago, when I first had the notion of a show based on Joyce's work, I mentioned it to Clive James, who knew her personally. His reaction was muted. This wasn't a reflection of his feelings about me, I knew that, and when pressed he would only say that the most resounding impression she gave was of her innate class. It permeated everything she did. This threw me, but only for a minute. We are a class-ridden society and no one feels this more than we Northern middle-class girls; but the one quality which transcends class consciousness is self-consciousness in its literal sense, the ability to be oneself in whatever company. I don't always have it but I'm engaged in a perpetual struggle for it. When a lady in Debenhams said to me, 'Ooh, you're just like you are!' I thought, 'Joyce would have liked that.' I was ready for the challenge.

The idea of a one-woman tribute was conceived five years ago, when larger-than-life director Bryan Izzard asked me to contribute to a Channel Four programme on the monologue called *The Eye Of The Little Yellow Dog*, starring, amongst others, the late Leonard Rossiter, Cilla Black, Alec McCowen, Diane Langton, Anita Harris and Ronald Lacey. I was to perform two of Joyce's pieces, the first being 'Committee', a deadly accurate re-creation of a Northern Ladies Choral Committee meeting convened to axe one of its founder members: 'Now, we don't want any unpleasantness, friendly is what we are and friendly is how we mean to go on ... but I think we all know there is one voice in the altos that did not ought to be there. And I think we all know to whom I am referring ...'

It came as near to cattiness as Grenfell could, and gently brought the house down. Reggie Grenfell was there for the recording. I'm not alone in maintaining that he is the second sweetest man on earth. There's nothing Jack loathes more than reading some publication in which I've referred to him as a saint and I'm sure Reggie feels the same way. But of course they are, and there is little doubt that neither Joyce nor myself could ever have achieved a tenth of the success we have without the help and support, not to mention the sheer selflessness and lack of ego, of the men who chose to

love us. There, I've said it on record and without recourse
to a single one-liner. It was another thing we had in common.
The list was growing.

Reggie seemed genuinely pleased with the idea of a tribute
to Joyce, and from that day forth gave me endless friendship
and encouragement. He lives, still, in the same Chelsea flat
with its pink and white striped wallpaper, geranium-filled
window-boxes, elegant chintzy furniture, and the myriad of
expressive original paintings which Joyce and he shared for
so many years. Her presence permeates the flat.

After the monologues were over, Bryan Izzard prodded
me to start writing the show for myself. I wanted to do it,
but every time I picked up the Bic, a job came up. I thought
about Joyce through predictable sit-coms, through wonderful *Wonderful Town* rehearsals, through Ayckbourn and
Shakespeare and Bennett and Bernstein. Finally I went to
James Roose-Evans, who'd adapted *84 Charing Cross Road*
for the stage and said, 'What are you doing for the rest
of your life?' I felt that he might be the person to bring
out the spiritual element in Joyce's life, as well as the
comedy.

The Phipps family were Christian Scientists and Joyce's
religion was central to her life. Her husband Reggie was not
a strong believer, and it was only at his persistent insistence
that Joyce sought medical advice on the eye cancer which
eventually led to her death. We were anxious that Joyce's
love of God and of Good, as one, would not seem pious,
which she would have hated. In a preface to one of my
favourite sketches, 'First Flight', Joyce wrote: 'Goodness is
almost impossible to show on stage. It calls for simplicity
that is neither dull nor empty and for humility that is in no
way false.' It became clear that the way to tell the story of
her life was through her work.

Over the next eighteen months, James Roose-Evans com-
piled a first draft based on her autobiographies and her
prolific letters. He called it *In Search of Joyce Grenfell*. The
opening was from a book called *Joyce, By Her Friends*, and
was a piece written by Verily Anderson which conjured up
an imaginary car ride with Joyce: 'Turn left any minute now
and then sharp right and straight under a low lying archway

with a very steep mews. Well, really not much more than a single mew, it's so small. Oh, I do so adore Good. Good and love and God are all the same thing, really. Quick, nip in where that taxi's johnny-head-in-airing along. It won't mind. Good girl! I think it rather liked it. It seemed to jerk it into a sense of purpose.'

It was mid-way between a sketch and a chat and I loved it. I had introduced Roose-Evans to Reggie and he gave James access to Joyce's study and to all her unpublished material and letters. I chose the sketches I wanted to perform and wrote an over-long introduction based on why I felt drawn to Joyce. Our intention was to slide seamlessly from Maureen to Joyce.

We met more and more frequently as the months went by, until we had more drafts than the windows of a stone cottage. The truth is that there is an embarrassment of riches in Joyce's work that it was what to leave out which posed the problem, not what to include. Sometimes James's accompanying letters were longer and more convoluted than the script changes, but it was becoming clear that the linking material would hinge around Joyce's letters to her mother who, when Joyce was nineteen, had remarried and returned to America. The letters were a real find and James went on to publish two volumes of them; they became immediate best-sellers. Joyce's continuing appeal never ceases to delight me.

From the day that Michael Codron became interested in producing the show, I felt the cutting take root. Michael began his career producing revues and went on to become London's most experienced and successful producer of new plays. We were all elated when he came on board.

As the day of rehearsals approached I got my usual attack of the 'I'll never do its'. This time they centred around the inability, on my part, to learn and remember two-and-a-half hours' solo dialogue, to *look* remotely like the woman I was playing, and to overcome the prejudices of the millions of Joyce-worshippers who were all sitting out there sticking pins in little waxwork Lipman dolls. This latter feeling was based on three or four rather malicious letters saying, 'Get your hands off our Joyce. *She* was English.' This first puzzled, then scared and finally amused me, in the light of Joyce's American lineage.

So, I went to see a hypnotist. Well, I would, wouldn't I? I went at actress Brenda Bruce's recommendation. She's had the self-same panic attack before starting a one-woman show. It stands to reason when you think about it – after all, we are trained to inter-relate with other actors. It's a gregarious profession.

The hypnotist, Gloria May, was very matter of fact. There was no swinging pendulum and no 'You are going into a deep, deep, deep sleep . . .', just a comfy leather recliner and a soft voice suggesting relaxation, confidence and clarity. I don't know how or why it worked, but I stopped waking up in a cold sweat.

Of course, one of the advantages of waking up in the night in a sweat is that you tend to have your best ideas whilst failing to get back to sleep. One such revelation was the title of the show. Four-thirty in the morning, as I was changing into a nice fresh pyjama top, it struck me blitheringly between the brows: *Re:Joyce*. What could better sum up Joyce's name, Joyce's qualities, and the feeling with which we wanted our audience to leave the theatre? I may not have gone back to sleep but I lay awake grinning.

Rehearsals were due to begin for myself and my accompanist/narrator John Gould, a shy, quirky, gifted musician whom I'd known for almost twenty years. John was selected partly because he resembled, in type, Joyce's accompanist Bill Blezzard. It was tempting to consider asking Bill himself to share the stage, but the consensus of opinion was that people might find the combination a little ghostly, a little too reminiscent, when all along my instinct was to convey the spirit and feeling of Grenfell, without resorting to mimicry.

Just before rehearsals began, James Roose-Evans announced that another of his adaptations, *The Best of Friends*, had suddenly had its production brought forward, due to the unexpected acquisition of Sir John Gielgud. Consequently James would be directing *The Best of Friends* for half the day and *Re:Joyce* for the other. It was not ideal but it was a fait accompli and one was fated to comply with it.

We were due to try out the show at Farnham, a 400-seater theatre, less than an hour from London. Michael had tried to book Guildford, but they would only offer us one week as they felt we couldn't guarantee an audience for longer. Farnham, on the other hand, gave us four weeks and sold out two months before opening night, for the whole run. Sweet.

My scrappy diary reads:

'First week of rehearsals *Re:Joyce*. We begin at "Soho Laundry" (our rehearsal space) at 4.45 pm. Very strange. I'm laden. Champagne, fruit, cake, plates and knife – laid them on table. Went to ladies just before quarter to five to find they've been removed. This is obviously not the time for celebratory gestures.

'Michael Codron arrives looking young and fit – lovely purple scarf. I attempt champagne again but am given but cursory attention from director. I feel wrong-footed, as though my timing is all off. Lovely steady Welsh stage manager, John Ormerod, on "the book" ... we gingerly start from the top. The lovely beginning won't work. We try and try again and abandon it. The links all feel over-verbose. Early days, but I feel boring. We work until 9 o'clock.

'Tuesday: We start "early", 3.30 pm, for music with John and the gentle, whimsical choreographer Geraldine Stephenson, who reveals she's from Hull and was at the same school as me, Newland High School.

'James is full of rather forced energy. I feel strained. We need personal reflections – it's just a string of sketches held tenuously together by far too many dates and places. I'm worried. There seems to be a rush to get on and we're papering cracks. Still no opening sketch.

'Jack and I talk into the night. In the morning he suggests a perfect opening sentence: "Good evening. This is John Gould and I'm – not Joyce Grenfell. But that never stopped me wanting to be." Told Michael on phone. Loved it. I collected more useful bits of linking dialogue from Reggie, from Ma and Pa and from her brother Tommy and her dearest friend Virginia Graham.

'Rehearsals 3.30. James likes the new material. Relief.

'Wednesday: By now we are in two camps. James constantly concerned about the set, and me constantly concerned over the script.

'Thursday: More "set discussions"; I'm dragging a chair on and off for each sketch: "Re:Pickfords", I mentally mutter. It seems that "munchkins" are going to push and pull the dresser on and off stage throughout. I keep thinking of Joyce's lovely airy, chintzy flat but any mention gets short shrift.

'8 o'clock. "Couldn't we have a second chair?" ventured John Gould, inciting the first major row: "We'll have to re-think the whole thing" says James "we'll have to go back to the very beginning and re-block it!"

'I rise to the challenge in his voice "But surely – I can make the changes tomorrow morning . . ."

' "You are destroying the whole concept."

' "It's not a concept. It's a chair."

' "I went home at 9.30, grey and scared. Woke totally stiff-necked. Funny that! Rang Gloria for a hypnotherapy session. I'm weepy. "Trust yourself" she says and gave me the best gift in the universe, one hour of total relaxation.'

On the Sunday evening I was to attend the SWET awards, and Ben Frow had produced a black and white spotted dress for me to wear. It was wicked. A short, plain black, strapless dress with a tailcoat top of bold black and white spots sweeping down the back to the floor. Standing in the wings, thudding, before my entrance, the line came to me. I walked into the centre of the stage, and said: 'Enter, large, ethnic Dalmatian, stage right.' It got a roar of appreciation which I can still hear, and afterwards Stephen Sondheim came over to ask me if I'd had the dress made to go with the remark.

Later, at Grosvenor House, the dress really came into its own. I was to be seated next to Prince Edward at dinner. This was good news, as I had met him after a children's charity evening and had found him shy, attractive and funny.

During the reception I made my first major mistake. I tried to go to the ladies' room. Now, I want you to know that normally I can do this unaided. No, honestly I can. But in a brand new fitted dress into which I'd climbed only two hours earlier, and in which I'd never attempted the sitting position let alone ... well to cut a long and visually absurd story short, I was about as likely to have a pee in that dress as I was to share a bagel with Adnan Kashoggi.

After a long, lonely, sweat-filled stay in a small cubicle of the Grosvenor House ladies' room, I wriggled the dress vaguely back into position and called out 'Help' in a voice that only a bat could hear. As it happens there was a Koo in reply. Koo Stark was out there in the powder room and seemed to identify with my predicament; indeed she promised to procure me a long thin-necked vessel and return. I waited eagerly, but the poor girl must have been hijacked by paparazzi because she never came back. Later, much later, when I'd refused at least seventeen attempts to ply me with drink, I found myself sitting at dinner, attempting to charm the ruling monarch's fourth child. Suddenly, up came Miss Stark, bold as brass and dressed in gold foil. She slid down the wall behind us to say 'Hello Sir' to the Prince. From nowhere there was a manifestation, a man-infestation of photographers, five-rows deep angled like a bas-relief of gabbling gargoyles.

'Would you kindly go away,' said Prince Edward in a voice which would certainly have carried across Rutland. And go away they did, only turning back to snap Koo whispering into my ear.

The photo said it all. The following Sunday, we were there in the 'Gaga' section of the *Mail on Sunday*. Koo whispering, Lipman listening, the Prince looking studiously away. The caption read 'Koo tells Mo the Royal Secret'. Little did they know that what Koo was in fact telling Mo was much more to do with the Royal Wee. 'Sorry I couldn't get the vase,' she breathed, 'did you manage?'

'Not yet,' I told her, 'I'll be OK as long as there's no running water in the cabaret.'

I could describe the run I took down our drive later that night, key in hand; the nature of my flight upstairs, twelve skips at a time and the sight of my mother's-help, helping this particular mother to find her pretty Victorian loo with a tight black sheath dress covering her head – but I won't.

Monday dawned, as Mondays will, and it was back to the

Soho Laundry. We did our first run-through for producers Michael Codron and David Sutton and there was, at last, a frisson of magic in the air. It was too long and the opening was still shaky but the second half was shaping up well. A 4.30 am brainwave worked. I wove four of Joyce's characters into one cocktail party scene, ducking in and out of each character in an attempt to fill the stage with people.

It required enormous concentration and a lot of physical changes – each one accompanied by different music. It was dead right but it gave me a tough act to follow and only Joyce's famous 'George, don't do that' would fit the bill. In a way this was the hardest to get right. I could almost always hear her voice in my ear throughout most of the sketches, but the subtlety of her nursery school teacher would often escape me. 'Lavinia, what do we do when we come back from the littlest room? We pull our knickers *up* again.' It was tempting to continue 'No, Sydney, no need to help her – she can manage on her own.'

By now it had become clear that the way to approach the show would be to do the linking material as near to Joyce's as I could, but to do the sketches very much more as I would approach them as an actress. Which would be to make them more dynamic, occasionally broader but always keeping the inner life of each woman as real and as simple as Joyce would herself have wanted.

The dresses which Ben and I pored over by phone and at snatched meetings were going to be sensational. He would arrive with scraps of fabric dropping from his waistcoat, bits of lining from his corduroy trousers. He sifted through junk shops for cardigans, jackets and hats for the sketches by day and pinned me into paper versions of the dresses by night. Gradually, a style of late fifties cocktail gowns, tight waisted, full skirted in jewel coloured silks was emerging and the ballgown for the 'Countess of Cotely' which would be performed in a cut-out oval shape like a John Singer Sargent portrait, was a breathtaking oyster satin with hundreds of pearls and the palest of pink roses sewn into the skirt. It was a miracle – if not of fishes and loaves, then of cast-offs and left-overs.

Happily, *The Best of Friends* was a critical and public

success. It starred, apart from Sir John, the late, great, Ray McAnally and the divine Rosemary Harris. Every day at rehearsals, James would tell us the distinguished content of the previous night's audience. 'Paul Newman and Joanne Woodward were *in* last night. Most complimentary. Veery Glamorous!'

We felt very small fry by comparison. There was no glamour in my evenings, just scissors, sellotape and a pen. One evening he turned a small chair over on its side and said 'While I'm gone, Geraldine, dear, could you work on turning this chair into a forest?'

John Gould was equally hard at work and spent hours tracking down Joyce's more obscure lyrics and tunes which we could try out in place of any songs which were too difficult for my limited vocal range.

Joyce had a natural, pure, clear soprano voice, which, in my car, or my shower, and occasionally in the rehearsal room, I could emulate. On stage, however, corseted and hypertense, sounds would emerge which would not have been out of place in the nest of a fledgeling sedge-warbler. Ian Adam, my singing teacher, was ever the confidence booster. 'Imagine you're squeezing a penny between your cheeks, dear,' he would burr in his soft Scots voice, and I can assure you he wasn't referring to the cheeks of my face. I don't know why or how it worked but it certainly took my mind off my voice. I knew that the throat mike would take the strain, I intended to wear it in the front of my hair, as originated by the cast of *Les Miserables*, not as Joyce wore hers – at the throat – as TV presenters wear them, on the lapel – which in any case was something I did not have. This way the battery pack sits in a pouch tied around your waist and the connecting wire goes straight up your back, up your neck and sits snugly in your fringe. Funny to think that the elegant cocktail dress, carefully applied make-up and coiffed hair, conceals a roll-on, a boned bra, flesh-coloured wire toupée-taped to the neck and a pouchful of wires, plugs and batteries. It marginally removes the glamour, doesn't it? Needless to say the weather was in the 80s.

Our final rehearsal before Farnham, however, delivered the cruellest blow so far.

The last number in the show was 'Olde Tyme Dancing', better known from years of being a Family Favourite as 'Stately as a Galleon.' Throughout the rehearsals our choreographer, Geraldine Stephenson, had often pleaded for a larger space than the laundry in which to practise the swooping choreography she had devised. We also needed space to rehearse the tender, waltzing end to Act II, where Joyce dances off into infinity.

The day before Farnham, Michael had arranged for us to use the Dean Street Synagogue, which has a huge, parquet-floored hall in the basement. I arrived there at ten-thirty to find an ashen-faced Geraldine hunched in a chair by the door. She was waiting for an ambulance to take her to St Thomas' Hospital. She had two broken wrists.

She had arrived early, as she always does, to practise the dances herself before putting my two left feet through them. She took a couple of steps on the highly polished floor and fell head over everything, put out her hands to break the inevitable fall, and heard the sickening snaps as she hit the deck. John, the stage manager, went with her to the X-ray department. I stayed to find out what had happened, took a few steps into the hall, and almost followed her example. The floor was polished to the consistency of Telly Savalas' head.

Gerry was out of action. Her wrists were reset and to this day, two years later, she is still seeking compensation. She came back a week or so later to Farnham, plastered, in the literal sense, and indomitable. She is brave, gifted, warm and ... well what can I say? She's a Hull girl. There's no higher compliment.

The stage at Farnham was a shock and a half. It was vast. I felt like a pea on a drum. I took one look at the set and an involuntary shudder caught my throat. A plain black backcloth, a plain black piano and – *la pièce de résistance* – a huge mock wooden dresser straight out of the transformation scene in *Cinderella*. Ben, his assistant Lucy, John Gould and I sat in amazement as Phyl, the rosy, cosy raven-haired lady who was to be my dresser, mounted an enormous step-ladder and began pinning on to the backcloth, yard after yard after metre after metre of off-white gauze curtaining. My stomach sank. It looked a bit like a touring version of *Orpheus in the Underworld*. There was tension in the air. You could have sliced it with a spatula. A moment came in the technical run-through when it erupted. Ben described my 'wobbly': 'You were bending down to tie your shoe-laces, dressed in the ENSA uniform and I turned to Lucy and said, "Wait for it. Here it comes."'

The stage was cavernous and empty and the wooden floor felt cheerless and cold. 'I can't work on this set,' I said, striving for control. 'Something has to be done. I'm not being difficult. It's impossible.' I left before the tears came, and the technical rehearsal was never finished. At midnight Phyl was still there sewing weights into the gauze curtaining to stop it flapping. I wished she could have done the same for me.

The show was on the floor, and the leading lady was flawed. The answer came in a roll. 'Carpet. We'll get you a carpet. I'm sure the carpet will make all the difference,' said Patrick Sanford, the director of Farnham. And he was right, the moment my shoes were in a defined area I felt better. When the giant dresser disappeared for ever I felt better still. And when Reggie sent a picture, hand-painted by Joyce, I felt best of all. I was ready. We opened.

The opening night came and went. It was too long by half an hour (running at two hours twenty minutes), the lighting was gloomy and the show was top-heavy in places and fluffy in others, but overall the magic of Joyce had prevailed. The audience was happy, they accepted my portrayal and they were moved to tears as well as laughter.

I stayed overnight at the Bush Hotel. James had left after the show, Jack had gone back to London, which just left Ben and some warm champagne and a plate of dryish chicken sandwiches to mull and bitch over till 2 am. Happily, the next day's local reviews were excellent.

John Gould and I had a tremendous rapport and the run was a happy one with constant 'House Full' signs up. We were tipped to transfer, but nobody mentioned when or where, and by the third week we felt despondent. The show couldn't and shouldn't end there. Michael was still enthusiastic, he felt the show needed changes but didn't specify

what they were. James came back to see it once, in the last
week of the run, but at the suggestion that a fresh eye – some
advice from another director – might be useful, he tendered
his resignation.

It was sad but inevitable. I'll always acknowledge with
appreciation his great contribution to the compilation and
the setting up of *In Search of Joyce Grenfell*. He will never
acknowledge my contribution to *Re:Joyce*.

In the final week at Farnham, Michael sent a new young
director to see the show. He came round to my dressing-
room afterwards and said, 'Well it was maaarvellous, love –
super ... but, I mean, was that it?'

'Sorry?' I smiled (it was running at 2 hours 20 minutes).

'Well, I mean – wasn't there anything else that happened
in her life? No more dramas?'

It was like complaining that Emily Brontë had never travelled outside Yorkshire.

'No,' I said, slightly crisply. 'No dramas. No scandals. No
flagrant passions, life and death struggles, tug of war babies
or front page revelations Just one marriage to the man she
loved from the age of nineteen until their Golden Wedding.'
'Just one writer, observer, philosopher,' I added to myself,
'one entertainer, pen-pal to thousands of known and
unknown friends, philanthropist, seasoned traveller, one
aficionado of music, birds, flowers, children, good God and
Life. A totally fulfilled member of the human race.'

'Sorry dear,' I concluded, 'but Piaf she 'ain't.' Never saw
him again. Funny that.

The greatest accolade came when Reggie came to the show,
bringing Joyce's closest friend Virginia Graham. Like most
people who knew Joyce well, she had been filled with trepidation at the prospect of seeing someone trying on Joyce's
inimitable footwear. By the end of the evening both she and
Reggie had given us their seal of approval. I was worried
that the evening and particularly the ending would upset
him. He said 'No. It was just wonderful to see Joyce again.'

No review, no trophy, no accolade in the world will ever
make me feel that good again.

And so to London. Did we have a West End show or not?
Well, both. In truth they wanted half the show. It's nobody's

fault that this is sometimes the cruellest business on terra infirma and the consensus of opinion was that the blend of John Gould and myself did not entirely work. If the show was to transfer then it would have to be with a new accompanist/narrator. I'd like to skip over this decision because it wakes me up in a sweat fairly often.

However, the mood was insistent. I would never find a better musician, his contribution to *Re:Joyce* was unquantifiable. Where the powers-that-be were probably right was that the show needed more contrast. More Radio 2, if you like, and less Radio 4. Everyone was passing the buck – no one would actually express to John what their feelings were. It was not a nice time.

Various suggestions were made for new accompanists, and a couple of meetings were set up. Nobody seemed right. Then, one night, on the phone, my close friend Astrid – who'd seen the show at Farnham – said 'Why don't you ask Denis?'

I was surprised and sceptical. Denis King, her husband, had been on stage with his brothers, Mike and Tony, as The King Brothers from the age of twelve. Indeed, we'd often hooted at a poster of a diminutive Den, aged six, which bore the words: 'He's six, he sings, he syncopates.' Their act had been incredibly successful in the fifties and they had shared the bill with Judy Garland and Sammy Davis Jnr. I had no doubts about his musicianship, his talent or his ability to tell a funny story funnily. All I doubted was his willingness to do so. Like *The Fabulous Baker Boys*, the King Brothers had broken up as much because they'd 'had it up to here' as because of the ominous advent of 'the group'. Den was now a successful composer and he claimed to hate performing.

So it was with some trepidation that I put forward the idea of his leaping back into the West End, twenty years after he'd gratefully left it. He laughed a bit and stroked his beard a bit. I told Michael he was thinking it over. Michael gave him a tape of the Farnham show. He played it in the car on the way from the meeting and was bitten. 'You will be beardless, won't you?' Denis and I agreed that we *both* would.

Alan Strachan was suggested as the new director. We'd never met and I wasn't very familiar with his work. We talked on the phone. He'd read the script and already seemed to be familiar with Joyce's published material.

The immediate problem was rehearsal time, as Denis was due to leave for Massachusetts any moment to spend the summer with Astrid's parents. There would only be a couple of weeks left when he returned before the opening at the Fortune Theatre on 17 September. It was a historic coup as Joyce had opened *Joyce Grenfell Requests the Pleasure* there in 1954. Previews were from 8 September. Time was at a premium. The solution was obvious. I did the only sensible thing any panic-stricken woman would have done under similar circumstances: I packed. For four.

Denis and Astrid met us at Boston airport, waving large federal flags and they transported us to Astrid's parents' home in Becket, Massachusetts. Denis and I worked on the show each morning and on our final evening we performed it in ninety degree heat for a deeply moved and even more deeply biased audience of mutual families.

On our way home via New York, some 'dear' friends (as in generous), fixed us a stretch limo to take us to the airport. As the kids lounged back against luxuriant leather, sipping iced coke from the built-in fridge and switching channels on the in-motor TV, I heard Jack mumbling. I turned to him to see that his face was white.

'What's wrong, darling – are you car sick?' I asked.

'In a sense,' he intoned, 'Look at them. The kids. What must it be like? I'd never even been *in* a car until I was twenty ... I'd never had a holiday till I was twenty-five! What must it be like to be them?'

For a moment I thought I was with Alan Bennett. I could almost hear the trombones.

Re:Joyce: Chapter Too

Back home and into rehearsals in a church hall immediately behind the Fortune Theatre. Alan Strachan seemed genuinely pleased with the work we'd done so far. And, likewise, I was overwhelmed by his contribution. He was well-informed, interested, intelligent, open-to-suggestions, creative, fun-loving and hard-working. Can you describe bliss?

Throughout the *Re:Joyce* period, I should point out that the evening job continued. I'd been writing a monthly column for *Options* as long as I'd been writing at all. I'd written it under hairdryers in TV studios, in mid-flight to sundry family holidays, from hospital beds and, occasionally, two weeks late, leaning on the fax machine in the local Pip-Pip-Pip shop. My editor, Sally O'Sullivan, was the first person to ask me to write anything other than my name on an Access receipt, and I would have followed her to World's End.

She was about to leave *Options* and start a new weekly magazine called *Riva*. I was to be its diarist. The idea of a weekly stint as well as a monthly one for *Options*, a daily one home in Muswell Hill and a nightly one up the West End seemed about as feasible as Lech Walesa assuming the management of Stringfellows.

'There are several reasons why I can't work regularly for *Riva*,' I told Sally over a sea-bass starter and a strong Campari in L'Etoile. 'For one thing it sounds like an overlapping full-back on the Juventus transfer list, for another my kids are asking if an appointment is necessary these days or should they start the row without me? Their teachers are treating Jack like a single-parent family! And there's the one-woman show. Sal – I'm the bloody woman!'

Suffice to say, I refused point-blank to be employed, and shook my head firmly up to and including the moment I said 'Yes'. The magazine was launched ceremoniously and seven weeks later was scuppered in as blatant an act of back-stabbing as Fleet Street has seen since Sweeney Todd set up shop there.

My weekly diary, however, is a welcome reminder of the build-up to *Re:Joyce,* Mark Two ...

'Tuesday: After rehearsals I drive home to be fed by my own loving mother, down South for the duration. (Note: There really is *nothing* more comforting than a chicken from the kosher butcher. Must remember this when tempted into the local hen shop.) 9 pm Ben Frow arrives to try on costumes for *Re:Joyce.* A choice is required between four samples of lilac fabric. With added input of mother and Yvonne (mother's help – no, mine, not my mother's), there are four different opinions. Ben finally produces fifth violet scrap from waistcoat pocket, on which we all violetly (sic) agree. Midnight I sink gratefully into insomnia.

'2.30 am. Amy creeps in with a worry. I'm thrilled to see her! We repair to the kitchen and blithely set off the burglar alarm searching for the cat to cuddle. Amy's worried about the cat. Vet says she could be diabetic. Pronounced her breath foul, her stools appalling and her stomach distended. Just what you want in a pet really. She's having a change of diet and a blood test. Amy confesses that she's concerned Pushkin might have Aids. I bark with laughter, arousing rest of family, including Adam who comes down for cornflakes. It's now 3.30 am. He says cats *can* get it, in cat form. I stop laughing.

'7 am. Still awake. Get up and drive to work. Breath foul, stomach distended, indistinguishable from cat really. No one notices, or if they do, they notice behind my back.

'In my lunchbreak I give an interview re *Re:Joyce* to a gentleman of the Street of Shame. It was a fiasco. He was a good journalist and one I'd known professionally for many years. He'd always seemed pleasant enough, if a little 'over-tired and emotional' on occasion.

'Today he came armed with an angle, as sharp as Elizabeth David's kitchen knife. Basically the angle was "What's a nice

'Don't look now, Harry, but that woman behind is a spy from Mercury.' Zelma's début in a British Telecom ad. *(Courtesy of British Telecom)*

'All my life I've been a good mixer...' *(Courtesy of British Telecom)*

Bottom: the head of Geoffrey Chiswick (Harry); *top:* the head of Richard Phillips (*not* hairy); *middle:* the middle of Grubby Foster masquerading as Miriam Margolyes. *(Ollie Ball)*

Beattie's sister Rose and husband (Clive Swift) wait for director Richard Phillips to tell them what they're doing 6,000 miles away from home. *(Courtesy of British Telecom)*

Re *Re: Joyce:* 'I don't suppose you remember me . . . Yes, that's right,
Lumpy Latimer. It's *too* ghastly, isn't it? *(Zoë Dominic)*

The Countess of Cotely. Born with a silver spoon in her mouth, but certainly not one with any chicken soup on it. (*Zoë Dominic*)

'I say, Commander, you've made me an awfully happy WAAF. *Do* call me sausage . . .' (*Zoë Dominic*)

Facing the music. The King and I. (*Zoë Dominic*)

'It's Beattie, Ma'am – would that be *your* daughter or *my* doppelgänger?'

'If you think you're going to get to that receiver before I do, you're a dead bear.' Beattie and one-eyed fluffy person on the Telethon line.
(*Independent*)

Jewish girl like you doing in a show about Joyce Grenfell?"
I was shocked. Into reticence.

' "How much does your Jewishness affect your life?"

' "Er ... how do you mean? ... why?"

' "I mean do you keep up all the traditions?"

' "Well ... what did you ... er ..."

' "Do you go to the synagogue? Do you light Friday night
candles? Are your children being brought up in the ..."

' "Look, I don't really want to answer these sort of questions."

' "Why?"

' "It's nothing to do with the play. I don't want to discuss
my religion."

' "Well, *I* do."

' "Then I might as well go ..."

' "Look, what are you afraid of saying?"

' "I'm not afraid. Do you ask Judi Dench why a Quaker
should be playing Cleopatra? Or Sir Alec Guinness 'As a
well-known Catholic actor, what right did you have to play
Fagin?' I mean. ..." And at this point reason failed me. I
choked up and, big daft girl's blouse that I am, burst into
tears. This makes the reporter contrite and the weeper
furious with herself. He hugs me and we fumble through the
rest of a dull interview. The photographer, a nice human
being, is embarrassed and the photo sympathetic.

'Little did I know that this was just the tip of an Iceberg,
frozen on chat shows, enlarged on British Telecom commercials and now floating treacherously towards me.

'Saturday: A full life. One week to go before first Dress
Rehearsal of *Re:Joyce*. Rehearsals every day in church hall
from ten till five-thirty. Then home for dinner and some
heavy worrying for remainder of evening. Sorry to sound
like Joan Collins, but the older you get, the harder it gets.
Last night I dreamed I used a chair at the hairdresser's as a
toilet and Maggie Smith was in the next chair. I took this to
be a dream of fear of exposure due to approaching First
Night, but Amy looked it up in her *Dictionary of Dreams*
under "defecate" (sorry about that) and she said it meant a
huge windfall (that too). Must check the Box Office to see
how business is doing.

'Sunday: Day off. Papers in bed. Dying seals from distempered oceans. Italian ship trying to dump toxic waste on Torbay and killer algae growing in polluted seas. I'm not being facile, but we came from the sea, we've dumped on it for years and it looks like it's getting its own back. This time I'm voting for Greenpeace. Is there a choice?

'Monday: Bank Holiday except for those doing essential services. Like actors. Drove into West End in twenty minutes as opposed to forty. More Bank Hols – that's what this country needs. I don't know why the fairs don't put up their tents on a permanent basis. They've no sooner packed up their waltzers into 150 segments than there's another bloody Bank Holiday and they've got to wheel round and re-assemble 'em again. I blame Harold Wilson.

'Tuesday: First run-through of whole show. Teeth gritted expecting disaster. Not too bad. Except when I get home. I collapse over my lamb chops and have to be put to bed. To rest. Instead, I write this. Adam pops his head in to ask "Did you know they've removed the word 'gullible' from the English dictionary?" I'm incensed! Till I hear him laughing all the way to his tennis-court (or my hallway, depending on whose anaglypta he's erasing).

'Wogan wants me on Friday. Heart sinks. Nothing to wear. My hair needs colouring, and which bit should I perform to entice the public into *Re:Joyce*? I *daren't* sing – people who've already booked might cancel their Access – and I don't know which sketch would compress into the thirty-four seconds I'll undoubtedly be granted. Like Scarlett O'Hara – or, in my case, Maureen O'Hara – "I'll think about it tomorrow" Or Saturday, even.

'Friday: Anyone who saw my appearance on *Wogan* that week could be forgiven for thinking I was serenely confident, chic-ly gowned and nicely made-up. That's how my mother said I looked. Beneath these accoutrements, however, the old aorta was pounding like a duck's foot, for at 6.15 pm, with a 7 o'clock live show ahead of me, I had nothing to wear. True, I had the somewhat grisly T-shirt and track-suit bottoms which had gamely seen me through a two-hour run-through, but they were in a state and could probably have walked unaided to the BBC on their own.

'Ben had been making a new dress for the end of Act I which he promised to bring to Shepherd's Bush by 5.45 pm, in time for my appearance. At 6.15 a taxi was dispatched to pick up the old dress – any old dress – to cover my confusion and my body. At 6.45 the taxi returned and Sally, my dresser, threw me into the dress. At 7 o'clock, as I descended the steps to the studio, Ben burst, bag-laden, through the door, burbling about tubes from Bounds Green. I gave him my least friendly look, he returned it and I sauntered on set looking serenely confident, chic-ly gowned etc ...

'Sunday: Kids are suddenly back at school tomorrow and have to be labelled. Where did the yawning acres of six weeks go? Adam's football kit is in the five corners of the house, stiff enough to wash itself. Amy will *die* if she's not in Mr Hill's class for English. I hide in the bedroom, pretending to work on my lines.

'Monday: Migraine. Ignore it – might go away – matter over mind. Oh, sod it, I'll take the Paramax. John Dunne Show, Radio 2, I'm plugging opening night. Six foot seven inches of nicest, brightest man on radio, cheers me up no end. "Have you based Beattie on your Mum?", he asks me. "No-o-o", I lie, and tell him her latest telephone pearl, which goes: ME: "Any news?" MOTHER: "Well, Olive's much better. Your Auntie Anna's moved house again. Oh, and I've got to have all the front re-pointed, isn't it shocking? No, that's all, really. How are the kids? Oh, I knew I had something else to tell you, your brother got married."

'Tuesday/Wednesday: Lighting, fitting clothes and eating polystyrene sandwiches till 11.30 pm. Nothing lights, nothing fits, usual story. Alan Strachan is a rock to lean on. Everyone treats me with the temerity usually afforded to expectant fathers and potential Messiahs. I feel very white and small. The set, by Peter Rice, who had worked on *Joyce Grenfell Requests the Pleasure,* is quite magical. Dove-grey walls, rose-pink carpet, elegant furnishings. Understated, delicate and perfect. Alan Strachan seems to achieve what he wants by osmosis. Michael Codron and his associate, David Sutton, are quietly confident, if not "Over the moon, Brian". The thing we all share is an overwhelming love of the show.

'Thursday: First preview audience. A sell-out. Denis, who hasn't been on stage for decades, hasn't a nerve in his body. As curtain goes up, my hands are shaking so badly I'm in grave danger of flight. Audience response is shattering – like a massive, roaring animal. They laugh, and clap everything. Feel like Ken Dodd at the Hippodrome rather than Joyce Grenfell at the Fortune. Huge relief. Bit of a camp house but they adore it. Towards the end of "Stately As a Galleon" I get cramp in both feet and they curl up under me like the last Empress's fingernails and stay cramped through waltzing finale, curtain calls and notes from director, friends and husband.

'It's husband's birthday. Our after-show supper is aborted by the Camden Bistro's opening pleasantry "We closed at eleven." It's not five minutes past. Jack opened his presents in the car and we head for home and a tin of lentil soup. My feet remain cramped. I curl up, literally, to sleep.

'Friday. Marvellous acupuncture, then shop at Selfridges for anti-wrinkle cream *with* liposomes, which flawless friend, Julia McKenzie tells me I should be using, "by now". Then into theatre for last rehearsal of new opening. 4.15, I undress, to discover small needle still in stomach. Highly irregular but seems to have had no ill effects.

'Second night preview more staid but better show. Haven't seen children properly for days. They leave me funny, loving notes on pillow accompanied by fluffy marsupials. I rearrange their bedclothes in the night, hoping they'll wake up and recognize me.

'Saturday: Just before the five o'clock matinée a note arrives marked "Urgent". I ignore it until end of show then read: "Mazeltov on your new show. My husband Barry and I are in Box B, and it's his birthday tonight so could you please wish him a Happy Birthday at some point during the show? I know he would be thrilled." The usual definition of "chutzpah" is a small boy peeing through someone's letter box, then ringing the doorbell to see how far it went. Or it used to be until I got that letter. Idly I wonder if she'd have done the same thing had the play been Shakespearean: "Now is the winter of our discontent . . . but leaving aside discontent for the moment I want you all to put your hands together for good old birthday boy Barry in Box B. All together now, Happy Birthday to you ..."

'Sunday: Blessed day of rest. Rest? After adrenalin used in four previews of "Re:Joyce", it's more like convalescence. I float round the house – Elizabeth Barrett Lipman. Daughter returns from overnight stay with friend. White face, dark circles and short temper – she's had a *brilliant* time!

'Monday: Producer rings to check OK for one critic to come night before Opening Night. I tell him – since this critic hasn't liked anything he's seen for about twenty years – it doesn't matter if he comes on a wet Wednesday with no R in the month and a tram strike.

'Tuesday: Wrap Opening Night presents. Happy audience – save one, of course, and he'll be writing about it.

'Wednesday: Re-wrap presents. Anchor in pit of stomach. Ring for cab to theatre at 1.45 on account. Phone call at 1.45 – they'll be five minutes late. At 2.05 I stagger out with boxes of presents and walkabout phone and attempt to flag down cab, passing Porsche, man on mule, baby buggy or Geoff Capes, whilst abusing cab-firm in voice only dolphins can hear – "How can you do this to me *today!* You can take your account and stuff it up your ..." At this point, mini-cab and black cab arrive together. I assault one and get in the other, phone still under chin, in perfect psychological condition for Opening Night.

'Dressing room like a cross between Interflora, Kew, and Barbara Cartland's bedchamber. Cards separated from bouquets – necessitating diplomatic thank-you's. Flowers from *Riva* – six feet across. Obviously one week's entire production budget on one overdue columnist.

'Sally, has been superb throughout thirteen rapid costume changes and the seamless and unobtrusive handing of props and costumes. She's an actress, black-haired and exotic-eyed, who shares my love of flamenco and loves to be in the theatre and look after people. She's also a friend and I'd be lost without her. Lost and naked, probably. Derek Easton came in to put up my chignon and "wire up" my fringe. He's a gentle sweet old-fashioned thing who'd do almost anything for me and I'm devoted to him.

'The tiny dressing-room played host to scores of strangers

and friends that night. Vivian Ellis of *Mr Cinders* and *Bless the Bride* talked enchantingly about Joyce, whilst Reggie and family and Simon Williams and other chums queued down the stairway for a hug and a plastic cup of champagne.

'Denis had been in good voice and fine spirits that night. I have no idea how I was, although Jack and my relieved director assured me that the audience had just been coolly first-nightish and we, the cast, had stayed calm and thawed them into real pleasure and ultimate Rejoycing. The old beginning "Hello songs" had been reinstated and were well-received and the second half seemed to take wings. Still a mite too long perhaps, but the laughs were all whoppers and the poignancy of the end of her life seemed to touch the audience into the most intense silence I've ever heard. You could've heard a critic smile!

'Thursday: Face of doom on early-morning husband. Critics good, very good, but not good enough for biased spouse. I'm thrilled – but for one which says I play Joyce Grenfell Jewish! I raise my eyes to heaven and scream for mercy. "If you bleed me – are you not a prick?" Box Office buzzing, houses full, all swell that ends swell. We play deliriously till Saturday. Eyes down for a full house and a long run.

'Sunday: Not even the worst monkfish in the worst Italian restaurant in North London can mar this glorious Sunday. A walk in Ally Pally, tea with a mate. *Jagged Edge* on video and bed by eleven. "And home by twelve?", do I hear you ask?

'Monday: The beginning of the show is often a trying time because of latecomers. A very delicate, spotlit recollection of childhood, with almost music box accompaniment, it didn't blend too well with gangway doors opening, light flooding into the darkened auditorium. Nor with the grumbling of people who didn't want to stand up when they'd just sat down.

'The boxes were the killers. The Fortune is a tiny gem of a theatre where the boxes sit very close to the stage. One night there was a very late entrance into the box involving doors and noise and much hissing. Someone's mother was obviously too shy to make such a visible entrance: "Psst.

Mother. Come on. It's all right. Come in." Voices off: "I can't. Ssh. No. I'll wait." "Mother *will you come in!*" (Fairly long silence – obviously a lot of head shaking was going on.) Daughter then gets up, goes to door of box and propels mother into box, mother pulling back and protesting. Loud sotto voce: "Mother I've told you. It's all right – sit down."

'By now the audience were watching the show as one watches Becker and Lendl. Mother took one tiny look down at all the people looking up – made a long, low moaning noise and fled from the box never to return. Meanwhile, Denis and I provided the background music for this particular "pack in the box" and much hissing was heard from me in the interval into the ear of our Company Manager Jeremy Adams. A compromise was reached whereby all the late-comers were allowed in, spontaneously, in one great gush after a particularly jolly sketch called "Lumpy Latimer", and they could all settle themselves down, remove their shoes, finish their sandwiches and consult the fellow next to them over what they'd missed.

'On Saturday: Two shows, half-an-hour in between. It's agony. Tonight Joyce Carey and Graham Payne are in to see the show. We met them afterwards on stage. Both worked with Joyce. She is very frail and beautiful and both were wildly enthusiastic. As I'm scrubbing off six hours' entombed make-up at 2.00 am I suddenly realize I'm incredibly happy. Those of you who know me kindly frame that remark.

'Saturday: Float home on cloud after two shows in sheer delight. I walk back to my car with friends, talking all the while, and fumbling my keys in door, fail to open it. I push, prod, drop keys and re-attempt entry in vain until I realize that the only resemblance between the car into which I was breaking and entering and my own car is that they were both white.

'Sunday: Papers in bed. Roast chicken in barbeque sauce and a walk round the Gainsborough Exhibition in Kenwood House with daughter. Relatives in evening – they get lost finding our house and drive past it. They phone me from car. I take walkabout phone outside into road and guide them back round roundabout to house. We have the technology.

Later Jack phones me from kitchen asking for directions to living room.

'Wednesday: Lunch out and watched the new Murray Arbeid collection for Hartnell. Correction: mostly I watched the women watching it. Fabulous – and their feet alone were a poem (English women dress well except they won't spend on their feet, says Murray). His collection was warm and witty and, to my layman's eye, wonderful. Spectacular silver panne velvet roses on black chiffon. Chantilly lace and lemon taffeta. I know! It sounds more like a good meal, indeed one's lips were watering, as I suppose would one's eyes if one saw the *prices!*

'One dress was called "Dying Embers" after a lady at a fancy dress party who'd claimed she was dressed as dying embers – and if someone didn't poke her soon she was going home!

'I walked back along Piccadilly towards the theatre for the evening show. Suddenly it p-p-plummeted down on my cream jacket and sent brand new cream velvet hat frisbeeing into sopping road. I'd left umbrella in restaurant, suede high-heeled shoes were under threat, and a taxi was as rare as an Osprey.

'I attempt Tube but am driven out again by gang of pubescent boys who want me to write my name on various bits of their exposed torsos. Suddenly the world seems vastly uncivilized. I totter into arms of actor chum Gary Waldhorn, who half-walks-half-carries me to stage door of the Vaudeville Theatre.

'Any chance of anyone passing me the odd anabolic steroid, this week? No one need ever know. Perhaps I'm too old, too tired and too tetchy for this "daily" decathlon.

'Sunday Evening: Off to Windsor for a benefit for Thames Valley Hospice. Den and I are Re:Joycing before Prince Edward and others. We sit nicely from 5.30 to 8.30 then do our bit – "The Cocktail Party" – which goes down royally. Two of my favourite and most loved leading men are there – Simon Williams and Nigel Hawthorne – and an immodest amount of hugging and shrieking of "darling heart" ensues. Honestly, you'd think we were amateurs.'

We played to capacity for fifteen weeks, made the top ten

shows in London, extended for another six weeks, and I never felt a single twinge of boredom. 'Aren't you exhausted?' was the question everyone asked when they came backstage. 'Ye-es'. But not in a tired way. Physically tired but mentally impatient to get back on again. I've never known anything quite like it. All down to Joyce and her motto: 'I am not interested in the pursuit of happiness, but only in the discovery of joy'.

Re:Joyce: Chapter Free

The following year, by popular request, we returned from a triumphant tour (a fortnight in Brighton) to the West End. Alan Strachan, Geraldine, Denis, Michael and I were nothing short of ecstatic to be together again, at the slightly larger Vaudeville Theatre. This time we were to follow up the three months with a twelve-week season at the Long Wharf Theatre in New Haven, Connecticut. I began to realize that I would probably – hopefully even – end up in my dotage, still playing Joyce from a wheelchair in a Home for Distressed Thespians.

This time we didn't have an opening night, we just opened. No critics, not too many nerves, no reviews and full houses for three months. Wasn't that a dainty dish for me and Denis King? Den suffered terribly from stage fright and had some real moments of crisis which of course never showed from the front.

My crises tended to be more public. There was a section at the top of Act Two where Joyce is supposed to be auditioning for some American producers. I used the audience as the producers, stepping downstage and asking 'Hello – is anybody out there?' One night a man stood up in the stalls, swaying slightly, and said with a slight Scandinavian accent: 'Hellooo. Yes. I am here. Hellooo. I am glad to be here. Hellooo.'

I ignored him and carried on with the cocktail party. Later on, in the nursery school sketch, he got to his feet again. 'Yes. I am still here. Enchoying myself very much. Ey em gled to be here with you still. Yes. I wish you good evening. Very nice.'

It was up to Joyce to respond accordingly. I fixed him with my most formidable stare.

'Now look here,' I/she said, 'this is the second time you've disrupted this evening. If you've got anything else to say, KINDLY keep it to yourself. Now SIT DOWN.' He sat down. We never heard from him again.

My contract ran until two weeks before my son Adam's Barmitzvah and we planned to spend Christmas in Massachusetts then drive down to New Haven to begin re-rehearsing for our American opening at the Long Wharf Theatre.

It was a gamble. It was Terry Wogan who put the question that was on all our lips. 'How do you think the American audiences will react to a show about Joyce Grenfell?'

'Well,' I responded, 'they don't know me and, for the most part, they don't know Joyce. It's an enormous cheek, but it may just work. If not, I'll come home.'

The Long Wharf Theatre was not a prepossessing sight. It is sandwiched between a row of warehouses and meat-packing factories on a wharf in downtown New Haven. Inside it is functional rather than decorative. The theatre is what is known as a thrust stage with raised seating on three sides and there are two corridor-like dressing rooms. Annie Keefe, probably the finest stage manager in two continents and the Eastern Bloc, had decked out these rooms with ancient portraits of the Royal Family, Union Jacks, Victorian table-cloths and the odd stuffed owl in glass. It was very touching. Annie elevates stage managing to an art form.

From the first day, I knew we were working with class. I have never encountered a better-run theatre. The chairs in my dressing room may have been hard but they were soft enough for Meryl Streep, Al Pacino, Tom Berenger, Julie Harris, Rosemary Harris, Joanne Woodward and Kathleen Turner. I wriggled into them, hoping something would rub off. From day one, in the Long Wharf's spacious airy dressing room, there was fresh coffee on the hob, hot butternut and squash soup, fresh bread and Pecan Danish standing by. We were captivated. I mean, it's extraordinary how much these little things mean when you're 3,000 miles away from Marks and Spencer's food hall.

Once again we changed, cut and adapted, both for an American house, and for the shape of the theatre. The first row of the audience were literally a few feet from my feet. It was going to be nothing if not cosy. With good reason, Oscar Wilde said that England and America are divided by the same language. Annie and her assistant Jim acted as language arbitrators. The Swedish diplomat's wife had to visit American tourist places instead of English ones so I had her saying: 'We are going to ze Rockingfellow Centre and ve are seeing Saks on 5th Avenue.' Wondrously, in the Scandinavian accent, Saks came out as Sex and it brought the house down. Joyce, I felt almost sure, would have approved.

When Shirl's girlfriend said: 'You know my boyfriend Norm? The one that drives the lorry with the big ears?', it became necessary for him to drive a *truck* instead. Her hair was put up with *rhinestone* forget-me-nots instead of diamanté ones and when her friend Mr Lewis says: 'might I divest you of your plastic mac?' the whole process shut down for an hour or so whilst six fairly literate people racked their brains for a 'mac' substitute. Not as easy as you might think – Joyce had the same problem. The fact is that the clackety-clack sound of 'plastic mac' is half the reason that it's funny. (If you want to get a laugh, choose a word with a 'k' in it, say the comics – knickers, knockers and – well, other such onomatopæic rib ticklers.)

The overheard comments from the audience were very slightly different, of course. One night, I flounced on in one of Ben's exquisite 1950s flavoured ball gowns to hear a man 'up in back' mutter 'Jeez, she's got tits!' Nice.

It's a funny business, comedy. Denis, who watched my part of the show every night, would often give me odd notes on inflections he'd have preferred done another way or phrasing he thought I could improve on. Often he was right, often I gave him a bad time for sticking his nose in. One issue became long-running and momentous.

'By this time,' (Shirley's girlfriend again) 'me feet were killing me, because, you know, I'd got Lily Piggot's shoes on and well, she's not my size for long ...' 'The audience always begin laughing early on and they miss the last line,' said Den. 'Why don't you pause after Lily Piggot's shoes – then you'll get two laughs.'

'Wrong shaped laughs,' I said without thinking.

'What? How do you mean? Shaped?'

'Er,' I'm slightly embarrassed. 'I don't want two square laughs. I want one big, er – sausage-shaped one.'

He was staring now. Speechless and staring.

'Er. It's hard to explain. If I get both laughs they'll be nice, neat laughs and that'll be that. If I drive the line through, preventing them from laughing, then the final laugh will be both laughs joined together, and some more – from relief.' I drew the er – sausage shape in the air for him. 'I haven't got the timing right yet – but I get it right about one night in three and it's worth it.'

Thereafter, because he patently thought my laughter geometry chart was the first sign of incipient lunacy, I would play the lines, then turn upstage and make a huge gesture demonstrating the sausage shape of the laugh, which never failed to roll him up.

Similarly, one of his best laughs came when, explaining about Bill Blezzard's eccentric act at the piano, Denis lay under the piano and played – hands crossed – 'How Much Is That Doggy In The Window?' One night, at home in the beach house he and Astrid, their son Alexander and I were sharing, Den had a few Scotches sitting around the piano and revealed a talent for playing 'Smoke Gets In Your Eyes' with his nose.

In it went. Well, why not – he was sticking his nose in everywhere else. After the upside-down act I would say 'nursery style': 'Denis, *don't* do that', and to the audience – 'Don't encourage him. Next thing you know he'll be playing "Smoke Gets In Your Eyes" with his NOSE.' He did. The audience roared. 'Honestly,' I'd say, 'he's very talented really. He plays entirely by ear.' Whereupon – you've guessed it. I hate to think where this particular gag might end up . . . .

During previews, in sub-zero temperatures, the audiences were thin and seemed a little confused. I rang Reggie in England. 'Go slower,' he told me. 'Joyce always slowed it down a bit for Americans – takes them a while to tune in y'know.' I did. They did. The word of mouth grew, so did the audiences. By opening night, they were ecstatic and it has to be said, the brightest, the best, and the most appreciative audience we'd played to.

And oh, we loved the intimacy of having them so close, close enough that when I rode my bicycle for 'Committee' through the 'vomitarium' separating one wedge of audience from the next I was able to steady myself by grasping the leg of a gentleman who had stretched it over the side. Everything was going so well. It was ominous.

We were due to open on Thursday. It was the Friday before when it happened. I came back to the beautiful beach house from shopping. I'd just forced myself to drive, for the first time in my life, in a country where they haven't the sense to drive on the proper side of the road. I was very proud of this. I did it out of necessity. When you live with another couple and they have a lively two-year-old, it is kind of imperative to make yourself scarce on occasion. Sometimes I'd just walk along the beach, sometimes I'd buzz into the tiny town and browse around the patchwork, dried flowers, and charming chiming doorbell shop. Today, when I returned to the house, Denis said: 'Jack rang. It's bad news love. You'd better sit down.' There's no other way of preparing someone but God how I hate those words. At least five tragic scenarios had gone through my head by the time he told me that Dad had died.

Nothing can prepare you for the shock. Nothing. I'd been through so many rehearsals of this moment in London. So many times I'd prepared myself and others for his death. Always with resignation and with grief but buffered by the knowledge that he would no longer be in pain and confusion, by the fact that he'd had a long and lively life – that he would be at peace at last. I'd been calm and controlled. And he would be at death's door – unrecognizable. Then he'd confound specialists and loved ones around him by recovering and being Moishe again. And I'd always been there, by his side.

Now he'd been and gone and done it. And where was I? I was 3,000 miles away, amongst strangers in a funny little town in Connecticut preparing to open a show which no one knew or cared about. I couldn't breathe properly.

Denis continued, 'Your mother is perfectly OK. She's taking it very well. Jack and the kids are going to Hull tomorrow. The funeral is on Sunday ... Jack says you're not to think about trying to . . .' They were both hugging me and I was crying the kind of tears which seem to come from a part of you which you never knew you had.

I phoned Jack in Hull. Dad had been improving daily – he was eating well, in good spirits and coming up to his eightieth birthday. Except we were always unsure when exactly his birthday was – the 15th or the 18th of January – he'd never really known. (The funny thing is that Jack's father never knew when his birthday was either. Believe it or not – his was the 15th or the 18th of January too.) Always prone to bronchitis, he had a slight chestiness, but was well enough to have his birthday dinner out at a restaurant. He was thrilled with his birthday cake and Mum and Rita – their sister-in-law and her son, had sung 'Happy Birthday' to him. The following day his chest got considerably worse and this led to his hospitalization. It was probably pneumonia although the death certificate said 'Septicaemia' for some reason. Once again we'll never really know. I couldn't speak. I've never felt so lonely, so helpless. I wanted all my arms around them. Wanted to talk about him, to be part of the mourning, of the cleansing ceremony. I spoke to Ma, who seemed calm. Compared to me, who just wailed like a baby.

'She's numb at the moment,' said my brother, 'she's frying fish patties – the house is full of people.'

'Geoff I've got to be there.'

'Mo, for once in your life, don't do this. Let me do it. It's time.'

I felt suddenly very sick. I dived into the bathroom and bent over the loo. The lid fell onto the bridge of my nose. I forgot the sickness and leapt around clutching my nose. Laughing helplessly.

Then I sat down and wrote my family a letter.

'You don't want to be sitting by Long Island Sound with the sun shining down on the water and the sky streaked with apricot when you hear the news that your Dad has died. But then where *would* you want to be?

'I'm lucky, really, because I'm with Denis and Astrid and they're real friends – good friends and their comfort is so welcome – but I'm in a foreign country so I'm alone, and what I most want to do is talk about Dad to people – which is why I'm writing this. The shock and grief are not of his death really, but more because of his life. I didn't expect it to hit me quite so hard, but when I think about it it's because I'm so bloody sad that the last fourteen years were spent in dying not in living.

'What I want to grieve is the old Maurice before he was laid so humiliatingly low by whatever it was – a stroke, a deprivation of oxygen, an act of God – we'll never know. But even at his most confused, the essence of Maurice was still there, and we loved him for it even when it drove us spare.

'I'm dedicating tonight's show to him – wherever he is I hope it's a good one for him. I wish you all Long Life – I'm devastated not to be there and am scribbling this in haste in my dressing room. Life goes on. I'll miss him. I love you.'

Somehow, once it was on paper, it was real. Then I took a walk along the suddenly alien seashore and tried to work out what to do. Edgar and Arvin had said they would leave it entirely to me. Should I get a car to NY and get on a plane tonight, or do tonight's show and cancel the two tomorrow. If I took Concorde and made the funeral on Sunday I could be back by Tuesday, ready to open on Thursday. I was drained. I lay down and tried to think ... my agent Anne Hutton phoned with commiseration, sympathy, and the times of the planes home.

Denis and I drove in to the theatre. He was compassion itself. At the theatre everyone closed in around me like a family. It was remarkable. 'You must do whatever you want,' said Annie. 'Not what you think is right or what anyone else thinks is right. Just sort your face out now and get through tonight.' I did. I don't know how.

For one thing, although I was ready for the challenge of the theories of life and death in *Re:Joyce*, it hadn't occurred to me how many references there were to fathers, including a beautiful sequence in the sketch 'First Flight'. In this the woman inadvertently mentions God and says to her fellow passenger: 'Oh, I do hope you didn't mind my saying that. Well, no, but a lot of people don't like you mentioning God. They get all embarrassed and start counting their buttons. But me, I'm used to it. My father talked a lot about God ...

Dutch double. Sightseeing in Amsterdam.
(*Esperanza Maldonado*)

Northern beau on *Northern Belle*. Jack on his hols.

It's the real thing . . . Coco the koala, Adam and Madam downunder.

The many faces of *About Face. Above:* standing by Michael Jayston in *Stand by Your Man; below left:* showing Patience in *Mrs Worthington's Daughter; below right:* Michael Gambon with his greatest fan in *Looking for Señor Duende.*

I thought the world of my father. I could do with having him here right now.'

Somebody was with me. I was once removed.

'Do the show for your Dad,' said Jennifer, my devoted, sisterly pillar of a dresser. I don't know if I did it for Dad or Dad did it for me. On top of everything, the sound system went AWOL and produced a continuous drone throughout the whole of Act I. Which, strangely enough, concentrated my mind wonderfully. It was, by common consent, our finest and most poignant performance. Something to do with Joyce, too. It's not the sort of material in which to be indulgent.

I awoke at dawn certain that I should go home. I phoned Shirley, a friend I'd made who ran a travel agency, and asked her to book me on the mid-day Concorde. I phoned Annie and asked her to cancel both performances today, and those on Monday and Tuesday. I phoned Alan and he gave me his love and support. I booked a car to New York. Robyn, one of the other stage managers, had given me some Hebrew books. I said the prayers as best I could. Then I packed.

The phone rang: Shirley. There was no mid-day Concorde that day. The only chance was to catch the overnight plane. Even if it landed on time, I would have the four-hour journey to Hull and it was unlikely that I would make it to the funeral. I felt dazed and a little crazy.

'Don't cry,' said Den, 'It's just not meant to be.'

He was right. I re:phoned *Re:Joyce* and cancelled the cancellations, then drove into New Haven to the Yale Synagogue. It was in the basement of the Yale rabbi's house. Very informal and Israeli in style. Women and men sharing the service and much erudite discussion of the Torah text. Moses and the burning bush. The young rabbi spoke about the tasks which God had given his prophet and Moses' reaction to them. 'Lord,' said Moses, 'I do not wish to be your agent.' My muddled mind smiled vaguely at the idea of Moses turning down such a long-running client. The service wasn't exactly what I needed, but it helped, and the young rabbi was kind and concerned. 'You know, as the daughter,' he told me, 'you have every right to ask for the funeral to be postponed.' It was hard to explain that things don't work that way in Hull.

Two previews later – it was blizzarding and they were less than packed houses – we drove back to Madison and I crashed out. 'I have always depended on the kindness of strangers', says Blanche DuBois in *Streetcar*. My strangers had all become my family. Several of the backstage staff, including Annie and Jennifer, had bought a space in the Chassidic Hospital in Jerusalem in my Dad's name and presented me with the certificate. Their support was magnificent. I lay there, my eyes and head swimming through the last forty years until sleep finally bailed me out.

That's all, really. No time will ever be harder than that time, or maybe it will.

We opened to mostly sensational reviews, which showed huge appreciation of Joyce's work and managed to compare me to Lily Tomlin and even Bea Lillie, but which also truly recognized Denis' talent and contribution to the show. Julia McKenzie and Jerry Haste, her actor/director husband, motored from New York for the opening, bringing *Home* while *Away*.

Amy wrote a stunning and final tribute to her grandfather. Geoffrey, my brother, did him proud at the funeral and the young rabbi in Hull was moving and personal in his eulogy.

The show went from strength to strength and played to full houses throughout. The one offer to transfer to New York came from Don Taffner, an American TV producer, who'd actually seen the show at Farnham. He rang me just before a show and said the words: 'Well, I intend to bring the show to New York. How do you feel?'

Can a heart rise and sink at the same time? Oh, I wanted New York to see *Re:Joyce*; yes, I wanted it a lot. I also wanted, fairly desperately, to go home. Jack and I spoke every morning my time, evening his. He was coping. Amy, with mock GCSEs, was coping. Adam was Adam. He was capability itself. And Jill, the housekeeper I'd employed just before leaving England, was just about holding the fort.

We went into New York one weekend to see the theatre Don Taffner had suggested, the Criterion Center. It was bleak and unused, a sort of complex of two theatres, bars and restaurants.

'I'll show ya round with great pleasure,' said the affable manager, 'but I can't think of a worse theatre than this for your show.' Perhaps not diplomatic but honest. And he was right.

Three months passed of glorious shows and intermittent homesickness. I ferried and drove to Great Neck one weekend to see Maggie, an old friend from the Sixties, who'd been through three husbands and several transformations since we'd first been King's Road freaks together. Now she's married to a New York lawyer and she's become an Orthodox Jewish wife. Gone was the flimsily dressed groupie with the ever-rolling joint, and in her place was a homemaker – a 'ballabosty' – in an elegant wig and demurely covering blouse and skirt, baking Chollah bread, making theme cakes, studying the Torah and, most amazing of all, performing the near-sacred duty of washing the dead.

She'd wandered into it almost by mistake. Someone had come into a study meeting and said 'Would anyone volunteer to do the washing?' Maggie had stuck up her hand and said, 'Sure. I'll do it, why not, what's a bit of washing when all's said and done?' Once over the shock, she'd actually begun to like her job.

'M'reen,' she breathed, 'I get *sooo* much from it, I can't tell you. I can feel people's souls. It's incredible.'

It *was* incredible. It was incredible that I'd ended up in her kitchen, too, because she was the perfect person for me to cry on – and she, knowing me from way back when, was a phenomenal comfort to me, explaining so much I didn't know about the Jewish way of death, about the absence of hell, about the soul. I came out feeling straight again. Unfurrowed. Dad was so frightened to go. Now I felt he'd be OK. He'd adjust. As we'd adjust to life without him.

The last verse of Joyce's song, 'Time', was almost the end of the show:

And now I'm an old, old woman,
So I want the last word.
There is no such thing as Time.
Only this very minute.
And I'm in it. Thank the Lord.

We all had a good cry and presents and kisses flew around

like so many midges. We were all well and truly bitten. I packed up three months' baggage and bought yet another case to bring home the excesses of my shopaholism, wrote down the addresses of many new friends and drove to New York to meet a really old one. Friend, I mean. Jack was there for voluntary Chinese Torture – or re-writing another Barbra Streisand movie, depending on which way you view it. Den and Astrid flew off to the Bahamas for a week. One week later I was home. Home. The best four-letter word in the world. Or maybe the second best.

About Face

About Face came about because Central TV asked me to do a comedy series. We had one of those dinners – eye to I in Joe Allen's. Head of Light Entertainment, John Schofield, my agent and me. I confessed my feelings about sit-com – that they are all sit and no com, and that I couldn't venture on to one more open plan kitchen sitting-room with Habitat furniture and a constantly ringing phone and doorbell, without recourse to nausea.

Pause here. Then, falteringly, an improvized idea about playing six different women, written by six different writers, all on film, and going for character rather than wisecracks. By the crème brulée we had the go ahead.

Everything went as smoothly as a TV series should go. Producer, Tony Wolfe, could scarcely have been more friendly and supportive. John Henderson ('Hendo'), the tallest as well as the most innovative of directors, came aboard and it was almost ominous the way we agreed on just about everything. We met with each of the six writers over the coming months, either chez Rosenthal or in Tutton's Café in Covent Garden before the eight o'clock curtain-up for my *Re:Joyce* show.

We had plenty of ideas for characters. My otherwise empty Filofax was full of them. Richard Harris, who wrote the much loved *Outside Edge*, was my first choice as writer for the flamenco character. I had wandered into the flamenco world via a couple of potter friends of mine, Susan Bennett and Earl Hyde, who coerced us into a flamenco 'Peña' one evening in Hackney. Jack was quite surprised when he heard where we were going. He's not averse to an evening out but not necessarily one where he might have to stamp a lot and shout 'Ole'.

It was revelationary. Not least because our host, Ron Hitchin, is a revelation in himself – and by that I mean a one-off case. Ex-boxer, ex-jiving champion, potter and flamenco fanatic, he lives in a terraced house which he's *hand-tiled* from cellar to chimney, including a four poster bed. This night the house was alive with flamenco aficionados, the air pregnant with simmering paellas, the small through-room vibrant with clicking castanets and Spanish guitars.

I was hooked. Fascinated. People just got up and danced sultry Sevillianos, skirting round one another, swishing their improvised flamenco skirts, their arms swooping and dipping, their fingers swirling and curling like tentacles. Every so often, Ron would materialize, suctioned irresistibly from the kitchen stove to put his athletic stamp on the small wooden floor. Bewitching. And I was twitching to join in.

What made the gathering extraordinary was its marked absence of Spaniards. Oh, there was the full quota of Spanish hairdos and Spanish shawls and Spanish song splitting the air. The odd thing was that it all came from Swedes and South Africans and ladies in hooped earrings from Ealing South. The only genuine Iberian beauty, with scraped-back jet locks and a magnificent mantilla, crept up to me after a particularly enervating Bullerias and gasped, 'I fawt it was you – I lave those Bri'ish Telecom ads – they're the best larf on telly' in Billingsgate cockney.

This had to be my first *About Face*. John and I met with Richard Harris. He liked the idea but felt it would suit him better if he transferred it to an obsession with Country and Western (or Bang and Twang as it's known), as he had some neighbours who left the house twice-weekly in stetsons and chaps.

'Just meet Ron and the girls,' I pleaded. 'It'll inspire you, honest!'

What I meant was, it'll seduce you, and by gum it did. One evening watching some sultry Southgate señoritas performing Allegrias and a few jars with Ron, and Richard was hooked in with us. Wonderful what lust can do for your writing hand.

Once the choreographer had shown me a few basics and

I'd got my mitts on a pair of castanets, I was lined and sinkered. I couldn't pass a piece of patio or lino or – be still my heart – a parquet floor without both feet lurching into thunderous action, both elbows flying up to their owner's earholes and both nostrils flaring as if they'd been lacquered. The week of the play, the heatwave began in earnest and half a stone dripped out of my leotard. My co-star was Michael Gambon – quite simply the funniest man in the land.

The second character was the politician's wife. I had spent a posh lunch at the *Sunday Telegraph* offices and studied the social behaviour of a certain ex-politician's wife throughout. What struck me much more than her fragrance was her cool toughness. A woman who knew where she was going, how and why. Why does such a woman stand by her man? Geoffrey Perkins came in and agreed to do some delving into the subject. Some weeks later he read us the first draft. Playing all the parts. It was funny and promising, and had a great part for Michael Jayston as the MFI politician – you know, one loose screw and the whole cabinet falls apart.

The third script, *Gracie*, came from a combination of an article about a cloakroom attendant celebrating twenty-five years' ablutions at Annabel's, and my love of the rather tortuous Cockney Cypriot accent of my neighbours in Muswell Hill. One day, an anonymous script called *Gracie* arrived relating one beautifully to the other. I phoned John Henderson.

'This is a very funny script. There's no name on it, I *love* it. Who wrote it?'

'Er – we did,' said Hendo, sheepishly. He and his partner Chips had written it on the quiet. Hendo manages to do roughly six jobs at once, has a vast brief-case jammed with complex electronic gadgets and does most of his administration on the car phone on his way to and from various offices and his beautiful country home and exceptionally understanding wife and kids. For their anniversary he carved, for his wife Dee, a wooden model of Stonehenge which, when a light was shone on the stones, reflected the words, 'I Love You' in shadow on the base. Is there a woman out there reading this, who doesn't feel a sudden desire to kneecap her husband?

Gracie was the first play we filmed. It had me leaping to
the Wine Shop on the Broadway in pursuit of Lizzy's mother
and her accent. Lizzy, who runs the shop, had kindly offered
me her mum as a guideline for the voice. So it was that I
drove, tape-recorder in hand, to Totteridge one Saturday
afternoon, to meet and record the true tones of Cyprus.
Lizzy's mum was enchanting. But very shy. And the tape is
a collector's item. Four minutes of me burbling on about my
trip to Paphos last year, followed by four seconds of Lizzy's
mum saying in a whisper, 'Yess . . . very nice.' I start gamely
up again about the sadness of Famagusta for another five
minutes, followed by 'Yess . . . very ssad.' Fortunately,
Lizzy's friend had a sale of rather smart suits that morning
so I was able to drop a cool £126 on the way out, rendering
my journey not entirely unnecessary.

Gracie had all the hallmarks of success. It was not till
editing that we realized there had been one major error,
which none of us had seen. An American movie-star, played
by Diana Weston, locks herself in Gracie's loo, refuses to
come out and ruins Gracie's special night. The character was
heard but never seen. Just a voice behind a door. On stage,
this would have been an innovation, but for an audience of
sophisticated viewers who've seen a camera introduced into
such spaces as the human blood stream and the nest of a new
born nightingale, it wouldn't wash. They needed to see the
star's point of view.

There were also a couple of fairly innocuous swear words;
one, from two floozies at the mirror, was 'I'll pull your tits
off'. Because of these the controller of programmes at Central
took a decision to pull the show off the air in mid-series and
reschedule it. I was incensed and I'm afraid I threatened to
pull HIS tits off. (Not for nothing did Jack threaten to leave
England if I signed up for a projected Assertiveness Course.)
Instead, the play was redubbed at the eleventh hour, loud
muffled clunks covered the offensive words, and the show
suffered because of it.

The fourth character was an American stage manager in
England. It was written by my friend Astrid Ronning, of
whom you'll have read much in these pages. *Mrs Worthington's Daughter* was a sharp, witty and satirical picture

of life in a provincial rep building up to a First Night. It was Astrid's first play, and Jack had acted as shoulder and listening post and dispenser of advice and coffee throughout its conception and birth. In some ways it was the hardest of the six characters, as Patience, the stage manager, was based on someone I know, was my own age and was 'acted upon' rather than 'acting'. Also Jack and Astrid were so close to it, and to me, I kept avoiding committing myself to it for fear of letting them down.

As it happened, the cast of the rep company was peppered with old friends from my past and it turned out to be one of my favourites of the series, not least because Sarah Grundy, make-up artiste par excellence, and her partner, Jane Kavanagh, worked some kind of maquillage magic on my face. She gave me the sort of glow which women are alleged to acquire during pregnancy. (Personally I just acquired stretch marks and a lump. Sixteen years later and lumpless, I had a bronze glow, freckles, frizzy red hair and, quite suddenly, a tendency to stop at every passing mirror, window and spoon and admire myself.)

Sarah and Jane's contribution was astonishing. To make someone with, let us say, as *defined* features as I possess, look so utterly different six times over six consecutive weeks, deserved two thumping great BAFTA awards. They were also the *best* fun, their make-up truck being a cross between a ladies' club and an alternative comedy store. The air in there was as blue as my feet in February, and the daily discussion on the four-minute warning competition (as in the person with whom you'd 'do it' if there were only four minutes left to live) left us paralysed with laughter, especially since the victim would invariably pop into the caravan that minute for a haircut. Don't you love the idea that if you only had four minutes to live you'd spend them '*doing it*' anyway? Personally I'd share fish and chips with my kids, but I wasn't going to admit it in front of 'the girls'!

I must confess that girls together are more sex obsessed and scatalogical, in my experience, than their male counterparts. Often in the dressing-room during *Re:Joyce* in New Haven, Denis would roll up his eyes in disgust and say 'You lot are appalling. I'm not staying in here to hear THIS!' (He did.)

He claimed that no men would ever discuss their carnal arrangements in the way that Annie, Jennifer and I did, most pre-show evenings, and I guess for the most part he's right. In the same way, with the obvious exception of your pub man, none of whom I know, the men in my immediate circle do not seem to need 'their little friends' the way my girlfriends and I do.

I could scarcely get through the day without a long rambling chat with a woman friend for no particular reason. Amy literally bursts through the door and immediately phones the friend she left at school twenty minutes earlier. Jack, on the other handset, would never ring *anyone* unless he had a reason to ring, and it would never occur to him to ring a friend and say, 'Maureen's in the show tonight – feel like having a meal out?'

Similarly, Adam's calls to his friend are truly household-management friendly. BT would hate them.

'Hi. Can I speak to Will, please? 'S'Adam. Hi Will, wanta game? OK. See you there. Bye.'

Gossiping Women and Business Men. For God's sake prove me wrong – I'm setting a cliché in cement!

Play Number Five was the most mischievous of my six-pack. To play Margaret Thatcher I would cross the Gobi desert on a Red Admiral. To play MT opposite John Wells' Denis was quite over-exciting. John Wells met us to discuss the politician's wife episode, but we got side-tracked into Maggie and Denis impersonations. The die was cast. And so were we. Hendo hired a small piece of land around a reservoir in Frensham for the episode which evolved farcically around the kidnapping of our most regal couple. It was hot work, bewigged, padded and hire-suited. At one point Maggie was required to berate Tony Slattery's self-made crackpot dictator straight in to the lake. Here's where the mischief came in.

'John?' I ventured. 'Might it be fun for Maggie to follow him into the lake – only, she *walks* on it?'

Here's where the joy of Hendo came in. 'Chippies – we need underwater scaffolding – let's go.'

It wasn't everyone's cup of tea, particularly Central's – too farcical for the intelligentsia and too restrained for the lefties, but on the whole it was, like most satire, sharp and funny in patches and as daft as a brush in others. I adored doing it.

The pièce de résistance was *The Bag Lady*, written by Jack with a mixture of pathos and humour and the kind of compassion which makes him the *truly* socialist writer he is.

The week of the Bag Lady the temperatures were in the eighties and mine was in the hundreds. I was wearing padding, nine layers of clothes, a dressing-gown, a plastic mac, two pairs of woollen socks, men's shoes, false teeth, contact lenses, a matted wig, a rain-hood and two warts made from freshly painted Rice Krispies. I looked super. Amy came with me to the filming one day and was told by an onlooker in the street, 'Ooh, don't you look like your mummy!' I told her that should the passerby pass by again she had my full permission to head-butt her. (Other passersby were more circumspect. One said to one of our camera crew as I lay in the gutter 'Who *is* that?' 'It's Maureen Lipman.' 'It isn't.' 'It is.' 'It isn't.' 'It is.' 'She looks terrible, what's happened to her?' 'Well, it's British Telecom ... Every time she phones Australia and gets it wrong, they make her pay for it.' Pause. Then, passerby: 'Well, I think that's absolutely disgusting. And I'm going to write to British Telecom and tell them!' Personally, I hope she does.

The great thing about the disguise was that I became totally invisible. The camera was concealed so many people were free to look at me (or away from me) in distaste. The more I shouted 'Bugger off wi' yer bandy legs!' the more total was the blank I received. Spotting a poster for the return of *Re:Joyce* outside the Vaudeville Theatre, I lurched into the box-office and shouted 'I want forty seats for the first night of *Re: Joyce*! Can I 'ave 'em?' The box-office manager stared for a hostile second and then shut the box-office in my face. Bliss. I felt liberated, and when in Mayfair I spotted a well-known and highly unpopular publisher, I was able not only to yell abuse at his terror-stricken back but also to chase him half-way down Curzon Street.

Outside the Brook Street Bureau in the Strand, our continuity girl spotted a sign: 'Telephonist wanted. Refined, well-spoken, used to dealing with people,' and dared me to apply. With my evil-smelling plastic bags I faced a roomful of interviewers and -ees, and bellowed, 'I've come for the job. For the telephn . . . telephon . . . telephi . . . the woman wot answers the phone!' Silence. A wall of disdain. I was invisible, untouchable (*well*-caste, if you like).

On the Saturday night, Amy and I saw a real bag lady, plastic mac'd and felt-hatted outside the Strand Theatre, and gave her some money. She took it with the same disdain that was meted out to her and I realized that, from her point of view, I didn't exist either.

The film was eleven minutes over when we finished but we thought we had a masterpiece. Some of us still do. When it went on the air Jack received more enthusiastic letters of praise than for any play he'd ever done, and people rang in droves and in tears.

'All in all,' I wrote at the time of filming *About Face*, 'a diverse few weeks. Even by my normal standards. As my son, whose repertoire of jokes is somewhat akin to being stuck in a ski-lift with Frank Carson, is wont to say, "Roses are red, Violets are blue, I'm a schizophrenic, and so am I."' On the sixth day of the seventh working week, at 10.30 pm in my stage manager's role, I had a funny turn on the stage of the Richmond Theatre. I expect they've had a few funny turns up there before, but it was *my* first. Just fatigue really, but enough to send me back to my caravan for a brief legs-up head-down. Adam was with me. We had a quiet chat about his forthcoming Barmitzvah, and in the darkened room he sang the bit he'd learned so far. And suddenly I remembered who I was. I felt all right then. And so did I.

So. What did we have? We had confusion. We had a comedy series which wasn't side-splittingly funny, which gave you no single character to cling to, and which changed style every week. Central were very excited. They rang me and told me how excited they were. Their press office rang me and told me how excited they were. Tony Wolfe bought me a magnificent brooch on their behalf and I bought plates printed with a still from *Señor Duende* for everyone involved.

Bag Lady came out last and received three of the nastiest reviews either of us have ever had, including one from Sheridan Morley saying my disguise was as convincing as Esther Rantzen's in *That's Life*. We were a bit stunned. In seven days out in the streets, dressed as a tramp, no one had recognized me. Was it because we were working together for one of the few times in our careers? Was it because the reviewers had been sent an undubbed copy to review? Or was it just our turn? 'C'est la vitriole.'

By the time you read this I'll be working on Series Two. I don't know why. Most of the writers will be different. The brief – the compromise – we'd arrived at was that the characters were up to me, but they must be funny on balance rather than sad.

So far I'm taking golf lessons and having my Scots accent honed, learning to sing 'Zadok the Priest' and watching tourist guides and dog-handlers with studied casualness. The rest is mystery. Watch this face.

4

Travel Log

A Fraughtnight Away

A couple of months back, I had a little holiday. Well, we all had one, really. Jack, the kids and me. All together in the same place (Cyprus) at the same time. I'm expecting Mr McWhirter and his bijou book of records on the line at any moment.

It was booked for us, at incredibly short notice, by Mrs Z Lipman, self-styled travel agent: 'Ooh, I *love* anything to do with brochures! I could be on this telephone all day long if I had a project!' During the time it took me to be an old lady who spends all day on a BT telephone, she had secured us two connecting rooms in a 4-star hotel in Paphos, with integral flights and a money-back guarantee of sunshine for fourteen days from the Lord. The only fly in the Ambre Solaire was that she seemed to have booked it with two different travel agents – both operated by men called Michael. This was her way of confirming that we'd got a holiday.

It was also *my* way of confirming the onset of dementia. Every time the phone rang it was a different Michael talking tickets and flight times and I had no idea which one she'd finally plumped for. Since the producer of *Re:Joyce* was also called Michael, it became even more confusing. There was a sticky moment when I asked him for an aisle seat for Jack on account of his leg and he said 'Isn't that a bit premature – we haven't got a theatre yet?'

The week before D-Day, when the suitcases were busy exploding all over the bedroom, Mother, glancing fondly through eighteen brochures, found a tiny sentence which sent us reeling to unpack. 'The Management regrets any inconvenience to clients during the necessary building works.' 'No!' said my mild-mannered husband, biting through a finger he'd formerly been chewing, 'No, no, no, no, no, NO! Not again! *Never!* WE'LL CANCEL! DO IT NOW!'

Some of the crowd of extras who inhabit my kitchen stopped in mid-tea and mid-conversation and raised their collective eyebrow at this uncharacteristic outburst. I explained about last year's holiday in Portugal. The one in Villamoura, surrounded on three sides by building sites, muck, dust and rubble and a 150-foot crane over the swimming pool. By the time we returned to Gatwick, my nerves were so bad that I queued up at the aliens' counter, because that's how I felt.

All three Michaels were summoned to phone Paphos, as was my cousin, Dave (who also has a brother called Michael but he doesn't work for Horizon). All four reported no building work, only landscape gardening. We shakily re-packed the unpacking.

The night before take-off, we heard that a friend of Amy's was feeling low because of a nasty hospital visit the next day. By mutual consent, we abandoned the cases – now in their third re-incarnation – and dressed up in extremely silly clothes to cheer her up. Jack appeared in long black wig, long red long-johns with a plastic parrot popping out of his vest. Amy transmogrified into a fully-made-up rabbit. Adam became a disturbingly convincing 1920s flapper, in turquoise shift and blonde bob. And I looked a perfect pillock in Adam's entire school uniform, freckles and cap. We piled into the Honda, wondering why we were doing this, and unpiled at the child's doorstep. Much excitement ensued and the family hamster was summoned to join in the fun. It took one look at Amy and leapt insanely through the air to land – claws first, teeth second – on her nose.

'Sorry to trouble you, Doctor. Mrs Rosenthal here. We're going on holiday today and Amy's had her nose mauled by a rodent. A tetanus injection? Oh, she will be pleased . . .'

Punctured but undaunted, we flew off to the Island of Aphrodite. Very nice, too. The sun shone. We played tennis, we swam, and all four of us did the *Independent* crossword and played 'Yes, I am not Botticelli' till the *real* cross words began. It was like a holiday.

Over pre-dinner dolmades, the kids took to ordering cocktails: 'I'll have a Singapore Sling, please and a Tequila Sunrise for my brother.' We let them have their fling and, sure enough, after a few stagily legless evenings in The Six Bells, they reverted to bottled water with a cherry in it.

One memorable evening I met a charming man from the Water Board in a bar, where I'd gone in search of a cake. He kindly recommended not only the cake shop but a visit to a local restaurant for some *real* Cypriot food. I jumped at the chance. He jumped, too. Backwards – when I produced a husband and two kids. Gamely, he agreed to take us all, then quietly suggested that he and I could skive off afterwards for a few dances. 'There's life in the old girl yet,' I thought, then settled for the cake instead.

Towards the end of Week One, a Kuwaiti plane was hijacked and allowed to land in Cyprus. The hotel was buzzing with it. A total stranger, English, stopped me in the main street: 'I might have known with trouble at the airport that *you'd* be here!' Back in England our friends were having roughly the same reaction: 'As soon as that plane started circling,' said Julia on the phone, 'I knew it was going to land in your hotel.'

Security was stepped up. We drove to Kourian to see the amphitheatre and saw instead what appeared to be a military coup. Soldiers lay in the grass pointing rifles. Lines of cars were stopped and searched. Quietly, we began to panic. Perhaps we'd seen something we shouldn't? But what? Finally, a uniformed officer asked us abruptly for our tickets. 'What tickets?' we burbled. 'For the military brass band!' he barked, 'people have come for miles to see this.' Apparently, we could still have scraped a ticket, but dinner with the man from the Water Board beckoned, and we had to 9-point turn our way out against the thousands of military personnel fighting their way in.

We did finally see a much smaller amphitheatre in Paphos itself. I watched, fascinated, as an elderly lady clambered up to the top row and thundered to her companion not thirty yards away: 'CAN? YOU? HEAR? ME?' 'Yes, dear,' said her friend, chattily. 'What veg shall we have tonight?'

Back at the hotel, people kept on complimenting us on our

kids. It was bizarre. '*So* interesting? *So* bright! *Such* good manners!' Our jaws fell open in shock. Then one night in a restaurant, someone prefaced a discussion on Russia by saying 'There's no such thing as Refuseniks. It's all propaganda.' Before Jack or I could say 'Glasnost' the kids were in: 'Have you any idea of the number of people in labour camps and mental institutions? Do you know the number of people denied the basic freedoms of life? Do you know that Jewish boys aren't allowed to have Barmitzvahs – and can only have them by proxy at an English boy's ceremony?' Oh, boy. Oh, girl. Where did we go right?

Later that night, we discovered that the little geniuses had been putting their dirty underwear in the waste-paper basket every night. Every morning the maid threw them out and there was now one pair of knickers between them for seven days. Imbeciles! Where did we go wrong?

The second week sped by as second weeks do. Patchy weather, much discussed in the hotel bar. Lots of sightseeing, oh – and I got bitten on the arm by a pelican in a café. It was more the shock than the bite itself, which was rather like being attacked by a pair of rubber gloves. All in all, Cyprus was green, floral, friendly, rather like England would have been had we stayed in it, but warmer.

So, 'Dear Mrs Lipman, Thank you for booking our holiday, it was lovely. We will definitely travel with your company again. Thanks also for house-sitting for us. The house hasn't been this clean since the builders left. In 1910.'

To Hull and Back

'Darling, it's the "freebie" to end them all and we immediately thought of you.' It was Jan from *Options* and her voice was brimming with Western promise.

'I'll take it!' I procrastinated. 'How long's the flight?' Well, you never know, do you, with places like Mauritius and the Azores? One doesn't want to be caught without enough boiled sweets for the journey.

Her reply was what I can only describe as a four-letter word. I repeated it aloud and the first eighteen years of my life passed painfully and pungently through my mind. 'Hull?' I murmured, 'You want me to go on a fact-finding tour of Hull?' She did, too. For the Great English Cities Marketing Group. On offer, one weekend touring and sightseeing the newly vamped old city in the company of a group of journalists. Had I a doubt in my diary, it was swung by the coincidentally arranged theatre production in memory of my late uncle, the ex-Lord Mayor of Hull. All this and Mother's cooking beckoned provocatively. Shin and bone soup! Perchance a drop of plaice on the bone? A stuffed monkey to follow? (Don't write in. It's a cake, not a diseased Primate). 'I'll still take it,' I told her, and somewhere in the silence that followed I thought I heard the sound of an assistant editor pivoting sideways out of an office chair.

Cleverly no mention had been made of our little friends, 'the late British Rail', otherwise I might have saved her the fall. I travelled Hullwards from a book-signing in Manchester. The guard told me to take the front two carriages only for Hull. When the train arrived it was a two-carriage only train and both resembled Berwick Street fruit market after a heavy Saturday's trading.

The cab-driver in Hull was as mystified as was I by the new

one-way system, but I must tell you that, having travelled one way around most major British cities this year, they've all been designed by the same man. He is also responsible for the clues in *Blankety-Blank,* the rules of *3–2–1* and the Barbican Centre. I glimpsed my father's old tailor's shop as we raced towards and almost into Princess Dock, and later learned that it is about to become the dockside entrance to a new shopping centre on stilts. Dad liked a tall storey.

The following afternoon I saw *A Christmas Carol* at the New Theatre, as performed by 150 citizens of Raleigh, North Carolina – twin city, naturally enough, to Hull. It was a three-hour pantomime, written, directed, produced, musicalized by and starring a certain Ira David Wood III. Good manners and the fact that the show that day was in honour of my uncle prevent me telling you more about it. Suffice it to say that Ira made Barbra Streisand in *Yentl* look retiring. I was also required to walk across the stage at one point and it would be useless to convey my embarrassment in black and white. 'He'll ad-lib with you – he's just brilliant,' hissed the stage-manager before pushing me on to a stage I last trod at the age of seven during David Whitfield's *Aladdin*. Four minutes or hours later relatively-speaking, he'd said not one word and I'd died and joined Dickens in heaven.

That night I had two dinners. One at home (fried fish) and one with the newly arrived journalists (grilled fish). Fresh as paint after a mere two-hour train delay, they fell into their dinners at the Georgian Hotel in the street eloquently named The Land of Green Ginger. Their tickets bore the phrase 'Golden Rail Holidays', the first and last words surely running foul of the Trade Descriptions Act.

On Saturday, we saw the pedestrianized city centre. As intended, it's very pleasant for the pedestrian and deeply malicious towards the poor motorist. We saw the *wonderful* Maritime Museum and the twenty-million-pound marina which made my eyes pop. There are plans for a Heritage Centre, caravan park, leisure centre and ice-rink. (Funny how ice-rinks have replaced the bowling alleys of yesteryear. The Town Planners' vision of the year 2000 seems to be people who watch movies all day with M&S bags on their knees and blades on their feet! Pearl and Dean meet Torvill and Dean.) No, I mustn't mock. The city is much improved, historically fascinating and very pretty in places. (It says here). No, it IS.

Whilst the rest of the press looked forward to a night out at *A Christmas Carol* ('You'll love it!' I told them), I prepared to join my parents at the seventieth birthday party of their friend, Joyce. I was unprepared, however, for the Hull tradition of all the men being at one end of the room and all the women at the other. For the whole evening! 'We always do it,' said my mother, 'What would we talk to them about?' At one point a man ventured into our charmed circle and, having said 'Hello, how are you?' seemed to vanish as though plucked by an invisible, but nicely manicured hand. It was, however, a lovely party and I know damn well on which side of the room my Jack would have spent it.

On Sunday we saw the historic market town of Beverley as 'splendid and precious' as the brochure said it was, and well-remembered by me as sporting the best ice-cream in the world. Whether it's still that good I can't tell you since the approach of anything cold these days makes my gums curl up.

Finally, we headed back to Paragon Station and a Sunday train journey. I know you'd feel better if I told you it was warm, pleasant and on time. So would I. But this is fact as well as friction. So I'll tell it like it was. A flight from Boston USA had been re-routed to Newcastle and all 500 passengers had been put aboard the train. Our reserved seats were gone. Old cans and old bodies lay resignedly on the floor of the closed buffet car, luggage and litter littered every corridor. We stood for one and a half hours and sat on our tote bags for the other ninety-two.

I have to tell you that a weekend break in Hull is a very good idea. There is much to see, much to learn and plenty to stimulate the senses. Just make the journey there by helium balloon, private jet or via Norway.

Are We Down Under?

G'day She-las everywhere, this is your friendly foreign correspondent fresh from two weeks in Sydney Oz courtesy of Qantas or Qaint Arse as it's lovingly called. I've lugged it, legged it, logged it and lagged it. Well no. Not strictly the latter because I've discovered the antidote to jet lag and it doesn't come in a bottle. It comes in a roll. A roll of brown paper. Let me expound – try and stop me!

Jack and I went to a Variety Club Ball where we met a certain Mr Robert Charlton. Now Jack seeing Bobby is like Maggie seeing Cecil Parkinson or Pamella Bordes seeing anyone. He becomes suffused with adoration and something touchingly close to bashfulness. I could bite lumps out of him! *And* Jack. No I'm being facetious and it's got to stop. We happened to mention to Bobby that we were about to fly to the land of the Billabong and that I was afraid that I'd be too jet lagged to work. (Yet another BT commercial – this time playing Beattie's Australian sister, Rose – she says 'helloy' instead of 'hello'). Bobby glanced at Henry Cooper sitting to his right and to a man they both said 'Brown Paper'.

My first thought was that they were suggesting I eat it, my second that I put a bag of it over my head, my third that they'd both overdone the Chardonnay. They explained that what you do is cut out the shape of your foot in brown paper and wear it next to your skin for the whole journey, whereupon jet lag becomes as likely a travelling companion as scurvy. Back home and deaf to the snorts of family and friends, I cut out innersoles, eight each, individually named them all and placed them in the relevant hand luggage. Then I put four years' worth of summer clothes on the floor of three bedrooms. Then I stared at it all. Then I put some of it away again. Then I took it all out again and added some more. Then I went to the pictures. Then after a couple of days of leaping 'roo-style' over piles of mis-matched and deeply creased linen sportswear (you buy it that way) in order to get to any part of the house, I phoned Denise Katz of 'Creative Organizers' and said 'I'm Maureen. Pack Me.' Mindless extravagance I hear you hiss? Well hiss off – it was worth it! I learned after forty-three crumpled years how to fill a suitcase. How to layer the floor of the case with bra and knicker-filled shoes and bags, how to cover each layer of clothes with polythene. And how to FOLD! I could do a summer season in Benettons now with no trouble. I stood back and the words 'I rest my case' passed my lips. I was faint with relief. For once I didn't need to lie across my luggage on top of my son, whilst his father attempted the traveller's equivalent of eating a chocolate éclair without allowing cream to squidge out of the sides.

'Have you packed your mac?' said my friend Lizzy when I reported my triumph.

'For Australia?' I hooted, 'it's 78 degrees there.'

'You can't possibly travel without a mac,' she persisted.

'Why?' I retorted. 'I never wear one here – why should I drag one 12,000 miles to not wear one there? I'll travel in my check blazer – if it rains I'll wear that.'

Old readers read on – your worst suspicions are merely understatements.

After tropical, near monsoon rain for eleven days out of the fifteen, I have now wrung out the check blazer for the last time. It's been dried out in Sydney, mangled in Melbourne and Tai-dyed in Thailand and I'll shortly be cutting it up as a rag to wipe the stains out of my new Australian Drizabone.

Seriously, I've never seen such rain. Long, dark, relentless rain, reminiscent of Wimbledon fortnight and Ingmar Bergman movies. The production company tried hard to keep morale high. They booked us a boat trip round Sydney harbour. at 8.30 am I phone, yelling over the sound of the storm to say hopefully, 'It is off isn't it?' 'Certainly not,' said Adrian, the producer. 'We wouldn't want to disappoint the kids, would we?' 'No, of course,' I said looking at the said kids, huddled in their beds mouthing 'We're not going on a blood-with-a-y-in-it, boat trip in this lousy weather!' We went. Me shivering in my check blazer and two layers of T-shirts. Jolly Jack and Amy huddled in the cabin in their cricket sweaters and Adam 'up aft' in borrowed sou'wester and cape looking for all the world like a tiny sardine advert.

Actually the kids didn't want to move out of the hotel at all once they'd heard that Kylie Minogue was staying there. They mounted a twenty-four hour siege on the lobby – leaving their posts only to stuff that old Aussie favourite 'Barramundi in vinegar glaze' down their mouths, while still craning round to see the entrance foyer. Then we'd have 'Pleasecanweleavethetab ...' as they de-materialized. Their patience was ultimately rewarded, I can report, in the shape of the Shiny, Tiny Mini-ogue (and I mean that in a caring way) who gave them a signed photo, a few words, and thus the 'back-to-school' story of the decade.

Furthermore, I got them on to the *Neighbours* set in Melbourne. Well, what kind of mother do you think I am? They were visibly moved. Adam made a small speech of the 'We want to thank you for having the kind of job which brought us to this miracle' variety. Beats me. These kids have been brought up surrounded by show-biz but nothing till *Neighbours* has reduced them to wobbly-kneed adoration. In fact one night, when we'd ordered dinner from Room Service, they rang through to check the order on my lamb chops and Jack called through to me in the bath – 'Maureen. Lamb chops. Well done?' To which Amy screamed from the other bedroom 'Has Mod won an award?'

The hotel itself was like Joe Allen's after a first night. Mike Parkinson, Janet Brown, Roald Dahl. David Puttnam, Denholm Elliott ('Why do you suppose his parents called him Denim?' whispered Amy in a restaurant one night gazing at his jeans). Yes, the great and the near great were there. There was even a carefully weird pop group called 'Stryper', whose manager benevolently deposited a publicity still of the lads (I think they were lads) on to my Minogue-spotting children, who were suitably appalled.

'Wait till I see Roald Dahl,' I muttered darkly, remembering the author's untimely attack on Salman Rushdie. 'I'm going to tell him exactly what I think of him.' As I spoke the lift doors opened and there he was, and there was I, the Emmeline Pankhurst of the soft left, saying 'Hellooo. How are you? How lovely to see you again.'

'There are times when I despair of myself,' I moaned to the company over dinner.

'Why?' said Adam, 'What's wrong with Roald Dahl writing to *The Times* about Salman Rushdie?'

I was incensed. How long will it take before my children understand that you support the underdog at all times if you've ever been a genuine *Guardian* reader. 'What's wrong?' I yelled. 'You think it's right to denounce a fellow writer at a time when millions of extremists are trying to kill him?'

'Oh, sorry,' continued Adam calmly, 'I thought the argument was about free speech. I mean if Rushdie has the right to write what he likes, then surely Dahl has the right to criticize it.'

There was a momentary pause and then I hit back with masterly supremacy. 'Yeah well – I mean that's one way of ... Oh SHUDDUP, smart arse!'

The first day's filming took place in a garden overlooking Sydney Harbour. The bridge was growing out of my shoulders and the Opera House looked like a hair ornament. I was wearing a fetching array of grey wig, blue contact lenses, pink sun visor, multi-national bermudas and a yard-and-a-half of padding. Oh, and I was sipping a cool guava juice. The only digger in the woodpile was overhead in the shape of plastic tenting to prevent the howling wind and blinding rain from blowing me on to Bondi Beach and massive arc lamps burning down to simulate Australian weather. We finally abandoned all hope about four o'clock, I shed the padding and about twenty years and headed back to the family, who'd spent the day in Sydney shark aquarium. Well so had I, in a sense. Wistfully I phoned England to be told that the weather was in the 70s and they were out having a barbie!

We did actually finish the shoot in decent weather and our end of term wrap party was held at The Last Australian Fish Restaurant. This meant a table for thirty in the Southern Hemisphere's noisiest joint. Juke boxes play 50s Rock 'n' Roll. Suspendered girls and grease-quiffed boys jitterbug in frenzied fashion. And the waiters are apparently hired by the decibel. All moustached, bicepy and decidedly macho – particularly the waitresses – they thump the tables and literally bellow 'Whaddyalldrinkiiiiiiiinnn?' I actually thought that some crazed Antipodean fundamentalist cult had wandered in and accordingly threw myself under the table. The kids were pulverized. Jack quietly pushed shredded serviettes in both ears. It was an experience.

Berry, the unit sound man, made it his business to jive with every woman in the room, regardless of shape or age. This included me. My body went into shock. It had been so long. In fact my legs continued twitching long after he'd thrown me back in my chair and right through the anaemic whiting and chips, which was banged down unceremoniously in front of me by a skinhead with a shogun top-knot and a nose-ring. So rude and loud was he that when he came back to scream 'Here's the vinegar y'arsked for' three inches from my left eardrum, I involuntarily screamed 'eff-off!' to his departing T-shirt (which, incidentally, said 'Save gas. Fart with a friend'), thereby totally alienating the nice Jewish family from Hendon, who'd just told me how much younger I looked in real life. My revenge came when the same waiter roared 'Gimme yer plates,' as he slammed past me. 'Here y'ar sport,' I retorted, tipping half-finished whiting and chips all over the table and handing him back an empty plate, 'Nice clean one for you.'

We left Sydney on a rainy day after an eight-hour delay at the airport, and headed for Bangkok. Guess what film they were showing? Yeah, *Rain Man*. We arrived at Bangkok at 5.00 am, which was daunting, and the Oriental Hotel, which some claim is the best hotel in the world, and in my humble but limited opinion, is. You won't be surprised to hear that our rooms had been cancelled by mistake nor that we ended up in the most magnificent suite. One probably normally reserved for passing potentates. The bowing and scraping was to die for: 'Hello I am Prassit – anything I can do for you? You want me unpack for you – bring breakfast?' ME: 'Thank you. Here is my check jacket. Can you press it, Prassit?' I felt rather foolish.

What a motley crew we looked with our tawdry luggage

still bearing the old Minorca stickers. Adam in his bush hat, hip-length Drizabone and shorts, looking like a cross between Paddington Bear and a flasher. Jack with his pile of Thai currency – 'Bahts' – or 'Lionels' as we called them – dispensing generous tips to all and sundry, which later turned out to be about forty pence each. They could only have assumed we were an eccentric group of travelling circus freaks or failed terrorists. Indeed a swarthy gentleman sitting by the lift on our floor refused to let us out of the lift as Amy and I returned rather bedraggled from the pool. 'No, no, no you go down,' ME: 'No, no, no, we stay up.' HIM: 'No, no, not this floor, you go back in lift.' ME: 'Oh yes, this floor! You mind own business.' It turned out he was a bodyguard to a princess staying on 'our floor'. He simply couldn't believe we could afford to be there. Who could blame him?

We loved what we saw of Thailand in thirty-six hours but it quite dis*orient*ated me. The people are so graceful. Such beauty and style. I want to go back there and see it properly through drier eyes. I'm home now and *gladdi* to be here. It's beaut! I've thrown away the brown paper innersole – and I've written a bright and perky thank-you letter to Bobby. It worked! I'm *still* trying to find places for the twelve Qantas toilet bags we gathered between us on the round trip and will personally dismember the next person who sees that Aussie commercial and says 'Struth that backdrop of Sydney looks a bit crook. Why dint you come eight here and do the thing properly – and get a bit of sun on yer Pommy face whoil yer adit?'

Italiantics

I've been on a little trip again. The Italian Lakes. And yes, they are very beautiful, and yes we had decent weather, and yes, we only moved rooms, hotel and resort once in two weeks (which is something of a record), and yes, I feel ever so much better for it.

The thing is, I'm supposed to be writing about it for a magazine, and herein lies the blub, because I am to the world of travel writing, what Derek Jameson is to the world of elocution, or what Sigmund Freud was to the world of French polishing. It's not that I don't like scenery, I do, it's lovely. It's just that I can't get excited about it properly. When I read Paul Theroux and he is getting on a train in China with his ticket clutched in his hot little hand, it is clear to me that the man is beside himself, and both of him are delirious, at the prospect of five days of bone-shaking travel and a steady diet of dead doggy. Likewise when I watched Dame Freya Stark's last expedition. I was mesmerized by the lady's indomitable spirits. Age ninety-six or something, off up the Himalayan mountains on a mule, God bless her. Ninety-six! I find it tricky to get out of the house for a sliced loaf. And she loved every minute of it. Every awful minute. Prised out of her tent by beaming Sherpas, unfrozen with bat's tea, she smiled and joked uncomplainingly all the way to the summit. Quite literally on top of the world.

Then, when I read the Sunday papers, anytime from Christmas onwards, there they are again, the Eric Newbys and the Fiona Pitt-Kethleys – mind you, that's one broad who really knows how to enjoy herself abroad. She gives a whole new dimension to the words 'package' tours, that one does.

Any road up (or down) they all wax lyrical about sunsets

and moonlight and moonsets and sunlight, and villages that
nestle, and roads that meander, and tiny roadside inns that
welcome, and sudden jewelled lakes inset into lavender hills.
Their breaths are collectively taken away from them at least
three times a day. They have quiet, contemplative moments
around scrubbed wooden tables over local yak's yoghurt.
They meet and are befriended by apple-cheeked peasants.
They exchange greetings with giggling natives. They sleep
in muslin tents 'neath diamond and velvet skies and learn
the secret initiation rites of the disappearing world. Theirs
is a charmed and curious journey which begins as an outward
bound and ends as an interior voyage of discovery.

What they *don't* seem to do is pack three more cases than
they need into a two door minicab with no roof-rack, hang
about in airport buffets eating listeria sandwiches whilst
French Air Traffic Controllers air their grievances, or fail to
acquire a syllable of the language of the country of their
destination then complain bitterly when the taxi driver rips
them off.

What they haven't packed is a different outfit for each
evening, so as not to disappoint the other people in the
dining-room, nor three enormous toilet bags, one filled with
make-up, one filled with make-up remover, and one filled
with flashy costume jewellery which will spend two weeks in
a hotel safe for fear of bent chambermaids. Neither do they
have with them an armchair lilo, an armchair lilo pump
inflator, two oars, two tennis rackets and a little Brother
computer.

More importantly 'they' don't concentrate on un-import-
ant things like 'Who's who' in the hotel foyer. 'Do you
suppose those two are married? To each other.' or 'Have you
noticed how that man shows off to other women and ignores
his wife?' or 'Why is that fat jolly couple always rolling about
with glee like a fat jolly couple in a Donald McGill?'

And it's always been that way. Bournemouth to me means
the waitress who exclaimed on seeing my mother 'Mrs
Lipman! How are you? How lovely to see you. Do you
remember me? I used to work in Hammonds in Hull.' Mother
showed equal effusiveness until the moment her old friend
left the table, then she said all in one breath, 'I've never seen

her in my life before, hasn't she put weight on?' That's Bournemouth.

And Florida means the waitress in a Jewish Restaurant who, after taking our order, said, 'You don't want soda water?' then said, 'Are you Jewish?' and on being told that we were, sat down at the table with us and said, 'You're Jewish and you don't want soda water?' The explanation involved large quantities of food and copious of gas, so I'll leave it to your imagination. That was Florida!

And Ireland – beautiful though it was – my over-riding memory has to be a harassed waitress again. 'Excuse me, can I have my coffee without cream?' 'I'm sorry sir – we don't have any cream, you'll have to have it without milk.'

As for Australia, well Australia will always be Steve the driver who pointed out every visible and invisible landmark on a thirty mile journey until he finally ran out of landmarks to be proud of and said, 'And as we round this bend, if you crane forward you can just see the back of the Tayo biscuit factory. Can you see it? I don't know if you have the Tayo biscuits in England, do you? It's a little sort of crackerish wafer about two inches across and you can have it with cheese or with something a little more sweet ...' And that was Australia.

So next time you're browsing in your local bookshop and you see John Mortimer's Tuscany, Melvyn Bragg's Lakes, Felicity Kendal's India, and Colin Welland's Barnes, just thank your lucky diamonds 'n velvet that you won't come across Maureen Lipman's World, because it would be awfully small, and if not overlooked, then most certainly overheard.

Where was I? Oh, yes – the Italian Lakes ...

Courtesy of the French Air Controllers' strike and the English Customs officials' strike, our plane touched down at Milan airport a mere two hours later than scheduled. It did so to a tumult of applause from the party of Italian teenagers who'd run riot throughout, as no doubt they had done during their two weeks in St Albans. They kissed each other, the stewardesses and the ground they finally alighted on. In baggage reclaim they finally realized their holiday was over and began to embrace and weep *en masse* with great dramatic

Lady of Spain. (*Annie Livings*)

'It's for Loo-oo-ooo!' Lady in waiting room.

Old bag lady and Iron lady – you choose which is which . . .

Enter large, ethnic Dalmatian, stage left. Definitely *not* a 'house-Frow'.
(*Dress by Ben Frow, photograph by Iain Philpott*)

effect. We were almost certainly in Italy.

It was nine-thirty at night and the pre-arranged taxi obviously had a previous pre-arrangement, so Jack and the kids and I fought our way through to another and peacefully drove the hour-long journey through the cool Milanese air scented with oleander and lemon. For this was to be an unusual Rosenthal holiday. One of tranquillity and calm, even at the height of August, spent in a white Victorian wedding cake of a hotel in Stresa on the edge of Lake Maggiore. In other words, this year there would be no rented villa with open sewerage and an empty pool. There would be no sweaty mattresses and bawling entertainments officer vanguarding you on to the floor to do the 'Birdie' dance.

No shopping in foreign supermarkets, so enchanting for the first couple of days, so interminable for the rest of your stay, and no sand – this year's suitcases would return home sandless – apart from last year's shingle!

We reached the hotel at 11.00 pm. It was sunk in gloom. Death Valley. 'Well, you wanted a quiet holiday,' I muttered to myself, and myself muttered back, 'If I'd wanted it this quiet I'd have gone to Highgate Cemetery.' We groped our way to the reception and thence to our rooms and thence back to reception to change them; Adam scrabbling through his phrase book in search of the Italian for 'poky' and 'Can we get poky room service?' In curt English we were informed there was no food in the hotel, in Stresa, or indeed in all of Northern Italy at this time of night. 'Grazie mille,' cooed the phrase-book-clutching boy as his mother marched the family imperiously out into the main street in search of pizza, and I don't mean the leaning tower of.

The town of Stresa, even to my bleary undernourished eyes, was a pretty sight. Basically it's a town front bordering the lake, with a busy winding town set behind a double line of trees bordering the café bars. At night the people gather in the square to sip cappuccino and eat gelati whilst swinging in striped banquettes. We found a vine-covered garden restaurant, overdosed on pizza Napolitano and wine and straggled back to 'Gloom City' for some serious crashing out. In an unusual burst of romantic folly Jack and I pushed our twin beds together, slept across them to avoid the gap and woke up unable to move a single limb between us.

The following day was grey and misty but the swimming pool beckoned seductively to a family starved of water since – ooh – last Friday's Radox bath. Very English round the pool in best boisterous tradition. A plethora of Kellys and Shanes were yelled at and a portly, life-and-soul-of-the-party from Pontefract sang 'The Rose of Tralee' under the poolside shower. Incredibly reluctantly we headed into town for a delicious pasta at the Pizzaria Bolongara and thence for a trip by ferry to the first of the Borromean Islands, Isola Bella. The lake was peppered with small white ferries, looking as Joyce Grenfell once wrote, like 'harmonicas at sea', and the three islands, plus Lovers' Island – a sharp rock sticking out of the ocean at an angle which only a lover could stand – are its greatest treasures.

Charles Borromeo was a rich, titled, seventeenth-century philanthropist whose statue dominates the Verbona Area – thirty-five metres high with an eighty-five metre nose and two of the most outstanding ears I've seen since Spock was last beamed up. He built the Borromeo Palace on Isola Bella in honour of his wife Isabella. It is extraordinarily imposing with mosaic marble floors, ravishing antiques, tapestries and paintings and an underground grotto decorated entirely in shells and stone mosaic. But it is the Italian gardens which stun you. Ten terraced levels down to the sea, white peacocks, an English flower garden, a garden of love and the stone-built folly of an amphitheatre in the uppermost terrace sporting unicorns and obelisks and giant stone statues with iron swords, each one fitted with a lightning conductor, necessary on Maggiore as the electric thunderstorms are sudden and dramatic. Wonderful white lasers snake down through a blackening sky and the thunder booms and bounces around the mist-covered mountains. How am I doing, Mr Theroux?

By our second week we had fallen in love with the little town of Pallanza across the lake, and moved lock, stock and barrel to its truly Majestic hotel, recently reopened after renovations. Built around a central atrium like a Roman villa, it has a fine indoor pool and quiet lakeside garden.

The tiny shingle beach about five metres across became the children's private property as they took to walking up and down like expectant fathers discussing – what else? – their school and their friends. Occasionally they swam across the thirty feet or so of water dividing the beach from the tiny island with one imposing Villa which was Toscanini's summer residence, but mostly they just walked and talked.

We ferried over to Isola des Pescatores for a delicious fish lunch, the first of many helpings of a deliciously moist local sponge cake, and a wander through the lovely, ramblingly haphazard cobbled streets hung with colourful curtains of real net – fisherman's style – hung out to dry. Then back on board with the other tourists to the third and perhaps the most interesting Isola, the Isola Madre, where the less formal gardens are dotted with azaleas, rhododendrons and rare plants and flowers from remote lands. Open-air cages hold every hue of budgerigar. Parrots fly free overlooked by a massive Cashmere Cypress tree which stands on the eighteenth-century Borromeo Palace with its puppet theatre and fascinating collection of antique puppets. The kids wanted to buy a holiday home on this island, and dragged us into every shop in search of real estate. Instead, we bought dried porcini, only slightly more expensive than we might have done at the St James' Deli in Muswell Hill.

In short, we *had* our restful holiday, and we will undoubtedly return there. Probably though I'd go to Lake Orta, a tortuous coach trip and boat trip from Maggiore, where the old town is even more like Shakespeare's Verona – the colours are calming to the eye and the hotels less discovered by people like us.

We spent out last evening in the Hotel Milano in Pallanza with our always helpful and amusing Horizon representative, Guiseppe (from Birmingham), eating one of the most memorable meals of our lives – Capanello – a mixture of vegetables and pine nuts, each roasted in its own juice. Words still fail me but I can taste it still. And to follow – a magnificent Chicken Curry!

When in Italy do as the Indians do ...

The Connecticut Connection

'Hi there folks my name is Maureen and I'm your American correspondent circa 1990. May I run through our list of specials? OK now, well are you familiar with our seedtray? And might I interest you in some of our homemade oatmeal and honey cranberry muffins without sesame? And would you like a waffle with your maple syrup? *You're* Welcome.

'As you may have have gathered, 1990 finds me East Coast Stateside, in the L S Lowry meets Edward Hopper port of New Haven, Connecticut. I'm here to try out my one-woman show *Re:Joyce* on unsuspecting Americans, united by their states of ignorance of either Joyce Grenfell or your cowering correspondent, Ms Lipman.

'We, Jack and the kids and I, spent two weeks with friends in Massachusetts, in their rambling white house, surrounded by three feet of rambling white snow. It was homely as *pie*. All our clothing was totally inadequate of course. When you hear that a place is eight degrees under, it probably isn't enough to pack three cocktail dresses and a change of thermal underwear. Well, how do you pack for a nine-week stay in three different parts of America? If you're me – badly.

'First off, I had attempted for the first time in forty-three years to have matching luggage. The old Minorca/Tenerife expandables had, for some time, had the look of being regularly made love to by a couple of newly-wed bisons, so I'd gritted my bridgework and headed for Wood Green shopping centre – which for me is tantamount to Lord Lucan heading for Bow Street.

'I'd easily attracted a salesgirl in the deserted luggage department of D H Evans by dint of lying on the floor shrieking "Help me! Help me! I'm a customer!" Eventually a salesperson took pity on me and sauntered over to reveal she knew as much about suitcases as I knew about trout-tickling in Tannoch Brae.

'Finally, having failed to open any of the cases I'd wanted to see inside, she sat down on them and grumbled, "*I* don't know, do I? I've 'ad 'flu!" Overwhelmed with guilt, I'd bought the cases from under her and managed to squeeze one-third of the clothing into two, an amount that I could have packed with ease into *one* old bison expandable.

'What I hadn't of course packed were ear-muffs, leg warmers or a parka. This showed a lack of forethought. Had I not promised my son that, if he behaved impeccably in a houseful of adults, I would go cross-country skiing with him? Well how was I know that he damn well *would* behave impeccably?

'Out I went into the eight degrees under. And down I went about thirteen times just on the way from the ski-lodge to the start of the trail. And since I was wearing roughly half the contents of one suitcase, getting up again was an act of sheer improbability.

'After a while I began to whimper into my anorak . . . Then my tears froze and I started to bleat. The scenario was that my uninsured ankles would snap – they already felt about as solid as a couple of prawn crackers – and I would be unable to do the show. This gave a whole new meaning to the salutation "Break a leg" as used in the UK on opening nights, and gave one elderly thespian the perfect reason to roll over on her back, unpadlock her feet from their absurd bindings and walk home shaken but not deterred.

'The next day I said a teary goodbye to my family who were flying home to England for the start of term, and my accompanist, his wife and I motored down to New Haven. Other than feeling car-sick, home-sick, child-sick and chap-sick (sic), I felt fine.

'And so far, three weeks in, even finer. We live in a beach house on the Long Island Sound and when the sun shines through the crisp clean snow I can almost smile when I'm told to "have a nice day" by the garbage man. I'm as homesick as a coyote in Castle Combe on some days, and as assimilated as an owl at a barn dance on others.

'It was pointed out to me this morning over corned beef

hash that I'm pronouncing weekend with the stress on "week" instead of "end", and that my new blue jeans (stress on "blue") with tan suede "chaps" are hardly what one expects from a fragile Englishwoman who shops in Muswell Hill and plays Joyce Grenfell seven nights a week. The Matching Jacket has suede appliqué trees, fringes and thongs, cost more than an apartment (flat to you), and I'm seriously thinking of embroidering MDL across the back. Not for Maureen Diane Lipman, but for "Mutton Dressed as Lamb."

'It has taken me six weeks to drive on the wrong side of the road and, having done it, I'm possessed by a wild exhilaration which must frighten the hell out of my fellow drivers. It means that I pootle down the freeway at 55 with a Jack Nicholson smile, feverishly bright eyes, and the occasional burst of manic laughter when I pass a billboard which reads "Hey! Have you tuned up your snow-thrower yet?"

'I've stopped being frightfully British in the drug store in the hope that they'll find my accent cute, and I'm learning to leave restaurants with a "Hound of the Baskervilles" bag containing enough residue food to feed the Italian population of Hoboken, New Jersey. I've also recovered from the TV announcer who prefaced my interview by saying 'She's best known in England for her series *About Faces* in which she plays six different Jewish Grandmothers, and she's going to tell us what makes her the funniest woman in England ...'' Correction – I've *nearly* recovered.

'The supermarkets here are lethal, the choice bewildering. There are twelve different kinds of *milk*. There's 2% milk, 4% milk, non-fat milk, fat-as-hell milk, non-dairy milk, non-cholesterol milk, *swimming in cholesterol* milk, and a product called "Jog", which I assume has been homogenized on the backs of the fruitcakes who belt past my windows all day long wearing Reeboks, glitter tights and ear flaps.

'Everybody here is a "foodie". Food, not religion, is the opiate (appropriate) of the masses. There are two distinct kinds. Gourmet and junk. At the theatre where I'm working, they favour the former but are not averse to "pigging" or "grossing-out" on the latter. Long discussions on recipes are the norm in the Green Room, amongst both sexes. The men make their own pasta!

'Then, at the cinema, you find your popcorn comes salt or sweet, with or without butter and in three sizes, huge, monstrously huge and "is there any chance of being wheeled to my seat please?" And the worst part is that you eat it! All of it.

'You know what else I'm in love with here? I'm in love with American Catalogues. Unlike the unpleasant "His & Hers Matching Monogrammed Pigskin Telephone and Bidet Cover" which drop uninvited out of every passing periodical, these have a real homesy, folksy appeal.

'Catalogues invite you to send for "all cotton American sleeping gloves, which allow your hands to breathe while you sleep." Isn't that the best? And while your hands are a-breathin', you can be a-wearin' the "All American Seersucker nightgown for an 'I want one' response!" And Please God you get one? Please God we all do ...!

'Then there's the Vermont farmers' "Bag Balm" for both sore hands and cows' udders. Presumably they can't get the cows to keep their sleeping gloves on, and the "strange-looking knife for cutting squishy produce ..." no I'm not scoffing, well I am scoffing – everything in sight. To the extent that I'm thinking of sending for the "all cotton, triple gusset garter belt and tummy controller in regular and *Queen* size!" As I write this I can feel the zip on my new blue jeans surreptitiously sliding down of its own accord. And I'm in the Post Office!

'But I'm not scoffing at our Colonial cousins for their dimity ways. As I said, I'm half in love with them. Their famed hospitality is no myth. It's a hit. In the meantime, if you should chance upon a plump-bodied, thin-faced, English actress, with a distinct twang, and a Jack Nicholson grin, driving on the wrong side of the road with her flies undone, you can more or less assume it's Thursday and the green, green grass of England has beckoned me Home.'

Going Dutch

When it's spring again I'll bring again . . .

The GCSEs had taken their toll. On my daughter, I mean, as well as me. Our little matching thin faces were a whiter shade of pale – 'blech' is the Yiddish word for it which conjures up a whole colour chart from beige to green. Also my adorable and petite Columbian housekeeper, Esperanza (every time I say that someone says Esther Rantzen? Who fits very few of those adjectives), was having emotional problems.

'Amsterdam,' I said, triumphantly, 'Let's go to Amsterdam. We'll see the Van Gogh exhibition. We'll go up the Red Light district. We'll do Anne Frank's house and we'll eat every herring in Holland!'

Amy's eyes looked up from her typewriter. '*Yeeah*' she beamed, humouring me all the while, and resumed typing her latest story of love and intrigue in the matriarchal Midlands.

I tried it on Esperanza who, when she's not beavering away for me, is in the middle of her photography finals, and she too, made encouraging noises in the certain knowledge that the discussion would be the last she heard of the trip.

Jack and Adam were watching the football. 'Lovely,' they chorused. 'Have fun. Pass it down the middle you selfish pillock!'

So I rang the Travel Company, inquired about flights and hotels and booked it for the next weekend. Like a grown-up. I was devilish proud when the tickets arrived and thrilled skinny when I saw the look of bewilderment and disbelief on the faces of my fellow travellers, one of whom had planned a weekend of serious study, the other a party at Tasha's house.

We were due to leave at 8.30am, Saturday. On Thursday night, after dinner at my friend Lizzy's, I mentioned the intended cultural foray and Lizzy's sister, Sue, said the immortal words: 'You have got tickets for the Van Gogh haven't you?' 'Tickets?' I laughed, 'No, I'll get them at the door, won't I?' Sue put me right. Contrary to lack of expectations Van Gogh, not *Miss Saigon*, was the hottest ticket in Europe and if I didn't sell my body to the concierge at the hotel immediately, I might as well stay home and look at some painting by numbers up Regents Canal.

I spent the following morning in my customary dialling position, grovelling and posturing to the Travel Agent, the hotel reception, Dutch Tourist board, and everyone but the Eurovision Song Contest committee, to try to wangle my way in. Nothing. I had more chances of playing vibes with Thelonius Monk at the Pizza on the Park than I had of penetrating the Van Gogh Museum this weekend.

I packed our case for rain and sun and arranged my face accordingly. Amy was despondent. She now wanted to see the exhibition more than life itself and a lilac mini. In a last shameless act of rank pulling I rang *She* magazine and wangled a fax from them claiming that I was reviewing the exhibition for their magazine.

We flew into Schipol at 9.16 their time, after a flight which no sooner got up than it came down again – a bit like life really. In the half hour taxi trip to the Victoria hotel I did the big tourist trick that you only see in movies about the Big Apple: I bought three tickets for a Tina Turner concert that evening from the cab driver, who just happened to have them about his person. The concert was in Rotterdam. 'It's only a half an hour on the fast train,' he assured the green-horns in his Renault who thanked and overtipped him as they checked into their rooms overlooking Central station and the back of one canal.

The first thing Amy noticed in the foyer were the words Sauna, Jacuzzi and Swimming-Pool. 'Oh no. I didn't bring a swim suit.' Her mother, who had, kept quiet out of guilt and neglectfulness of child although in fact child was too busy to pick out clothes the night before because best friend was staying.

We strolled out into the sun-streaked main street, Damrak, in search of a pancake lunch and wound up in C&A's basement spending our colourful guilders on Lycra 'cozzies' for 'the girls'. 'I can't believe we've flown to Amsterdam and we're in C&A's!' I kept saying. 'I'm turning into my mother in leaps and bounds. Next thing I'll be queuing up at Kostomservis, Monday morning, trying to take them back. After they've been worn!'

The recommended Pancake Factory was in Princengracht number 171. I can't tell you how immoral it felt to be walking past the queue outside Anne Frank's house, in search of a pancake. The canals, streets and tram lines of Amsterdam criss-cross the city like a perfect spider's web and it's intricate enough to walk anywhere or to jump on a tram when your new sandals start cannibalizing your corns. The biggest danger to the meandering pedestrian is the cyclist – who abounds in plenty and stops short for no man. If you dive away from the cycle lane you're likely to be run over and if you leap away from the road to avoid a car you're likely to be TRAMMED to death. Drowning seems the best bet because the houseboats look so inviting with their brightly painted doors, and bursting geranium-boxed windows.

After walking miles down the wrong side of Princengracht we reversed our sandals, and taking care to pass the same queue outside Anne Frank's house, finally happened upon the basement pancake house in an old sheltered warehouse. There was seating for hundreds and about six more staff than customers. We ordered our pancakes and waited whilst the staff had the most jovial time amongst themselves. After half an hour (and I *know* how long a pancake takes to cook) I ventured to ask where they were and suggest they might like to bring them in this decade. The pancake maker's reply – in the same perfect English we encountered all over the city – was a collector's item.

'So. Next time you come to Amsterdam – why don't you cook your own pancakes?' Nice one, Hans!

We strolled/limped or leaped our way back to Damrak by way of the most wonderful narrow, boutique-lined streets and I was relieved painlessly of enormous quantities of bright yellow Dutch currency by the compulsory purchase of two short and stylish cotton macs for myself and Amy.

There was just time to catch the Rotterdam train, see the first group and get a decent seat. I was panicking inwardly because a) I was convinced the tickets were fraudulent and we'd end up in an empty Rotterdam stadium explaining our predicament to several chortling Dutch policemen who took us for English hooligans, and b) under normal circumstances, much as I admire her, I wouldn't take the 134 into Tottenham Court Road to see Tina Turner.

We were on the train to Rotterdam for one-and-a-half hours. It was obvious, even to our damp English brains, that this was not the *fast* train. But what a joy to tell your predicament to a Dutch guard or fellow passengers and have your every word understood and your every joke howled at. Imagine the predicament of a Dutchman in the same position on his way to Milton Keynes.

The train finally pulled in and disgorged all Tina Turner ticket holders on to another train to Rotterdam stadium. It was a short trip and a merry one as the whole train was Tina Bound and Mexican waves were already in rehearsal.

The huge stadium was buzzing with action. Esperanza's complex camera equipment was ticketed and confiscated straight away. The 'stockbroody' and 'slagroom' stalls were doing brisk business. Herrings on paper plates, burgers and onions, frites and franks filled the gaps between pancakes and lack of room-service, and over everything came the relentless vibrations of the very bad sound system of a heavily routine rock group.

Amy was fraught with premonitions of danger. Her face even more 'blech' than when I'd phoned the travel company. Apart from an irrational hatred of pop music, she was convinced we were going to be stampeded/robbed/mugged and, worse, miss the last train back, so it would be too late to ring Melanie and find out if anyone got kissed or pissed at Tasha's party.

We took our seats in a strangely vacant section of the otherwise packed stadium and tried to accustom ourselves to the grinding bass cords which tremelloed through our major organs. The spirits of the crowd were high and the standing-room only chaps, caged in the converted pitch area, were well into the swaying, clapping and inflatable-banana hurling stage, whilst two Englishwomen and a Columbian sat glumly wondering what in hell's name they were doing there.

At which point the entire stadium began doing the Mexican wave, and this particular Englishwoman got seriously over-excited. It looks so marvellous and I've always wanted to do it. I could hardly wait for it to reach my section. It did. Three people stood up. The rest of the section stayed seated. Three people sat down sheepishly. And the Mexican wave swept on.

After one-and-and-half excruciating hours, the tannoy system announced that there would be a forty-five minute interval whilst Miss Turner's equipment was set up. Try that one in the legitimate theatre and you'd have a riot on your hands and a ransacked bar. Here in the balmy Nether regions, they just applauded and threw the odd fish in the air.

Finally, oh, finally, the stage went dark, a large screen lit up, a floor to ceiling staircase came gliding on and the spotlight illuminated the luminescent Ms Turner, glamorous granny and megamomma rocking on her own assets fit to bust. In seconds we were standing on our seats (if we hadn't we might as well have been plugged into a Walkman) and stamping and hooting along with the throng.

Suddenly a thought struck me: basically, people in crowds tend to look threatening – particularly if we don't share their reasons for being there – but even more basically what people want more than anything else is the chance to have a singsong. I mean nobody *does* it anymore, and it's one of the basic needs of personkind. Our twice yearly gathering around Denis at the piano is positively therapeutic and I've seen strong silent, party-hating men transformed into lives-and-souls-of-the-hearty in the tinkling of an 'Ay-ay-ay-ay- we are my favourite people'. The crowd knew every word Tina was singing and like the audience of the Rocky Horror Show, sang right along with her. I pretended I knew them too.

We left, cleverly we thought, at the height of the euphoria as she launched into 'True Love', to pick up the cameras and be at the station before the 19,997 other people. 'You not coming back?' inquired the guard at one of the exits. Smugly we replied in the negative, and made our way to the locked and barred station. Only Princess Amy really fully enjoyed the taxi ride back into Rotterdam.

The following morning we arose bright and early (at 9.45!), too late for our swim, but well in time for the canal boat ride, the Portuguese synagogue, Anne Frank's house, several hopeless calls to the Van Gogh museum – our only hope it seemed, was to queue from 7.00 am at the bank behind the museum – sounds double Dutch to me but ... I'd have queued up at C&A's if I'd thought it would get us in to Vincent. Maybe we'd say we went to Amsterdam to see Van Gogh and saw the Turner exhibition instead.

We were guided to the Portuguese synagogue by a delightful Dutchman who just happened to be already guiding a very frail old couple to the same area, when I stopped him. It seems that he owned the local coffee shop where the old couple took coffee each day of their stay. '*We'll* drop in for a coffee afterwards,' I said as I thanked him, and he said, 'Please – be my guest. It is the most unusual coffee shop in the world.' I was intrigued. 'Well perhaps we'll come for brunch – do you have cakes?' 'Oh yes,' he said, 'we have hashish cake, hash brownies, all kinds of cannabis cake – please come along and see us.' No wonder the old couple were coming every day for coffee! I bet they talked about nothing else when they got home either. 'Amsterdam, oy, did we we have a piece of cake in Amsterdam!'

Esperanza, now resigned, gave up her camera once again in the Portuguese synagogue, as no photographs were allowed, a fact which was particularly at odds with the artefacts being sold inside to raise money to save the beautiful old building and the video playing full time commentary by the ark. The Jewish Museum was moving and illuminating, and by the time we reached Anne Frank's house I was feeling querulous in the face of the past and qualms of all kinds about the future.

The Frank hide-out is a painfully cramped reminder of the past. The stairs up to the concealed bookcase-entrance are steep as a loft-ladder, and each room feels claustrophobic and memory clad. Anne's eloquence filled me with aching sadness, doubled by the fact that my own sixteen-year-old was by my side, henna-haired, bonny and full of life. The Frank family hid for two shuttered years and, once found, were put on the last train which ever went to the death camps. We shuffled out into the sunlight, eager for air and grateful for our lives. It was hard to watch West Germany beat Holland that evening on TV.

Desperate for that swim, we donned our new swimsuits and went in search of saturation and steam. All we found were signs pointing the way to the leisure centre, but no leisure centre as such. Finally, we returned to our rooms and rang down to reception:

'Can you tell me where the swimming-pool is?'

'Oh, yes. Not yet.'

'Pardon?'

'I'm sorry. Not yet.'

'You mean you can't tell me yet or you haven't got one yet?'

'That is right. It is not yet built until the summer.' (This was June).

'Thank you and goodbye.'

Still, we all needed a new swimsuit to go with the eleven we'd jointly left behind.

So, drier than we'd anticipated, we went in search of an indigenous Dutch restaurant. It took a while to find one, but not long to realize it was closed. That night we ate late. Indonesian late. And for dessert, we took a cab ride round the Red Light District with a jolly and exceedingly handsome cabby who found the three of us unbelievably quaint. Amy, of course, didn't want to get out and walk for fear we'd be mugged, raped, gagged, trampled or employed. The hookers sit in the windows like waxworks, occasionally stirring to lick an unlascivious lip or two. For the main part, they are vastly overweight, scantily clad and as bored as the face on a fish. The surrounding area throbs with razzmatazz, fantasy and false hopes. But then, who doesn't?

Late to bed and up at 5.30am, raring to queue. We reached the bank at 7.15 and joined the half-dozen earlier birds, in the light, drizzly Dutch daylight. Esperanza found some Spanish-speaking punters – it was their third morning of unsuccessful queuing – and, glumly, Amy and I read *Vanity*

Fair from cover to cover, including the adverts for clawfoot baths and cosmetic lifts.

At 9.30 the most powerful woman in Europe got out of her M-registration Fiat, more full of herself than that old sport Colin Moynihan disembarking somewhere in Europe, and opened up. Ten minutes later we had bought five tickets – two for the Spaniards and three for us – and were knocking back buttered croissants in the Korner Kaffe Shoppe.

Then followed two hours in the most emotionally charged, beautifully realized art exhibition I've ever been privileged to plod slowly round. We plugged into a marvellous commentary on Van Gogh's life and work. Don McLean said it all: 'Vincent, the world was never meant for one as beautiful as you.' Just to watch his incredible promise through trial and terror, through struggles with styles and fashions until he found his own, inimitable genius. The prolific outpouring of pain and self-doubt on starry, starry canvas made my brain hurt and my eyes swim, not least because it made me yearn for the books which Anne Frank never wrote.

Laden with the T-shirt, the posters, the chocolates, the cheese, the worsht and the clog with cactus in it, we caught the plane home. It felt more week than end and put me in touch with emotions I never acknowledged I had. And the source? Hollandaise?

5

Shaggy Togs Story

The Columbian Fisherman

There was once a Columbian fisherman. His name was José. He fished by day and by night to eke out his miserable existence. One day a miracle happened. José won the sweepstake. A million dollars. His life was transformed. He left his boat, his nets and his village and bought a one-way ticket to the South of France. The peasants and fishermen crowded around his hired car as he waved them goodbye. And a few tears ran down his old fish-stained smock. He winged his way to Cap Ferrat with one thought only in his mind. La crumpet Française.

All his life José had kept a tattered photograph of Mlle Brigitte Bardot on the wall of his abode. By the flickering light of a candle he would gaze at her luscious pouting lips, and he would dream of possessing such a woman. Now the dream would become a reality. He patted the wodge of dollars in the pocket of his ragged, sun-bleached trousers, and as the plane came in to land his heart was filled with the promise of a new dawning.

He checked into the first hotel he saw. He had no luggage, and his appearance (and his smell) caused some consternation in the lobby. But his money was real, and, to the French 'c'est tout'. One more eccentric South American millionaire in a Mediterranean paradise of millionaires.

Scarcely able to conceal his excitement, José set off for the beach. He couldn't believe his eyes. Such breasts, such skin, such lips, such breasts ... such curves, such breasts. 'Jesu Maria!' he breathed as he walked among them. With mounting joy and expectation, he thrust his hands deep into the pockets of his filthy, fish-strewn trousers, pulled out his money and, in a strange sing-song voice called, 'H'I godda meellion dollars! H'I godda meellion dollars! H'I godda meellion dollars ...' Louder and louder he called along the strip of flesh-coloured sand.

As one, the women turned their heads in disgust. As one, they viewed his massive, mud-splattered legs, his matted hair, his tangled beard, his blood-and-gut-strewn clothes. As one, they wrinkled their pert noses at the stench which accompanied him as he flaunted his crumpled fortune in their direction. As the sun set, José found himself alone and shunned, watching the big waves break against the bodies he so longed to clasp against his own.

Some distance away from him, surrounded by a bevy of squealing sun-maidens, an elegant Frenchman watched our poor hero. In tiny, black bikini trunks, dark shades and a waterproof Rolex, he was the epitome of casual glamour. As he stood to take his leave he bade his companions au revoir and was folding his Gucci towel into eighths when he felt, or rather smelled, the approach of José. 'Pardon,' growled the Latin, 'I notish h'all dese beautiful weemin arounda you – me, I 'ave a meellion dollars and no weeman she look h'atta me. Per que?'

The Frenchman hid his smile behind the smoke of a fresh Gauloise, inhaled deeply and regarded the wreck of a man before him. 'Ur ... well, m'sieur ... I ... ur ... sink mebbe you must change your image a leetle,' José nodded like a patient child. 'You must 'ave an 'aircut ... and ... ur ... a shave ... ur ... wit ze 'ot towels.' He smoothed his own bronzed jawline in pantomime, 'and am afraid you must 'ave a longue shower and ... ur ... use a grett deal of eau de toilette.' Again, the poor fisherman nodded attentively, committing every detail to memory. 'And ... ur ... zen you must srow away zese 'orrible clothes wheech smell so – ur, pardonnez-moi, so deesgusting and you must buy a small pair of ... ur ... ze bikini trunks like mine – et voilá! Ze weemin will lurve you complètement!'

José was wreathed in smiles. It was so simple. The next day he had his hair cut and styled, his chest hair trimmed, his whole body shampooed and perfumed, and in his tiny, black trunks he took one giant step forward on to the beckoning beach. Several nubile mademoiselles looked towards him with interest, but immediately his face split into a pumpkin grin and he lurched forward, crying 'H'I godda meellion dollars! H'I godda meellion dollars!' as one, the women turned their bronzed backs. 'H'I godda meellion doll ...' he petered out. Something was wrong and José knew not what.

For the rest of his empty, lonely day he watched Pierre le français at play with his sultry playmates. As the sun set, he sheepishly approached him. 'H'I am so clean like bone, my friend ... h'I smella so good like pimp, no? H'I godda bikini trunksa, like you tell me! H'I godda meellion dollarsh – but you know what else I got, eh? No weemin is what I got! Whassa wrong?'

Pierre stroked his chin and narrowed his shaded eyes. 'My friend,' he murmured, 'I sink mebbe tomorrow you must go to ze market zere you must buy ... ur ... a *potato* and ... ur ... zen you must put ze potato in your bikini trunks.'

José was still. He gazed at his friend and mentor in silence. Then he rose, laid his hand on the Frenchman's shoulder and departed. With dignity. His quest was over.

The following day he went to the market and followed his friend's advice. Then, with the potato in his trunks, he once again laid siege to the burning beach. Heads turned as he marched up and down. Heads turned away as he called out, in the only manner he knew, the language of the fish market, 'H'I godda meellion dollars! Who wanta piece of dis?' Fruitlessly. Again, as the sun set, José was alone.

Pierre regarded his protegé's approach through blank-mirrored lenses. 'H'I do as you say, my friend! H'I bought a potato! H'I put heem inna ma trunks h'and steel no weemin! What do I do wrong? I beg of you – what I do?'

The Frenchman shifted his weight minimally on the striped Gucci towel and shrugged as only a Frenchman can ...

'Mon ami,' he said gently, 'I sink mebbe ... ur ... tomorrow you should come to the ze beach again ... and ... ur ... mebbe zis time ... you should try ... ur ... putting ze potato in ze *front* of your trunks.'

6

Epilogue

'WHAT WILL THEY SAY ABOUT HER WHEN SHE'S GONE'
– BY MARIANNE PLUME AND ANNA GRAM

We first became aware of Miss Lipman's remarkable blend of charm, chutzpah and – well, what's the opposite of laid-back? – versatility when we saw her in a LAMDA production of *Mandragola*, playing a nine months pregnant French whore. She was a big girl in those days with a corseted bosom on which, as I recall, she had laboriously painted a coach and eight horses, two of which kept apparently nose-diving in and out of her not inconsiderable chest. The song she sang was called 'He had a way with him', and by the end of it we were convinced that we were in the presence of something which was biggish.

Over the next twenty years her career plummeted upwards, whilst her weight soared downhill into what she described in her first book *How Was It For You?* as a sort of 'animated scrag end'. Her performances in *Outside Edge* as a large, fur-coated, predatory, brick-laying earth mother, and her subsequent appearance as the tipsy spinster in *See How They Run* won her numerous awards, not least of which were the 'Bendiest Body Since Nat Jackley' and 'The Shamelessly OTT and Attempted Play Stealing Award'.

She was the first to admit to being a bit of a minor bird, in that her love of mimicry made her Joyce Grenfell an aristocratic eccentric and her Kitty McShane a convincing colleen, although one cynical and food-loving critic was moved to write: 'Asking Maureen Lipman to play Kitty McShane is like asking Barbra Streisand to play Mother Teresa' (interested producers stop here).

Her television work varied from the statutory loony sit-coms, which revolved, as all sit-coms do, around her zany put-upon-persona, to a composed and competent Princess of France in *Love's Labour's Lost* (Shakespeare's first encounter with a Jewish Princess). She effortfully livened-up many a quiz and chat show and once told a joke concerning a vase on the *Parkinson* show which was so risqué that it risked both their careers. Her film career was limited to cameo roles, which grew steadily smaller after an auspicious start in *Up The Junction*. She put this down to having an agent who doesn't know any film people and a largish nose. Always there with the speedy, self-deprecating quip, she claimed to have half a huge ego, a quarter of a pound of self-esteem, an infinitesimal amount of self-respect, a charisma bypass and a side order of talent. Those who worked with her, and are still alive, claimed she was waspish, witty and professional. At least three of the directors who worked with her more than once, say they would certainly have worked with her again and their cheques are in the post.

As a wife and mother she left a medium amount to be desired. Although her children, when we reminded them who she was, claimed to have found her work very funny and her 'Carribean Fricassee' unforgettable. Her husband, Jack Rosenthal, remembers her cold feet and her warm disposition, and says she's left a place in his appointment book that can never be filled.

Her final word on herself was to request her own epitaph: 'Better Late Than Ever ...'